Blessed are they
who believe.

Luke 1:45

# God Forgive Us for
# Being Women

# FRAMEWORKS

## Interdisciplinary Studies for Faith and Learning

Previously published
volumes in the series:

*What's So Liberal about the Liberal Arts?*
*Integrated Approaches to Christian Formation*

Paul W. Lewis and
Martin William Mittelstadt, editors

*Christian Morality: An Interdisciplinary Framework*
*for Thinking about Contemporary Moral Issues*

Geoffrey W. Sutton and
Brandon Schmidly, editors

# God Forgive Us for Being Women

*Rhetoric, Theology, and the Pentecostal Tradition*

## Joy E. A. Qualls

PICKWICK *Publications* · Eugene, Oregon

GOD FORGIVE US FOR BEING WOMEN
Rhetoric, Theology, and the Pentecostal Tradition

Frameworks: Interdisciplinary Studies for Faith and Learning

Pickwick Publications
An Imprint of Wipf and Stock Publishers
199 W. 8th Ave., Suite 3
Eugene, OR 97401

www.wipfandstock.com

PAPERBACK ISBN: 978-1-5326-0202-3
HARDCOVER ISBN: 978-1-5326-0204-7
EBOOK ISBN: 978-1-5326-0203-0

## Cataloguing-in-Publication data:

Names: Qualls, Joy E. A.

Title: God forgive us for being women : rhetoric, theology, and the Pentecostal tradition / Joy E. A. Qualls.

Description: Eugene, OR: Pickwick Publications, 2018 | Series: Frameworks: Interdisciplinary Studies for Faith and Learning | Includes bibliographical references.

Identifiers: ISBN 978-1-5326-0202-3 (paperback) | ISBN 978-1-5326-0204-7 (hardcover) | ISBN 978-1-5326-0203-0 (ebook)

Subjects: LCSH: Pentecostal women. | Christian leadership—Pentecostals. | Pentecostal churches—Doctrines. | Women in church work—Pentecostal churches. | Sex role—Religious aspects—Pentecostal churches.

Classification: LCC BV676 Q8 2018 (print) | LCC BV676 (ebook)

Manufactured in the U.S.A.                    05/29/18

# Series Preface

WE AFFIRM THE VALUE of a Christian liberal arts education. We believe that lifelong development of a Christian worldview makes us more fully human. We attest that engagement in the liberal arts contributes to the process of integrating Christian spirituality with a broad range of disciplinary studies. This integrative process requires that we explore and reflect upon biblical and theological studies while learning effective communication, pursuing healthy relationships, and engaging our diverse global community. We believe that the convergence of academic disciplines opens the door to the good life with enlarged promise for worship of the living God, development of deeper communities, and preparation for service and witness.

Our contributors are dedicated to the integration of faith, life, and learning. We celebrate exposure to God's truth at work in the world not only through preachers, missionaries, and theologians, but also through the likes of poets, artists, musicians, lawyers, physicians, and scientists. We seek to explore issues of faith, increase self-awareness, foster diversity, cultivate societal engagement, explore the natural world, and encourage holistic service and witness. We offer these studies not only as our personal act of worship, but as liturgies to prepare readers for worship and as an opportunity to wrestle with faith and practice through the arts and sciences.

In this series, we proclaim our commitment to interdisciplinary studies. Interdisciplinary studies involves the methodological combination of two or more academic disciplines into one research project. Within a Christian worldview, we address complex questions of faith and life, promote cooperative learning, provide fresh opportunities to ask meaningful questions and address human need. Given our broad approach to interdisciplinary studies, we seek contributors from diverse Christian traditions and disciplines. Possibilities for publication include but are not limited to the following examples: 1) We seek single or multiple author contributions that address Christian faith and life via convergence of two or more academic disciplines; 2) We seek edited volumes that stretch across interdisciplinary lines. Such volumes may be directed specifically at the convergence of two or more disciplines and address a specific topic or serve as a wide-ranging collection of essays across multiple disciplines unified by a single theme; 3) We seek contributors across all Christian traditions and encourage conversations among scholars regarding questions within a specific tradition or across multiple traditions. In so doing we welcome both theoretical and applied perspectives.

The vision for this project emerged among professors at Evangel University (Springfield, MO). Evangel University, owned and operated by the General Council of the Assemblies of God (AG), is the fellowship's national university of arts, sciences, and professions: the first college in the Pentecostal tradition founded as a liberal arts college (1955). Evangel University is a member institution of the Council for Christian Colleges and Universities (CCCU). Consistent with the values and mission of the AG and CCCU, Evangel University exists to educate and equip Christians from any tradition for life and service with particular attention to Pentecostal and Charismatic traditions. Evangel University employs a general education curriculum that includes required interdisciplinary courses for all students. The Evangel University representatives for this series continue to participate in the articulation and development of the Evangel University *ethos* and seek contributors that demonstrate and model confessional integration not only for the Evangel University community and Pentecostals, but all Christians committed to the integration of faith, learning, and life. We offer this series not only as a gift from the Evangel University community to other Christian communities interested in the intersection of intellectual integration and spiritual and societal transformation, but also as an invitation to walk with us on this journey. Finally, in order to ensure a broad conversation, our editorial committee includes a diverse collection of scholars not only from Evangel University but also from other traditions, disciplines, and academic institutions who share our vision.

## SERIES EDITORS

- Paul W. Lewis (Associate Professor of Historical Theology and Missiology at Assemblies of God Theological Seminary)

- Martin William Mittelstadt (Professor of Biblical Studies at Evangel University)

# EDITORIAL BOARD

For every woman who has known the call of God on her life but is denied her place simply because she is a woman: The God who calls is faithful and blessed is she who believes that what the Lords has promised will be accomplished.

And for Blakeley, my girl, who knows this call in your childhood. May the voice of the Spirit remain as clear and sweet to you always as you walk out your call and as you bear witness to the world the Salvation given to us through Christ alone. I love you.

# Contents

# Acknowledgments

MY SCHOLARLY JOURNEY BEGAN over 20 years ago when I came to what was then Southern California College as a small-town girl who longed for the bright lights of the big city. It was here that all I thought I knew, all I believed and everything I had put my faith in was shattered into a million little pieces, then lovingly and with great care and thoughtful prodding was put back together again. Only this time, it was truly my own. Scholars, teachers, and God-fearing mentors who saw in me what I did not know surrounded me existed and slowly allowed a love of the art of scholarship to be birthed in me.

I am so grateful for the role that Dr. John and Mary Wilson played in giving me a North Dakota home away from home and instilled a love of history in me that taught me as much about the present as it does about the past. To Drs. Alison English, Elizabeth Leonard, Sheri Benvenuti, and Kelly Walter-Carney who encouraged me to seek out my heritage and embrace the study of women because our stories and voices need to be heard if the narrative of history is to be fully understood and completed. Mary, Elizabeth and Shari have both gone on from this life and their presence is missed in mine. I honor them with this book.

However, it would be an understatement if I did not give due honor to the man who provided the foundation for this work, Dr. Thomas J. Carmody, who invested more in my life that any amount of tuition could have paid for. Tom encouraged me to look beyond myself and learn to truly become a rhetorician. He taught me to become more thoughtful and to be one who engages in a hermeneutic of suspicion while putting on the full armor of God and honoring the Lord with my mind. The dream of a Ph.D. was birthed under his guidance, his constant encouragement and prayer. Today, that dream is a reality. Tom, thank you.

My scholarly journey moved to Regent University where I was again surrounded by a group of mentors who truly exemplified the commandment to love the Lord with all their hearts, souls, and minds. Drs. Robert Schihl, Michael Graves, William Brown, John Keeler, Benson Fraser, Norman Mintle, and Marc Newman all used their unique gifting's to instill in me a broad spectrum of learning as worship. Dr. Mark Steiner, my fearless dissertation chairman, who believed in this project and saw its potential long before and beyond what I was able to envision on my own. Thank you for pushing me and leaving me with open ended questions that I was forced to answer even when I did not want to go there. Your passion for a faithful witness inspires me and challenges me. Thank you.

I am living my dream serving as a scholar and professor. I am grateful to colleagues and friends who have made this work possible. Presidents Robert Spence and Carol Taylor Carol Taylor and the community of Evangel University, you gave me a firm foundation for my work to thrive. Drs. Marty Mittelstadt, Bob Berg, and the entire Frameworks series team, thank you for creating space for me to publish this in your series. Dr. Diane Awbrey, I would not be where I am today either in my career or in my writing without your efforts and belief that I was meant to flourish. Your work on this project is priceless. Thank you for being my friend and my champion. President Barry Corey and the community of Biola University, most especially my department, Communication Studies, thank you for choosing me and for believing that I could lead and serve. I have come into my own because these two Universities gave me the opportunity to live out my call.

When you engage in research such as this, you are dependent upon those who have come before you and those who are the keepers of the history. I am eternally grateful to Dr. George O. Wood, former General Superintendent of the Assemblies of God for his time and transparency. Thank you for being intentional in your championing women and changing the face of the Assemblies of God. There used to be a quota system in the Assemblies of God: white and male. No more! This is your legacy and I am grateful. Darrin Rodgers and the entire staff of the Flower Pentecostal Heritage Center who spent hours pulling files, allowing me to hold frail and brittle documents and touch history with my own hands. Great discussion and a lot of good debate also contributed to this project. I am eternally grateful for your help and friendship.

Women who have remained constants have surrounded me. Wherever I am and no matter my state of mind, these women are my rock of equilibrium and a shelter from the storm. Cheryl, you have been this rock and shelter for the longest of any. You can look beyond me and straight into my soul. You speak with the voice of the Holy Spirit because you allow him to inhabit every fiber of your being and you take me for who I am broken and tattered and make me want to be that practical woman in impractical shoes. I love you.

I have not received any greater blessing in my life than the love of a family. I am doubly blessed because I was both born and later married into families that have a faith that can move mountains and a belief in the power of God that is unmatched. The entire Qualls family: thank you for embracing me as one of your own. The extended Anderson tribe, you are many and as such I know that I will never want for love or care. The men in my life: my brothers, Jeremiah and John, who know my deepest faults and love me in spite of it all. My grandparents, Leonard and Peggy Anderson who helped to raise me and brought me up to believe in the power of prayer and a steadfast belief that hard work and trust in the Lord is an unbeatable combination. Grandpa, I wish you could read this version cover to cover, too. I miss you and your unwavering belief in me.

Abraham Lincoln is credited with stating that all he was or ever hoped to be was owed to his mother. This is my story; this is my song. All I am or ever hope to be I owe to my mother, Marilyn Andrick, who taught me what it means to be a woman who is velvet covered steel: strong, yet beautiful and rich. Mom, we have walked together through the depths of despair, the streams in the desert and the mountaintops of bliss. You are the woman the writer of Proverbs had in mind when he penned the 31st chapter and I, your child, rise today to call you blessed.

Kevin, you are more than just my husband. You are my very best friend. You love me deeper and more fully than I ever thought was capable by another human being. Thank you for the adventure we have journeyed these last twelve years and I look forward to the adventures yet to come. I love you does not express fully what my heart sings for you. Blakeley Elisabeth, my beautiful daughter who is already so tuned to the voice of the Spirit. This work is all for you, Baby Girl. Soren Ray Anderson, you feel deeply and wear your heart on your sleeve. You are my kindred spirit and there is leadership in your bones. Your mama loves you both.

Finally, I am so thankful for the scores of nameless, faceless woman who gave all they had on this earth, who often left families, material possessions, comfort and security to follow the call of God. So very few are mentioned here, but there is another book where their names are written and in the Lamb's book the names of these servants are made famous. I cannot wait to sit at the Starbucks of heaven and hear of your testimony to the faithfulness of a God who calls. Sitting among you is a woman whose heart epitomizes what the sacrifice of the call truly means. Karen Kay, the

Lord has welcomed you into the great cloud of witnesses. Well-done, good & faithful servant. I miss you deeply. Save a place for me.

Lord, I stand before you today on Holy Ground. I do not possess the earthly qualifications to bear your name to the nations. Who am I that I should speak for you? Yet, as in the days of Moses who stood before your presence in a burning bush, I hear you say to me, I will be with you. When they ask who sent you, tell them, "I AM." You are my I AM the same today, yesterday and forever. Blessed is she who has believed that what the Lord has said to her will be accomplished.

I Believe,

Joy Elizabeth Anderson Qualls

# 1

# Introduction

*. . . but for God-fearing, intelligent, Spirit-filled women, upon whom God has set his seal in their ministry, to have to sit and listen to men haggle over the matter of their place in the ministry is humiliating to say the least. . . . God almighty is no fool—I say it with all reverence— Would He fill a woman with the Holy Ghost—endow her with ability—give her a vision for souls and then tell her to shut her mouth?*

—Mae Eleanor Frey, Letter to J. R. Evans, 1928

THE EXASPERATION OF A woman on the saw dust trail of ministry is clear in a frail copy of a letter written on hotel stationary dated September 3, 1928. Mae Eleanor Frey, a female evangelist, wife, and mother wrote this letter and numerous others over a twenty-six-year period to Assemblies of God General Secretaries John Welch, J. R. Evans, and J. Roswell Flower. In a revealing look at the life of an early pioneer of Pentecostal ministry in the United States, Frey's letters detail her experience with male pastors, her encounters with the Ku Klux Klan and local ministers, her frustration with policy, and her extraordinary dependence on advice from the fellowship's headquarters. While the leaders of the Assemblies of God publicly endorsed Frey's work, she served at a time when the movement's constitution and bylaws denied women a role in the office of pastor. However, the leadership saw no reason that Frey could not pastor and actively sought opportunities for her to translate her work into a more pastoral role. Most outstanding in their correspondence is an astonishing disregard for the challenging dynamic of placing a woman in a district that they knew did not want her and their open challenge to the fellowship's official policy.[1] Historian Edith Blumhofer, who first published Frey's letters, suggests that this correspondence reveals wide discrepancies between policy and practices.

What could have been a dramatic showdown on the role of women in pastoral ministry was saved by the death of Frey's husband, which allowed her to continue in the less controversial work of evangelism.[2] Even so, she is continually encouraged to persevere in spite of the opposition of the governing body that she esteems so deeply. After one session, Frey states, "At this last Council I felt like a criminal as they brought up this foolish woman question again. . . . One felt like asking God to forgive us for being women. There is nothing in the word of God that forbids a woman from preaching the Gospel or conducting a work."[3] What Frey may or may not have known then is that her struggle goes beyond her movement and speaks to a stained glass ceiling that confronted her sisters before her and continues to confront her daughters after her.

Questions about a woman's place in the ministry of Christianity are not unique to the Assemblies of God or the Pentecostal movement. One only need examine the position of the Roman Catholic Church or the Southern Baptist Convention to discover that women have been and continue to be limited in the leadership roles they are allowed to play in the church. However, the Pentecostal movement created a space for the service of women that set precedent in a time when women had very little in the way of rights or freedoms within societal or church culture.

Pentecostals in the early days of the movement valued the testimonies of God's mysterious new work in women's lives. They believed that God could choose to manifest the gifts of the Holy Spirit including by infilling any believer with miraculous signs and wonders: men or women. These premises, according to Blumhofer, assured women a seat at the table of Pentecostal belief and gave them some voice in sharing the Pentecostal message.

The narrative of women's involvement in this movement is, however, as Blumhofer states, "complex and confusing."[4] She concludes that for the most part Pentecostal denominations have not embraced women as pastors, thereby excluding them from institutional positions for which full ordination is mandated while at the same time affirming their roles as evangelists,

1. Blumhofer, "Women in American Pentecostalism," 20.
2. Ibid.
3. Frey, Letter to J. R. Evans, September 3, 1928.
4. Blumhofer, "Women in American Pentecostalism," 19.

missionaries, and even pioneer pastors of new churches. The Assemblies of God is both the exception and the rule in the story of American Pentecostalism, and its relationship to women.

Blumhofer warns that no single thread but rather a grand tapestry weaves the story of the role of women in Pentecostalism. For every story of affirmation, another of frustration and repression emerges.[5] Wide-spread discrepancies exist. Assemblies of God Missionary and Professor of Theology Barbara Cavaness concurs: women pastors, evangelists, and missionaries are often celebrated in the sermons of Assemblies of God leaders, while these very leaders express reservations about women in private discussion and in the hiring and credentialing processes.[6]

What is the impact of these disparate messages faced by women in the Pentecostal tradition? These discrepancies and the resulting tensions are profoundly rhetorical. They are primarily rooted in the way people use words, language, and symbols. The historical, cultural, and theological context in which the Pentecostal movement emerged contributes to this discourse and permeates the formation of ideology and practice that creates dissonance and tension both within the fellowship and to the outside observer. The tension points to several key issues.

First, women have played and continue to play a prominent role in the Pentecostal movement. Historian and theologian Harvey Cox concludes that Pentecostal ministry is unthinkable without the work of women. Former General Superintendent of the Assemblies of God George O. Wood stated that allowing women to serve in ministry roles including those of pastor and elder is simply "who we are."[7] Pentecostalism of the modern era disrupted mainline practices in more than worship style and expression. Likewise, the role of women in leadership within the Pentecostal tradition goes beyond a question of feminism and garnering women a seat at the table. Rather, empowering women to lead in the church reconceptualizes how we approach the work of the church in our culture and quietly subverts centuries of religious identity and ideology.

Second, the inclusion of women in leadership positions within the Assemblies of God is doctrinally as distinctive as their pneumatology, their biblical doctrine of the work of the Holy Spirit. The shift the Assemblies of God made in their unique theological position concerning the "finished work" creates a greater rhetorical space for women in the church. If the "Baptism in the Holy Spirit" is an empowerment for service and the Spirit

5. Ibid.

6. Cavaness, "Biographical Study," 1999.

7. Wood in discussion with the author, November 2007.

pours out on daughters, what are those daughters empowered to do in their service? Theologically and rhetorically, the early fathers of the Assemblies of God saw it both ways. Theologically, the Spirit was available to these prophesying daughters, but when it came to creating both physical and rhetorical space for women to serve, their previous theological leanings and current cultural norms weighed heavily against granting women a new place in the emerging hierarchy of the fellowship.

Third, the Assemblies of God lost sight of its unique cultural and religious identity. Despite a radical beginning and a unique approach to theology, as the Assemblies of God grew and developed into an institution, strategic choices were made that precipitated rapid growth and development in the United States and around the world. In the process, however, these choices sacrificed distinct elements of their unique history and ideology. These choices contributed to the tensions faced by women who desired a calling to church ministry and leadership. This book builds upon previous scholarship in sociology and theology, which argue that the Assemblies of God sacrificed its moment in time to be a catalyst for the changing role of women in the church and in American culture. It centers on the rhetorical dichotomies that assisted in a missed opportunity.

Finally, these issues faced by the Assemblies of God mirror broader rhetorical problems in the evangelical community. As in the early days of the Assemblies of God, the world is an uncertain place. This uncertainty is driving questions of the role of religion in the public square and ramping up religious fervor. Women in church leadership challenge religious convention and American culture. Several voices compete over the role women have to play within the home, the society, and the church. At the same time a number of evangelicals supported the nomination of Alaska Governor Sarah Palin to the Vice-Presidency of the United States, other evangelical leaders were removing magazines from their bookstores that featured female pastors on the cover. According to Richard Land, former President of the Southern Baptist Ethics and Religious Liberty Commission, the Convention has no disconnect or inconsistency in its position on the role of women. Land states that leadership in public office is different from leadership in the home or the church.[8] This book examines the role evangelical rhetoric plays in creating and shaping both policy and perception on the place of women in public, private, and religious spheres even among Pentecostals.

American Christians should heed Blumhofer's warnings and at the same time expose and address the rhetorical underpinnings of the discrepancies that have existed and continue to permeate the role of women

---

8. Baker, "Southern Baptists Back Palin," October 3, 2008.

in American religion and church leadership. However, the vast narrative history cannot be ignored. Therefore, this book addresses the rhetorical beginnings of the Assemblies of God as a microcosm of the history of the Pentecostal movement in the United States in general.

Rather than engaging in a feminist analysis of patriarchy and power, I focus on the ways women negotiate and renegotiate rhetorical space. I examine how they used and became symbols as they conceptualized their theology and practiced their faith in the Pentecostal movement, trying to do proper justice to it as they engaged in public life.

## HISTORY AND SCHOLARSHIP

Historian Lewis Wilson notes that the Southern Baptist line, "We're too busy making history to take time to write it," only partially applies to Pentecostals. He asserts that a low priority on scholarship, rather than a high priority on history-making, produced few trained historians to write their own history and non-Pentecostals in academia were slow to recognize it as an appropriate subject for serious research.[9]

Prior to 1958, no scholarly history of the movement existed. This deficit began to change when Klaude Kendrick published *The Promise Fulfilled*, and Carl Brumback published *Suddenly . . . From Heaven* in 1961 followed by John Nichol's *Pentecostalism* in 1966 and William W. Menzies's *Anointed to Serve* in 1971. Wilson argues that while scholarly work increased over the next thirty years, Pentecostal historiography remains spotty. "Because of the limited publications, personal papers, church records and demographic studies available for the early days," he wrote, "it is tempting to allow some resources to be more representative than they were."[10]

While specific women who became known in Pentecostal circles, such as Maria Woodworth-Etter and Marie Burgess Brown, are referenced in these first histories, no formal discussion of the role of women in the Pentecostal movement or in the formation of the Assemblies of God exists. For example, Menzies notes that Evangelist Blanche Brittain was "a mighty instrument" used by Holy Spirit to start many churches and as a result of her ministry, over 100 ministers entered the ranks of "the Lord's Army" including G. Raymond Carlson who received salvation under Brittain's leadership in 1925.[11] However, at that point, the discussion ceases to be about Brittain

9. Wilson, "Book Review: *Restoring the Faith*," 119–22.
10. Ibid., 122.
11. Menzies, *Anointed to Serve*, 159.

or her work and focuses rather on Carlson, who would first receive credentials at age 16 and eventually move into national leadership in 1969.

This type of commentary is consistent in other historical anthologies of Menzies's era. Women are certainly not excluded from the discussion and are honored for their work, but the fact that women were present and participated in the ministry work of the new fellowship does not receive focused attention or discussion. One exception occurs in the work of Pentecostal historian and theologian Vinson Synan's *The Holiness–Pentecostal Tradition*.

First published in 1971, *The Holiness–Pentecostal Tradition* gives a brief description of women serving in ministry positions as an act that "varied from the norm of other churches."[12] The majority of the discussion centers on one specific woman. Maria Woodworth-Etter is the first woman to gain fame in the United States as a preacher, according to Synan, who also claims that Woodworth-Etter was an ardent feminist who did much to further the cause of her gender long before women earned suffrage in 1920. In both this text as well as several other treatments, Synan presents the most sustained history of the world-wide streams of the Holiness and Pentecostal traditions, their formation, and their adoption in the United States.

According to Lewis Wilson, no one deserves more credit, however, for attempting to rectify the lack of quality Pentecostal historical scholarship than Edith Blumhofer.[13] Blumhofer offers by sheer volume one of the more sustained analyses of the Assemblies of God as well as Pentecostalism as a whole. Specific to the role of women in the Assemblies of God, Blumhofer fills in a great deal of historical data including a lengthy discussion of how the role of women was first addressed in the forming of the movement. In addition, she writes focused chapters in several texts on the specific contributions of women as well as their struggle for recognition and support within their movement. Strikingly, Blumhofer distinctly advocates for the recognition of women and their role in the birth and the formation of Pentecostalism and critiques the lack of recognition for their efforts from both the leadership of the movement and the rank and file.

In the last decade, more texts like Blumhofer's have been written outside the confines of sanctioned histories from specific denominational standpoints. Church historian Grant Wacker notes that early Pentecostals were furious writers who produced a prodigious amount of text (mostly in the form of periodicals) and much of this material has not been read or examined by scholars. In *Heaven Below*, Wacker attempts to rectify this lack of critical examination and give both an in-depth account of Pentecostalism, but also

12. Synan, *Holiness–Pentecostal Tradition*, 190–91.
13. Wilson, "Book Review: *Restoring the Faith*," 119.

engage with how this belief system played out in everyday life. He notes the disproportionate role played by women in the early days of the movement while addressing the conflicting pressures faced by women from the movement's inception and states that the question simply remains "why?"[14] He concludes that while the nature of Pentecostals was to defy worldly convention, their pragmatic approach too often reminded them of the cost of this defiance. Few early leaders were willing to admit to themselves or anyone else that these conflicting attitudes battled for dominance.

Religion scholar Harvey Cox provides an outsider's perspective on the Pentecostal movement. His *Fire from Heaven* includes a chapter that evaluates the role of women in the movement. While others note the unique role of women or the silent tensions over their role in the church, Cox comes to a much more definitive conclusion. The Pentecostal movement would not have become what it has in the United States or around the world, he declares, had it not been for the exceptional contributions of women. He also cites both clear biblical and doctrinal evidence for the remarkable display of feminine leadership found in Pentecostalism.[15] More so than other writers, Cox highlights that despite the tensions and often-direct resistance to women's leadership, Pentecostal women found ways to keep preaching their message and thus sustained their role in the movement and possibly the movement itself.

Another historical treatment of the Assemblies of God is offered by the late Gary McGee, Professor of Church History and Pentecostal Studies at the Assemblies of God Theological Seminary. *People of the Spirit* offers accessible historical scholarship, making it appealing to both scholars and laypersons. Almost encyclopedic in its approach to telling the story of the Assemblies of God, McGee's *People of the Spirit* offers a more personal insight into the characters and personalities of those who have contributed to the leadership and development of the Assemblies of God. The oral histories and commentary by those present at various significant events provides a necessary link to what documents and personal papers do exist.

*Philip's Daughters*, an edited volume by Pentecostal scholars Estrelda Alexander and Amos Yong assembles twelve conference papers from a colloquium held in 2006. The "Women in Pentecostal-Charismatic Leadership" colloquium was sponsored by the Regent University School of Divinity and focused on the historical and theological perspectives of women in the Pentecostal movement. This compilation centers on the study of women in Pentecostalism, but it includes further critical analysis by Assemblies of God

14. Wacker, *Heaven Below*, 176.

15. Cox, *Fire from Heaven*, 124.

theologian Barbara Cavaness Park with regard to women missionaries as well as a history of Hispanic women in the Assemblies of God by Claremont McKenna Professor of Philosophy and Religion, Gaston Espinoza.

Yet, apart from Espinoza's brief refutation of a "Golden Age" for women in the Assemblies of God, few have examined the disconnect that has existed and continues to exist in how the role of women is communicated and practiced. This book builds on existing and emerging scholarship, by highlighting the rhetorical practices that have shaped and reinforced the dissonance surrounding the role of women in the Assemblies of God.

The role of women in the church speaks directly to believers' view of the nature of God and his relationship to his people. If women are excluded from key roles in sharing the gospel of Jesus and serving his people, then they are relegated to secondary status in their spiritual communities and put at a distance from the very inner workings of the Spirit in human life This book necessarily redresses the weaknesses in previously limited coverage and reconciles competing accounts theologically, historically, and most importantly, rhetorically.

The role of women in the Assemblies of God is symptomatic of greater issues at play within the Pentecostal tradition. These issues include the theological influence of earlier affiliations, a desire for greater acceptance amongst the evangelical community, and a reaction to the secular women's movement, which was perceived as an assault on the family and traditional values. In examining the issue of women, the book develops a nuanced critique of the movement itself in order that we might thoughtfully deal with the rhetorical challenges that exist not only within the Assemblies but also throughout the evangelical community.

While it seems as though the Assemblies of God exploded onto the world's stage in the early twentieth century, it actually grew out of a number of streams including the Keswick tradition in Europe, Scandinavian pietism, and Methodist revivalism. These scattered revivals came together to create a new social and religious movement that altered the religious landscape in the United States. Seeing the Assemblies of God in its historical and theological contexts highlights a specific rhetorical identity that begins to emerge. Out of this rhetorical invention comes inherent tension and dissonance with regard to the role of women. This tension and dissonance began from the movement's inception and continues to resonate and challenge the Assemblies of God and the women that long to be among the ranks of the called.

## A Brief History

The story of Pentecostalism reads like the best of American success stories: a movement of humble, yet mystical, beginnings weaves itself into the fabric of American culture and beyond to become the largest Protestant religious movement in the world. It is the best of all real-life fairytales.

The root of Pentecostal history and belief is that faith and experience are grounded in the biblical witness of God's engagement in human history.[16] The Old Testament prophet Joel speaks of God's promise that in the latter days of human history God himself would pour out his Spirit upon all flesh and this outpouring would be marked by dreams, visions, signs, and wonders. His proclamation of all flesh included the prophesying of both sons and daughters. We see an example of Joel's prophecy later in the New Testament scriptures where on the Day of Pentecost the Holy Spirit, the promised Guide and Comforter, descends upon the disciples and all those gathered with them, including women. This event is marked in the scriptures by the visual of "tongues" of fire manifesting over the heads of these believers. They were filled with the Holy Spirit through what is described as speaking in languages other than their own. Throughout the next couple of millennia, history would record various religious outpourings that included excited speech. In each example, these outpourings have been marked by miracles, healings, prophecy, and the supernatural gift of "tongues." These tongues can be an earthly language the recipient has never studied (*xenolalia*) or what has been described as a heavenly language unknown to anyone on earth (*glossolalia*).

In the latter nineteenth and early twentieth centuries, these relatively rare events became more frequent. For some, the onset of the American Civil War was such an event. The war was viewed as judgment for the sin of slavery and many turned to a personal and national repentance and reconciliation. Some people viewed God as a benevolent judge who demanded personal righteousness, even holiness, as a condition of blessing. Out of this belief grew the "holiness movement." This movement emerged primarily from the Wesleyan tradition and found a home within the Methodist Church. Edith Blumhofer notes that while holiness movements appeared within many denominations, the Methodist branch became the seedbed for the Pentecostal movement.[17]

What set "holiness" Methodists apart was their belief in a "second work of grace." The first work of grace was a sinner's justification, which

16. Medhurst, "Filled With the Spirit," 556.

17. Blumhofer, *Restoring the Faith*, 11–42.

comes from accepting Christ's salvation as a result of his atoning sacrifice at the cross. The holiness movement focused on a second work termed sanctification. This work was necessary to cleanse and purify the believer who had been saved. Some leaders differed on this position and argued that sanctification occurred with justification, and rather than as a second blessing, the outpouring of the Holy Spirit was evidence of empowerment. Pentecostal historian and theologian William W. Menzies, distinguishes the two factions this way: "Although both groups believe there is a definite crisis experience subsequent to the regeneration taught in the Bible, the Holiness understanding is that this experience is for sanctification of the believer, whereas, the Pentecostal understanding is that this experience is primarily an enduement [gift] for service."[18]

Regardless of some of the theological differences, the holiness movement began to grow, and its teachings spread through camp meetings by revivalists such as Dwight L. Moody and Charles Grandison Finney. Not all Methodists accepted the holiness message, however, and in 1894, the Southern Methodist church rejected the theology of holiness. Nearly 25 different groups left the movement. Those groups that split from the Southern Methodists included those who would form the Church of God (Cleveland, TN), the Church of God in Christ (COGIC), and the Pentecostal Holiness Church.

On the first day of the New Year and the first day of the twentieth century, January 1, 1901, the course of the Pentecostal movement changed dramatically.[19] Bethel Bible School in Topeka, Kansas, founded by former Methodist minister, Charles Fox Parham, witnessed a group of students praying for an outpouring of the Holy Spirit when a young woman named Agnes Ozman asked to be prayed over specifically for the gift of the Holy Spirit. When those around her laid their hands on her and began to pray for this request, Ozman started to speak aloud in words that were not English. Parham identified this gift as one that signaled the last, end-time revival before Christ would return to earth. Many believed that this was a new Pentecost and that God was giving them new tongues so they could go into foreign lands as missionaries. They believed that this gift of another language

18. Menzies, *Anointed to Serve*, 10.

19. While this day is consistently cited as the first outpouring of the Holy Spirit that sparks the modern Pentecostal movement, Assemblies of God Historian Darrin J. Rodgers argues that outpourings such as this were occurring concurrently and with more consistency in the Dakotas and Minnesota amongst a group of Scandinavian pietists. These same itinerant preachers and evangelists would eventually lead the Pentecostal movement and the Assemblies of God to grow exponentially in this part of the country, effectively challenging the notion that Pentecostalism is a distinctly Southern import. See also Rodgers, *Northern Harvest*.

was given so that lessening the need for foreign language training would shorten the road to missions.

Following the events at the school in Topeka, Parham set out on an evangelistic tour teaching and preaching on the events of January 1901. Eventually closing the Topeka school, Parham moved his Bible training school to Texas where he would encounter a young man named William Joseph Seymour. As an African-American student, Seymour was not permitted in the classroom with the white students, but Seymour was determined and hungry to learn. So, Parham allowed him to attend the school if he would sit outside the door to receive his lessons. Within weeks, Seymour was offered an opportunity to minister in Los Angeles at a house church led by Julia Hutchins. Seymour took the offer because one of the members of this church, a woman named Lucy Farrow who had once been employed by Parham, had played an integral role in introducing Parham and Seymour.

Shortly after his arrival in Los Angeles, Seymour was dismissed from the house church for preaching Parham's doctrine of what amounted to a third blessing in the gift of tongues. Seymour was not simply "fired" from his position but Sister Hutchins, as she was known, padlocked the door to keep Seymour out. Unfortunately for her, most of her followers stayed out as well and moved with Seymour to the home of a skeptical but curious man named Richard Asbery who lived at 214 Bonnie Brae Street.[20] Undaunted, Seymour continued to preach and within days many in attendance, including Seymour himself, spoke in an unknown tongue.

The group quickly outgrew their surroundings and eventually moved into an abandoned livery stable at 312 Azusa Street. The Azusa Street Revival introduced Pentecostalism, with its raucous worship and ecstatic utterances, to thousands of worshipers from both the United States and Europe. Many of those who came to witness for themselves would go on to found or mentor some of the major Pentecostal denominations and fellowships. Among these were Charles H. Mason, co-founder of the holiness Church of God in Christ and William H. Durham. Durham's revised theology of the doctrine of sanctification would launch the Assemblies of God. Also present was Ernest S. Williams who would later become a General Superintendent of the Assemblies.[21]

While many of these denominations existed prior to Azusa Street, they became more Pentecostal in orientation when their leaders themselves experienced what was now being termed "the Baptism of the Holy Spirit." The one exception to this pattern of development is the Assemblies of God.

20. Synan, *Holiness–Pentecostal Tradition*, 96.

21. Synan, *Century of the Holy Spirit*, 123–48.

In the spring of 1914, a group gathered in the old Grand Opera House in Hot Springs, Arkansas. While most were from the American Midwest, some also came from 17 additional states, Egypt, and South Africa. Following three days of sustained prayer, preaching and fellowship, they prepared to consider proposals to "facilitate cooperation for extending their movement."[22] The purposes around this gathering were five-fold:

1. To gain a better understanding of what God would have them teach,

2. to know how to best conserve the work that it would be built up and not torn down,

3. to understand the needs of the foreign field and how to place money for these efforts,

4. to charter churches so as to stop the fissures within the growing Pentecostal movement and

5. to form a Bible training school with a literary department for the people.

From a theological standpoint, all of the other churches that were once holiness and moved Pentecostal following Azusa Street retained their theology on sanctification as a distinct second blessing and added the Baptism in the Holy Spirit as a third blessing. The Assemblies, however, adopted the "finished work" theology of William Durham. They held that a believer was sanctified and justified simultaneously—a finished work—and that all that remained was the Baptism in the Holy Spirit.[23]

Due to some hesitation about a central organization and the establishment of creeds, this first gathering declared that participants were part of the "General Assembly of God" and the gathering itself was called the General Council, which was taken from Acts 15.[24] Out of this body, an advisory board was established known as the Executive Presbytery. Among the first were some of the most prominent in Pentecostal circles including E.N. Bell, J. Roswell Flower, Howard Goss, Daniel W. Kerr, and John Welch. A total of twelve men were chosen strictly in an advisory capacity to serve God and the saints in a fellowship of like-minded believers, or the Assemblies of God. Only two additional issues were taken up at this first General Council and both would prove to have longstanding implications: divorce and the rights and offices of women.

22. Blumhofer, *Assemblies of God*, 198.

23. Synan, *Century of the Holy Spirit*, 123–48.

24. Blumhofer, *Assemblies of God*, vol. 1, 202. See also Blumhofer, *Restoring the Faith*, 117.

Over the course of the next century, the Assemblies of God would become the largest and arguably the most successful of Pentecostal fellowships. According to the most recent General Council (2016) statistics, the Assemblies in the United States numbers nearly 3.2 million adherents including 1.8 million registered members.[25] Overseas, the numbers are even greater. According to the same report, nearly 68 million adherents worship in 200 countries and territories including the United States.[26] Blumhofer states: "The real story of the Assemblies of God is the story of hundreds of thousands of unnamed women and men who sustained it at the local level and carried its message around the world. "[27]

Blumhofer later argues that Pentecostalism emerged as a protest against dry denominationalism and is rooted deeply in Anglo-American radical evangelicalism. She continues that early Pentecostals were separatists and exclusivists and were not primarily concerned with theology but rather with perceived carnality. All of the trappings of the modern world along with a declining church attendance did nothing more than convince these adherents that the church had lost all spiritual power. Rather, a Pentecostal's faith centered around a series of defining encounters between an individual and his or her God that was regarded "as the hallmark of true Christianity."[28]

These early Pentecostals were adversarial toward other Protestants and defined themselves against what they perceived as the mainstream. Early Pentecostals did not just disagree with mainstream congregations, they denounced them. These attitudes were reinforced by countless testimonies given in Pentecostal missions by people who had come from traditional denominations but who had not truly "found God" until they encountered Pentecostalism. These attitudes and actions became a consistent part of an emerging rhetoric.

Church historian Grant Wacker argues that the founders of the Pentecostal movement sparked a period of "rapid symbol formation." The ideas, practices, and institutions they set in motion lasted long after their deaths and continue to define patterns in American religion that remain into the twenty-first century.[29] Pentecostals and their distinctive understanding of the human encounter with the divine included both primitivist and pragmatic dimensions. A primitivist or restorationist approach includes a desire

---

25. Bradford, "Summary Statistical Report."

26. Ibid.

27. Blumhofer, *Restoring the Faith*, 8.

28. Blumhofer et al., *Pentecostal Currents*, x.

29. Wacker, *Heaven Below*, 8.

to return to the first things or fundamental things and a yearning to be guided only by God's Spirit.

While Blumhofer describes a desire to avoid the contamination of culture, Wacker notes that pragmatism, as seen in Pentecostals' remarkable willingness to work within the culture of their age, was more prevalent. He states that too often it seemed they were holding their proverbial fingers in the wind to calculate where they were going, where they wanted to get to, and how they were going to accomplish these goals.[30] This pragmatism is no more apparent than in the ways Pentecostals have dealt with and continue to treat the issue of women.

## The Rights and Offices of Women

To the outside observer, Pentecostalism offered more hospitality for women in general and for preaching women specifically than its mainstream counterparts. However, with increased examination of the Pentecostal movement, a different picture is emerging: one that conflicts more than it conforms to that view. The theological justification for women's leadership in the church dates back as far as 1894 when Boston minister A. J. Gordon argued that Joel's prophecy served as the *Magna Carta* of the Christian Church. Gordon was deeply critical of conventional thought and practice that reduced women's roles to preparing coffee and sandwiches for church socials.[31]

Leading up to and following Azusa Street, Pentecostals challenged conventional wisdom and pressed the issue. Women such as Florence Crawford left Azusa and established a sect known as The Apostolic Faith in Portland, Oregon, and Ida Robinson led an African-American fellowship, which featured women as bishops and elders. Carrie Judd Montgomery was miraculously healed through the ministry of Elizabeth Mix and began to travel around the country giving testimony of her experience. She would go on to preach, teach, write, and work in social ministry establishing an orphanage and a missionary training school. Maria Woodworth-Etter, an evangelist, is probably one of the best-known preachers of her era. She began ministering in 1880 and following her Spirit baptism in 1912 began a worldwide evangelistic ministry promoting her message of salvation, holy living, and faith healing. In 1818, Etter founded and pastored a church in Indianapolis, Indiana, until her death. The church

---

30. Ibid.

31. Ibid., 160.

still exists as Lakeview Christian Center, which boasts a congregation of well over one thousand members.[32]

Almost as quickly, however, challenges to a woman's place were mounted. While the power of Joel's prophecy created space for women, what stumped these saints and created a sense of doubt was the right of women to speak officially from a prescribed position. The authority to speak carried with it the right to exposit Scripture, which in turn meant teaching men. As organizations developed, this authority carried with it the right to speak in business meetings and adjudicate disputes among men and between men and women. It also meant the right to administer ordinances, which included officiating in marriages, funerals, and serving Communion, putting men in the role of recipient. While many had no opposition to the female voice speaking for the Holy Spirit in prophecy, the priestly role for women contained the question of usurped authority. Nowhere is this played out more than within the Assemblies of God.

Immediately upon convening the business portion of the gathering at Hot Springs, the role of women in the Assemblies of God would be challenged. While nearly 20 percent of the delegates present at that first meeting were women, the body immediately determined that they would not have a vote on matters of business.[33] When it came time to deal specifically with the rights and offices of women, the statement bears the unmistakable imprint of E. N. Bell, Chairman of the first General Council.

According to Blumhofer, Bell had developed his views long before the formation of the Assemblies of God. Bell considered most women "busybodies" who had a tendency not to settle down, and, therefore, did not accomplish anything of considerable worth. While he could not deny the contributions of women to the Pentecostal movement, he accepted no biblical foundation for women to serve in the office of pastor. Bell also acknowledged that women had the right to prophesy and that prophecy was broader than preaching. His objection was against women who "forsook all other callings and devoted their entire time to gospel ministry." He insisted that men were "better adapted to rule and govern assemblies" and that God wanted to "take these heavy responsibilities off women's shoulders."[34]

The official minutes recorded the mixed signals of the men in the "Rights and Offices of Women" resolution. While it acknowledges the

32. Lee and Gohr, "Women in the Pentecostal Movement," 1–5.

33. The report in *Word and Witness*, an early publication of the Assemblies of God, states that 120 ministers signed the list as delegates, but the only extant list has 110 including twenty-two women, or 20 percent of the delegates. See "Hot Springs Assembly," *Word and Witness*, 1.

34. Bell, "Women Elders," 2.

mighty hand of God on the women for proclamation and prophecy, it admonishes them to subjection and "helper" status. The resolution reads:

> The Conference Committee recommended to the GENERAL COUNCIL that whereas the hand of God is mightily upon many women to proclaim and publish the "good tidings of great joy" in a wonderful way, that the GENERAL COUNCIL of the ASSEMBLIES OF GOD submit the following Scriptures for consideration.
>
> 1. In Christ, that is the matter of Salvation, the lines of sex are blotted out. Gal. 3:28.
>
> 2. Women are commanded to be in subjection and not to usurp authority over the man. 1 Tim 2:11–15.
>
> 3. They are called to prophesy and preach the Gospel. Acts 2:17. "He that prophesieth speaketh unto men to edification, to exhortation and to comfort." I Cor 14:3.
>
> 4. To be helpers in the Gospel. Rom 16:30.
>
> Therefore be it resolved, that this Council recommend to the ministry and Assemblies of God, that we recognize their God-given rights to be ordained, not as elders, but as Evangelists and Missionaries, after being duly approved according to the Scriptures.[35]

Later on that year at the request of Hattie Hacker and Jennie Kirkland who were serving overseas in India, women missionaries were given a greater right over their sisters in ministry domestically when they were granted permission to administer "baptism, marriage, burial of the dead and the Lord's Supper when a man [was] not available for the purpose.[36] This same privilege would not be extended to women domestically until 1922.

Barbara Cavaness rightly points out that this ambiguity "of accepting women ministers into the fellowship on one hand and denying them a vote and congregational leadership on the other" established a tone and a pattern of rhetoric toward women ministering in the States.[37] Menzies makes no mention of the action regarding women in the "Birth" chapter of his history of the Assemblies, nor does he even mention that women were in attendance at early Councils. This lack of attention to the role women played

35. General Council of the Assemblies of God, General Council Minutes, 7.

36. General Council of the Assemblies of God, Executive Presbytery Minutes, 1914, 23.

37. Cavaness, "Biographical Study," 106.

from the earliest days is an example of the pattern of rhetoric Cavaness Park cites and reinforces the ambiguity between the discourse and the recorded history of the actual role women played.

At the fifth General Council in 1917, Elizabeth Sission, a highly respected evangelist, delivered the keynote address, but in an ironic twist the official minutes note that "Some time was spent in discussing the question of whether the sisters present should be requested to vote, but it was finally decided to leave them on the same basis as in former Councils, namely, as advisory members, with the privilege of participating in all discussions."[38]

Throughout the course of the next decade and into the 1930s the General Council would address the question of granting women, more rights and privileges, only to reverse the policy at the following Councils. In the 1930s, two significant policy changes would impact the role of women. The first, in 1931, partially reversed earlier policy by stating that women were limited in ordination. Their ordination was only as evangelists and not in the office of pastor. The revised policy also removed the prior authorization to officiate Communion even when there was no man present to administer the ordinance.[39] In 1935, the Council reinstated the policy of granting full ordination to women as evangelists and pastors, including the right to administer the ordinances of the church to women who were at least twenty-five years old, a restriction not imposed upon their male counterparts.[40]

While the issue would continue to be debated and the exact meaning of the changes to the Assemblies of God Constitution and Bylaws in 1935 would be interpreted differently over the course of time, the official position on the rights and offices of women has changed little since this date. Article VII, Section 2(l) currently reads:

> The Scriptures plainly teach that divinely called and qualified women may also serve the church in the ministry of the Word (Joel 2:29; Acts 21:9; 1 Cor 11:5). Women who meet the qualifications for ministerial credentials are eligible for whatever grade of credentials their qualifications warrant and have the right to administer the ordinances of the church and are eligible to serve in all levels of church ministry and/or district and General Council leadership.[41]

Rhetorical dichotomy has plagued the Pentecostal movement and the Assemblies of God from the beginning and has highlighted tensions in belief

38. General Council of the Assemblies of God, General Council Minutes, 1917, 9.

39. General Council of the Assemblies of God, General Council Minutes, 1931, 18.

40. General Council of the Assemblies of God, General Council Minutes 1935, 112.

41. General Council of the Assemblies of God, Constitution and Bylaws, 2007, 31.

and practice. Were they restorationist or was this something brand new? Did the movement need to eschew culture or embrace it as a means to spread the Pentecostal message? Was the gift of tongues a further means of spiritual growth or was it an empowerment for service—or both? If the Holy Spirit could be poured out on daughters as well as sons for prophecy, did that translate into this empowerment for service and what did that look like?

## PENTECOSTALISM IN AMERICAN CULTURE AND RELIGIOUS IDENTITY

To answer these questions fully it is necessary to place the Pentecostal movement and the Assemblies of God in proper context. Historical theologian and ordained Assemblies of God minister Zachary Michael Tackett argues that the Assemblies of God emerged from the cultural, ecclesiological, and theological margins of American society and over time moved to the center, middle class of society.[42] In its progression to middle class acceptance, the Assemblies of God changed its perspectives on Scripture, millennialism, and the roles of women. In the early years of the movement, Pentecostals were committed to including all people as equal participants and especially the marginalized. Women, the poor, those with little formal education, and people of color as well as people of financial means and cultural status had a place in the spreading of the Pentecostal message.

Theologian Cheryl Bridges Johns summarized the radical nature of early Pentecostals in her 1993 presidential address to the Society for Pentecostal Studies:

> In the era of the war to end all wars, Pentecostals were pacifists. In an era when women were excluded from public voice, Pentecostals were ordaining women as ministers. In an era of the KKK, Pentecostal blacks and whites were worshiping together. This subversive and revolutionary movement . . . had a dual prophetic role: denouncing the dominant patterns of the status quo and announcing the patterns of God's order. Because of its ecstatic religious practices and its "abnormal" social behavior, Pentecostalism was opposed by the society at large and by the established churches.[43]

For Pentecostals to be accepted in the larger culture, they would need to make some compromises and accommodations to the culture. I contend

42. Tackett, "Embourgeoisement of the Assemblies of God," 1.

43. Johns, "Adolescence of Pentecostalism," 4–5.

that this is exactly what they did. In the process, however, the choices they made continued to have a dramatic impact on the role of women and amplified tensions that had already been established.

According to sociologist Margaret Poloma, the story of women in Pentecostalism as told by historians and theologians provides a good case study to "assess how religion may inadvertently act as an agent of change when it is in its 'charismatic moment' only to revert to reactionary measures once the institution is firmly in place."[44] Poloma argues that early Christianity did much to enhance the role of women and only later cultural ambivalence toward women created a situation in which women were "clearly second class citizens."[45] Likewise, the Pentecostal movement, instead of openly creating a place for the role of women in religious ministry, chose to stay with their brothers (and sisters) in more conservative Christianity and be a reactionary, rather than a revolutionary, movement in American culture. She contends that Pentecostalism could have sparked an alternative to the secular feminist movement (much like their Evangelical suffragists in the early nineteenth century), but Pentecostalism was quickly robbed of its "moment" and its prophetic stance as the institution became more entrenched in the culture.

From a sociological perspective, Poloma makes several observations that are relevant to the rhetoric surrounding women in Pentecostalism. First, there is a disjunction between what is promoted as "ideal" and what is "real." In other words, the movement promotes the ideal of equality in gender roles but in reality, this ideal is far from what is actually lived out.[46] Second, Poloma argues that the discrepancy between what is real and ideal was minimized in early Pentecostalism, and finally, she observes that the conjunction between what is ideal and what is real was promoted by a prophetic message found in Acts 2. Revivals mark a time of urgency; a job needs to be done regardless of gender roles. The intensity and urgency of this message diminished as Pentecostalism took on a more institutional form. As the message diminished, a greater disconnect between male and female roles emerged, and the male-dominated culture took over.[47] When asked what factor contributed most to the challenges that women have faced in the Assemblies of God, General Superintendent George O. Wood replied, "Culture. We tended to succumb to the prevailing culture."[48]

44. Poloma, "Charisma, Institutional and Social Change," 245.
45. Ibid., 245.
46. Ibid., 247.
47. Ibid.
48. Wood, discussion with the author, 2007.

In an earlier study, Poloma observed:

> The very success of the Assemblies has paradoxically made it
> more difficult for charisma to flow—particularly should the
> Spirit choose to rest on women. The countercultural mental-
> ity of the early Pentecostal, which allowed them to be open to
> women in ministry, has been replaced with an embracement of
> a certain segment of culture and a rejection of another. . . . this
> marriage . . . is moving the Assemblies of God away from its
> historical ambivalence toward women in ministry and toward
> silencing its prophetic daughters.[49]

I contend that while Poloma's finding of institutionalization is a key factor
in the discrepancies over the role of women, the root of both her findings
and the challenges presented by Blumhofer and others is in how the issue
has been communicated. The rhetoric of early Pentecostals created the dichotomy between policy and praxis that still exists today. The ability for the
movement to institutionalize and to embrace a more culturally acceptable
position for women and ministry is rooted in its rhetorical history.

The Assemblies of God stands today at a critical moment in which the
role of women in ministry is again at the forefront of denominational policy
and discourse; how it handles the situation rhetorically will help determine
whether the dissonance felt by women who are currently serving or considering service in ministry will continue or the counter-cultural revolution of the
past will be redeemed. Therefore, the significance of this book goes beyond
describing the historic place of the Assemblies of God and the greater Pentecostal movement and seeks a new rhetoric surrounding the role of women in
Pentecostal ministry for the present and into the future.

### Previous Scholarship on Women and Religious Identity

In addition to Poloma's studies, some secular rhetorical scholarship addresses the role of women in the church and the religious life of Americans.
These studies are useful for laying the ground of precedent and for providing additional historical data on the role women have played in American
religious life regardless of denominational or doctrinal background.

Literary scholar Elaine Lawless has done a substantial amount of
writing on women in Pentecostal circles with a specific emphasis on their
folk stories as means of religious participation.[50] Several book reviews by

49. Poloma, *Assemblies of God at the Crossroads*, 119.
50. Lawless, *Handmaidens of the Lord*, 61–75; Lawless, *God's Peculiar People*.

rhetorical scholars also touch on the subject of women as pastors or religious leaders including reviews of Lawless's ethnographic study of Pentecostal women preachers in mid-Missouri as well as others who examine the history of women's religious rhetoric in colonial America and in the Quaker tradition.[51] Rhetoric scholar Michael Casey studied some of the earliest women speakers in America (1630–1840). His study focused on what he states are four primitivist beliefs that prompted women to step outside their cultural sphere and speak in public. These beliefs include the prophetic persona, biblical precedent, oppressive practices such as patriarchy and racism (a cause to fight against), and the establishment of a particular vernacular that placed an emphasis on orality rather than literate preaching.[52] Certainly, Casey's work is a foundation piece that contributes to similar arguments made by Pentecostal women nearly a century later. Sharon Chambers-Gordon examines the folk culture and oral traditions of Pentecostal women through an ethnographic study of women's liberation in a Jamaican Pentecostal/Revivalist church. Very similar to the studies conducted by Lawless, Chambers-Gordon's work uses the Pentecostal church as her backdrop to study women's liberation through oral tradition and the feminine network.[53]

The practices of the Pentecostal movement and the Assemblies of God are uniquely centered around tensions between their assumptions about humanity's ability to experience God versus a history of restorationism, revivalism, anti-elitism, and counterculturalism unique to the tradition. Historian Nathan Hatch has noted that the strength of evangelical movements has been in their identification with people and their passion about communicating their message.[54] Pentecostalism is democratic in structure and spirit and therefore belongs to the people rather than to the .powerful Pentecostals tend to measure the importance of an issue by its popular reception or the adequacy of a method by the number of people it attracts; therefore, they place a greater value on the quantity of the response rather than on the quality of the message.

The focus of my work revolves around this tension and how women have worked through it to create and maintain rhetorical space in spite of the dissonance. The role of women in the Assemblies of God is centered in the pull between what is popular and what is possible. The tension exists in

---

51. Larson, *Daughters of the Light*; and Brekus, *Strangers and Pilgrims*; both reviewed by Campbell, "Book Review," 194–98.

52. Casey, "First Female Speakers in America (1630–1840)," 1–28.

53. Chambers-Gordon, "'Liberated in the Spirit,'" 52–56.

54. Hatch, *Democratization of American*, 214–19.

the rhetoric of the Assemblies of God and its prophesying daughters past, present, and future.

While scholarly research in the area of Pentecostalism is increasing, many areas remain untapped. One significant untapped area is in the rhetoric of the tradition. Challenges are created, shaped, reinforced and naturalized by how people in the early days of the Pentecostal movement talked about them and by how present-day members of the Assemblies of God talk. Pentecostal rhetoric has demonstrated the following results:

- It has created dissonance with regard to the role of women in leadership positions.

- It has damaged the ability of the movement to continue as the vanguard of restorationism.

- It has created a mistrust within its own organizations as well as in the greater culture it is trying to reach with its message.

Rhetorical history is a clarifying lens for describing and assessing actors, events, and cultures within the Pentecostal movement generally and the Assemblies of God specifically as they wrestled to shape their theology and witness in the American religious landscape. Rhetorical history concerns itself with the role of persuasion and looks closely at people engaged as actors of persuasion. Examining specific discourse and utilizing textual analyses of letters, personal papers, speeches and archival material in primary source collections reveals evidence of motives, methods, beliefs and values. Rhetorical history assesses the theological and cultural legacies of those who have led in Pentecostalism as well as those who have found a way to navigate the tensions to create rhetorical space for women who desire to participate in the work of spreading the Pentecostal message.[55]

## RHETORICAL HISTORY

What is rhetorical history and how do we evaluate it? To answer this question, we must first grapple with the question, "What is rhetoric?" Aristotle defined rhetoric as "the faculty wherein one discovers the available means of persuasion in any case whatsoever."[56] This definition does not imply that

55. Much of my research in rhetorical history has yielded studies that focused on political figures or situations, but I believe the nature of a movement like Pentecostalism shares many aspects of its rhetoric with those in the political world. I found Steven R. Goldzwig's arguments on rhetorical history significant in developing my own engagement with rhetorical history. See Goldzwig, "Civil Rights and the Cold War," 144.

56. Aristotle, *On Rhetoric*, 36.

a rhetorician will persuade all people all the time. Rather, it means that rhetoricians understand and use available means of persuasion in their given circumstances.

Aristotle stresses that rhetoric is closely related to dialectic, which is defined as discussion and reasoning by dialogue as a means of intellectual investigation.[57] The relationship between rhetoric and dialectic manifests itself in a number of ways: rhetoric is the counterpart to dialectic, rhetoric is an outgrowth of dialectic and the study of character, and rhetoric is a part of dialectic and resembles it. For Aristotle, rhetoric must be grounded, through investigation, on what is persuasive and what is not. So while rhetoric is not limited to a specific subject it is a legitimate artistic pursuit.[58]

Rhetoric in the Aristotelian tradition deals with arguments from accepted premises, but persuasion is not only about arguments and proofs, but about credibility and emotional attitudes. The three sources of persuasion that fall within the art of rhetoric are the character of the speaker (ethos), the disposition of the audience toward the speaker and the matter at hand (pathos) and the speech itself (logos). Epistemologically, Aristotle held that good rhetoric is based on objective truth and includes "what happens usually." Opinions on what is probable tend to be right on the mark as rhetoric is the same faculty that allows one to grasp what is merely apparent as to grasp what is true.[59]

Rhetorician Kenneth Burke expanded the understanding of Aristotle's definition to the broader category of "symbolic action." Burke shifted the focus of rhetoric from persuasion and highlighted the psychological component of rhetoric by concentrating on the analysis of motive. He notes that people assess the human situation and shape appropriate attitudes by constructing their concepts of the world around them. By starting with humans as they react symbolically to their environment, Burke arrives at the basic function of rhetoric "the use of words by human agents to form attitudes or actions in other human agents."[60] In other words, rhetorical action is one person trying to get another person to behave, feel, or think differently. Rhetorical practice is neither mystical nor scientific, but rather artistic, part of the human drama generated by language that is both recurrent and continually being reborn.

Burke attributes the following characteristics to human beings:

57. Merriam-Webster Online Dictionary, "Dialectic." http://www.merriam-webster.com/ dictionary/dialectic.

58. Conley, *Rhetoric in the European Tradition*, 14.

59. Ibid., 16.

60. Burke, *Rhetoric of Motives*, 41.

- symbol using,

- symbol making,

- symbol misusing,

- the inventor of the negative,

- separated from their natural condition by instruments
  of their own making,

- goaded by spirit of hierarchy, and

- rotten with perfection.[61]

Burke describes human society as a dramatic process that includes the elements of hierarchy, acceptance and rejection, and the experiences of guilt, purification and redemption. Hierarchy generates the structure of society. Power endows people with authority. Authority, in turn, establishes relationships among people that reflect the power they possess. As people accept their role and the hierarchical structure, bureaucracy is formed and with it comes order in society.[62]

Acceptance and rejection is another element of Burke's dramatic society. Burke's theory of rhetoric is rooted in humanity's propensity to accept or reject their situation and their attempts to symbolize these reactions. The negative, which is not inherent in nature, results from language or the separation of a symbol from what it represents. Language enables people to accept or reject their position within the hierarchy or even the hierarchy itself. According to rhetoric scholar Bernard L. Brock, "Acceptance results in satisfaction and order, whereas rejections results in alienation and disorder."[63]

The concepts of guilt, purification, and redemption complete the dramatic process and represent the effects of the acceptance and rejection of hierarchy. When hierarchy is rejected, guilt is felt. In every social institution, such as family, religion, or politics, hierarchy emerges, and when two of these hierarchies conflict, one will be rejected. Because humans cannot prevent this conflict, Burke believes that we are saddled with perpetual guilt.[64]

Guilt sets off a psychological reaction: it reduces social connections and makes people feel fragmented, so they strive for redemption from guilt. Purification, Burke says, comes through mortification and/or victimization. Mortification is an act of self-sacrifice that relieves guilt, while victimization

61. Burke, *Language as Symbolic Action*, 16.
62. Burke, *Permanence and Change*, 282.
63. Brock, "Rhetorical Criticism," 185.
64. Burke, *Permanence and Change*, 284.

purges guilt through the use of a scapegoat. The process of purification must equal the degree of guilt if one is to receive redemption.[65]

Central to understanding persuasion or other communicative acts is another key component of Burke's philosophy: the concept of identification or consubstantiality. He argues that interests or perceived interests join one person with another.[66] Speakers, whose attitudes are reflected in their language, will accept some ideas, people, and institutions and reject others; the audience will to some extent both agree and disagree. To the extent that audiences accept and reject the same ideas, people, and institutions, identification occurs. Identification is the critic's key to understanding the speakers' attitudes and the dramatic process.[67]

In answering the question, "what are people doing and why are they doing it?" Burke introduces what he calls the dramatistic pentad as a means of understanding the many layers of symbolic action. While some disagreement exists about the nature of the elements of the pentad as well as what they represent, a simple explanation for this study answers five questions: what took place in thought or deed (act), when or where was it done (scene), who did it (agent), how did they do it (agency) and why (purpose).[68] These terms are key to assigning human motives because motives, as Burke states, "arise out of them and terminate in them."[69] The pentad (act, scene, agent, agency, and purpose) along with the notions of identification and the inherently dramatic nature of society provides a vocabulary and theoretical structure that allows the critic to describe humans as they respond to their world.

Using Burke's pentad, we can easily see that women like Mae Eleanor Frey were and continue to be agents who desire to act by spreading the gospel in the context of ordained ministry wherever and whenever possible through preaching the Gospel for the purpose of winning the hearts and minds of "the lost" to their message regarding "the saving knowledge of Jesus Christ." To listen to their male counterparts argue over the matter creates a rhetorical tension that challenges women's identification with men as ministers and vice versa. I believe that applying Burke's theory of identification is central to our understanding both the urgency of the Pentecostal message and the tensions created by those attempting to share that message.

65. Brock, "Rhetorical Criticism," 186.
66. Burke, *Language as Symbolic Action*, 20–21.
67. Brock, "Rhetorical Criticism," 187.
68. Burke, *Grammar of Motives*, xv.
69. Ibid., xv–xvi.

Rhetorician Barry Brummett addresses another aspect of rhetorical inquiry by stressing the social dimensions and the functions of rhetoric, which are important to this argument. Brummett argues that rhetoric needs to be seen as the "social function that influences and manages meaning."[70] Rhetoric is not, in Brummett's eyes, merely an object or an act, such as giving a speech, writing an essay, or choosing a metaphor, but rather, framed within the social context and culture, rhetoric is the management of meaning and is just one dimension of countless acts and objects that make up a cultural environment. These acts are nothing more than manifestations created by people, which in turn express social identities and create values.[71]

Rhetorical scholar Lloyd Bitzer argues that the questions that typically trigger theories of rhetoric focus on the method of discourse or the discourse itself, rather than on the situation that "invites the orator's application of his method and the creation of discourse."[72] He asserts that rhetorical works obtain their character from the circumstances of the historic context in which they occur. So powerful is *situation* that it could be considered the very foundation for rhetorical activity. To say that rhetoric is situational, according to Bitzer, means:

1. rhetorical discourse comes into existence as response to a situation;

2. a speech is given rhetorical significance by the situation;

3. a rhetorical situation must exist as a necessary condition of rhetorical discourse;

4. many rhetorical situations mature and decay without giving birth to rhetorical utterances;

5. a situation is rhetorical as it needs and invites discourse capable of participating with situation and thereby altering its reality;

6. discourse is rhetorical as it functions as a fitting response to a situation that needs and invites it; and

7. the situation controls the rhetorical response.[73] It is not the rhetor and not the persuasive intent, but the situation that is the source of rhetorical criticism.

Rhetorical situation, then, may be defined as a complex of persons, events, objects, and relations in which speakers or writers create rhetorical

---

70. Brummett, *Rhetorical Dimensions of Popular Culture*, xii.

71. Ibid., 38.

72. Bitzer, "Rhetorical Situation," 2.

73. Ibid., 5–6.

discourse. Prior to the creation and presentation of discourse, Bitzer, requires three constituents of any rhetorical situation: exigence, audience and constraints. The exigence is an "imperfection marked by urgency" or something needing to be done. An exigence is rhetorical when it can be positively modified or assisted by discourse.[74]

Rhetoric always requires an audience. A rhetorical audience, according to Bitzer, "consists of only those persons who are capable of being influenced by discourse and of being mediators for change." [75] In addition to exigence and audience, every rhetorical situation comes with a complex system of people, events, objects and relations that have the power to constrain a decision or an action. Constraints can include beliefs, attitudes, policy, traditions and other motives. These constraints fall into two categories: Similar to Aristotle's artistic and inartistic proofs, Bitzer's constraints are those created or managed by the rhetor and those that are situational. Bitzer argues that the world presents "imperfections to be modified by means of discourse"—opportunities for rhetorical investigation.[76] Rhetoric is, then, not merely the craft of persuasion but a legitimate means of inquiry.

These rhetorical theories are directly linked to our investigation of the role of women in the ranks of Pentecostals. The holiness and later Pentecostal revivals created an exigency or a sense of urgency: to spread the discourse of Jesus as Savior, Baptizer, Healer and soon-coming King. This sense of urgency created a space for women and provided empowerment for service. However, within their gatherings was an audience bound by varying constraints of what ministry looked like and who could legitimately present the discourse. These constraints are central to this study and play a significant role in the social construction of Pentecostal culture and discourse.

A more fundamental theological exigence appears in the Pentecostal movement. The tension between radicalism and conservatism is an ongoing exigence that also needed to be negotiated and renegotiated. The result is a constant and very fundamental "imperfection" that exists almost inherently among core denominational distinctives and in the larger movement that requires a continual rhetorical effort to engage—whether to ameliorate the imperfections or to strategically amplify the imperfections so as to increase pressure for some sort of social or theological change. This tension is central to Pentecostalism's relationship with the larger evangelical community as well as to American religious culture.

74. Ibid., 7.
75. Ibid., 8.
76. Ibid., 14.

In order to examine fully the constraints and social construction of Pentecostal discourse, the rhetorical critic must reconstruct the goals, strategies, and vision of the tradition through a careful study of the surviving artifacts of the participants. As David Zarefsky argues:

> What distinguishes the rhetorical historian is not subject matter but perspective. The economic historian might view human conduct from the perspective of the market, the political historian from the mobilization of interest and power, the intellectual historian from the standpoint of the evolution of ideas and the rhetorical historian from the perspective of how messages are created and used by people to influence and relate to one another.[77]

By engaging in this perspective, this study provides an insight into how the adherents to the Pentecostal movement and the founding fathers and mothers of the Assemblies of God used rhetoric to both open a space for women as active participants in ministry while at the same time creating a dissonance by the dichotomy of policy and practice. The delicate dance between those who favor a greater role for women and those who favor a more traditional approach to women's involvement is inherently rhetorical. Rhetors, including ministers at the local level as well as denominational officials, used rhetoric to ameliorate the theological tensions in the Assemblies of God by closing and/or preempting those same spaces.

It is time to put down the mirror of reflection and engage the rhetorical situation so as to see what has been, what is, and what can be. The rhetorical historian has the same subject matter as any other historian, but the perspective focuses not on facts and figures, but on the messages created by early Pentecostals and used by them to both influence and relate to one another.

As a historian approaching texts from this perspective, I seek to view history as a series of rhetorical problems that call for public persuasion to advance a cause or overcome some impasse. How and how well did people in these rhetorical situations invent and deploy messages in response to the situation? Zarefsky argues that studies of this type may offer a powerful answer to the elusive "so what?" question. "By studying important historical events from a rhetorical perspective, one can see significant aspects about those events that other perspectives miss."[78]

---

77. Zarefsky, "Four Senses of Rhetorical History," 30.
78. Ibid., 30.

## Pentecostal Rhetorical Invention

If perspective plays a crucial role in examining rhetorical history, then it is important to identify principles of rhetorical invention inherent to Pentecostal thinking and in turn, Pentecostal talk. Rhetorician Martin J. Medhurst, himself the product of a Pentecostal upbringing, has identified a set of rhetorical principles that represent the life and teachings of the Assemblies of God.

As with Pentecostal theology, Medhurst argues that Pentecostal rhetoric is also informed by experience and thus these experiences and beliefs affect the way Pentecostals communicate. While Pentecostals share a common adherence to doctrines such as creation, fall, and redemption, they have also created a self-identity and public personae through a system of interrelated enthymemes and examples. In enthymematic form, Medhurst presents five premises:

- First, God is in control, for in Rom 8:28 "all things work together for good to them that love God, to them who are called according to the will of God."

- Second, pray without ceasing as 1 Thess 5:17 says "this is the will of God in Christ Jesus concerning you."

- Third, expect a miracle for in Isa 53:5 we are told that "by his stripes we are healed."

- Fourth, trust and obey as is stated in Heb 11:6 "without faith it is impossible to please Him."

- Finally, work, for in John 9:4 the scripture tells us that "the night cometh, when no man can work."[79]

Notably, in each instance a quote from Scripture appears. This reference is necessary as the Bible is the authorizing agent of the Pentecostal worldview and is guaranteed by God. Medhurst argues that these premises are inexorably linked and because Pentecostals live in the constant expectation that God will act in history, even from outside the norm of everyday experiences. Pentecostals live with a constant awareness of God's presence and power, and it shapes the way they think and approach everything. No matter what the situation, God can change it.[80]

The primary task for the Pentecostal is to trust and obey. This attitude includes an unfettered trust in the Bible as the inspired word of God. It is

79. Medhurst, "Filled With the Spirit," 565.
80. Ibid., 567.

not only the grand narrative of salvation, but it also offers specific promises to mankind from God. Pentecostals are also taught to trust and obey those in authority including the local pastor. Because God ordains this authority, one risks relationship with the divine by questioning or disobeying the pastor's instruction.

The fulfillment of obedience is found in the fifth premise: work. More than anything, the Pentecostal is admonished to work. Pentecostals from the earliest days of the tradition were to be about the Father's business and use all of the available means of persuasion to spread God's Word before it is too late. Medhurst argues that a sense of urgency pervades all Pentecostals' works. Time is running out and the work must be done before it is too late.[81]

The first act of rhetorical invention is to invent the Self. Medhurst affirms Kenneth Burke's contention that we invent language and the negative and they in turn invent us. This formation takes place over many years and establishes a worldview with a set of assumptions, beliefs and expectations. The worldview guides not only thought but also problem-solving. How we think about things and the motives that lead us to embrace them are critical to the invention of Self and the way we will engage in rhetorical practice.

I cannot deny that these five areas of Pentecostal rhetorical invention are central to my own worldview and rhetorical practice. I come to this work because I too have been trained in this tradition to view the world. I am drawn to the rhetoric of the Assemblies of God because it has played such a direct role in shaping my own ideology and identity.

Interest in this subject grew out of my experiences as a fourth-generation member of the Assemblies of God and my undergraduate education at an Assemblies of God University. Raised in a small Assemblies of God church in Crosby, North Dakota, I often looked at the portrait of Blanche Brittain, the itinerant pastor who set up a tent in my hometown in 1925, but knew nothing of her experience in pioneering a movement that would birth a General Superintendent out of my very own congregation.[82] I saw many family members, both men and women, enter the ministry as pastors and evangelists and knew nothing of the challenges to their calling by others within our own ranks.

Not until I entered an Assemblies of God institution of higher learning was I challenged to discover that women were not so readily accepted within the ministry of the church. There, I was educated in our history and doctrine more than I had been in any Sunday school classroom. The haunting realization that a chasm within our fellowship existed not in policy, but

81. Ibid., 568.

82. Rodgers, *Northern Harvest*, 119.

in practice, never left me. The voices of our fellowship's foremothers had to be heard, and I was convinced that the chasm of this dichotomy was rooted in the rhetoric of our tradition, not simply in our doctrine.

Finally, the Assemblies of God is my ecclesiastical home, by choice, not simply by birth. The Assemblies of God is not just where I attend worship services; the Assemblies of God has made me who I am. This book provides me the opportunity to analyze my tradition both sympathetically and critically. Finally, it allows me the ability to advocate for Pentecostals and help them move toward a new rhetoric of women in ministry for the future.

While numerous histories have been written (both those sanctioned and unsanctioned) and some have made the argument of the unique contribution of women, no one has argued for women as urgently as General Superintendent George O. Wood. At a gathering of Assemblies of God women ministers, Wood made the claim that the role of women in the Assemblies of God is as distinctive as the Assemblies' doctrine of pneumatology.[83] If the role of women is as unique as the distinctive doctrine of speaking in tongues then more focused study on the subject is warranted.

## *Problem*

Multiple challenges exist with regard to women in the Assemblies of God. First, many current members perceive that a "Golden Age" once existed for women in ministry as Charles Barfoot and Gerald Sheppard describe in their serminal article "Prophetic vs. Priestly Religion: The Changing Role of Women Clergy in Pentecostal Churches."[84] While the numbers of women, per capita, serving in the fellowship may have been greater in the formative years of the movement, contradictions in message still existed regarding their role, abilities, and freedom to function within the organization.

The tradition of the Pentecostal movement and the Assemblies of God is full of multiple narratives and competing messages, which produce the second challenge facing women: The nature of the organization itself. The lack of a strong central organization makes the Assemblies of God unique within the greater Pentecostal tradition and allows for dissonance between the theological and cultural practices of the organization.

Third, the culture in which the Assemblies of God exists also provides challenges to the role(s) of women. The Assemblies of God is relatively young in the story of American religion and has entered into a not undisputed alliance with Evangelicals. Even more so than within the Pentecostal

83. Wood, "Everything We Ever Wanted to Know."
84. Barfoot and Sheppard, "Prophetic vs. Priestly Religion," 2–17.

tradition, the Evangelical movement has a long history of rejecting women in roles of leadership, specifically leadership outside the domestic sphere and especially within the church. How the Assemblies of God has functioned and continues to function within the greater Evangelical community demands our attention.

Finally, as Poloma has noted, the Assemblies of God and the Pentecostal movement as a whole was at one time a counter-cultural social movement that challenged the notions of the secular culture as much as that of the religious culture. What role did the rise of secular social movements such as modern feminism and the "religious right" play in creating a reaction to women's roles within the church?

Blumhofer warns scholars not to seek a single narrative, so this book searches the Pentecostal rhetorical cacophony to tease out rhetoric focused on the role of women. In spite of the varieties of narrative, a unified voice emerges, that of women who have experienced both a distinct call to ministry and an empowerment for service via the theology of the Assemblies of God. This voice is not demanding a chance to rule, but rather, in the words of Beth Grant, National Chairperson of the Assemblies of God Network for Women in Ministry, it urges opportunities for women to take responsibility for their calling and to be poured out in their service to God.[85]

The story of Pentecostalism and the story of the Assemblies of God is a story of the discontented. It is the story of those who are dissatisfied with the way religion and the world in general is working. When people believe that the future will be different, their perception about the present changes.[86] The narrative of the Pentecostal movement is about concrete personal experience not abstract religious ideas. As Harvey Cox was examining Pentecostals at the close of the last century, he noted that it should come as no surprise that in a time of social and cultural disarray, Pentecostalism is burgeoning nearly everywhere in the world. We are again at an uncertain turning point in history.

Since the tragedy of September 11, 2001 brought global terrorism to the forefront and the world back to war, with the potential for nuclear proliferation and the fear of the power of a rogue leader in turning the political and social tides, we are once again at a time when religion and religious fervor are being examined. We live again in a time when the social and cultural fabric appears to be in disarray.

With so many other seemingly more "important" social and cultural issues, why study the role of women in an organization that has become

85. Grant, "Celebration and Commitment to Community."
86. Cox, *Fire from Heaven*, 15.

more mainstream and more mainline than its radical inception? Who cares what is happening in the Assemblies of God or what role women play in the ministry of the Gospel of Jesus within a Pentecostal tradition?

First, like the movement itself, women within the greater Pentecostal movement, and the Assemblies of God specifically, operated in a capacity that blew apart the culture of their day, yet their language sounds surprisingly familiar in the discourse concerning the role of women today. Some argued that the very fabric of the family, the foundation of society itself, would crumble because women dared to proclaim their message and live their calling. Others championed the cause of the change agents and their work to restore the church on earth, to usher in Christ's return, and to establish a New Jerusalem. Over a century after the founding of the Assemblies of God and nearly a century after women earned the right to vote in the United States, the church is still debating the place of women while the secular world promotes them to presidential candidates and mainline churches ordain them bishops.

Second, what began as a movement counter to the culture has been absorbed by the culture and the politics of today. The Pentecostal people of the Assemblies of God held positions that were radically opposed to mainstream practices in both religion and politics. Today, they are fighting for relevance amongst the competing voices of the religious right and for a place in the culture and amongst their own people who question the necessity of the movement at all. The implications of this struggle are numerous. Is the Pentecostal message still relevant in a post-modern, post-denominational culture? What should the role of the Pentecostal voice be in the public square?

Yale scholar Stephen L. Carter addresses an area significant to this question: the role of prophetic resistance. Carter argues that the prophetic religious voice, calling us to account, pointing the culture in the direction of God's will is very different from the one telling us who should be in charge. The Old Testament prophets simply presented the message of righteousness; they never had a hand in the building of kingdoms or the downfall of those who did not heed their message.[87]

The prophetic voice is inherently subversive to culture and politics. Carter argues that the church must avoid the temptation to join its authority to the authority of the state.[88] The way believers deviate from the cultural norm is the measure of religion's subversive power. The American political system is not adverse to those who are radical in their message.

87. Carter, *God's Name in Vain*, 32–39.
88. Ibid.

Rather, the American political system invites radicalism in order to tame it and refocus its energy from restructuring the culture to minor triumphs within the political system. This co-opting is only possible, however, when the radicals are willing to be co-opted. Once the decision is made to become a part of the system, the power of the prophetic is lost. As Carter declares, if you are in the business of endorsing candidates and pushing for their election, you can hardly stand outside the corridors of power and call the nation to righteousness.

I contend that the Assemblies of God is facing the choice Carter presents. By aligning the fellowship with the National Association of Evangelicals and embracing a more conservative political position, the Assemblies of God has sacrificed the prophetic nature of its message and diminished the impact of its role in the culture. What could have been an opportunity to challenge the culture on how God views women in the family, society and the church became a reaction to the culture's embracing women's roles calling it a means of subverting God's plan.

Third, what began as a small religious sect, has grown into a worldwide religious movement. While it was once a movement against the things of this world, it has become a movement very comfortable with "worldly" things like financial resources and American conveniences. What at first brought hope to social outsiders, many of those today who represent the Assemblies of God and the Pentecostal movement are amongst the wealthy and the elite. A movement that reviled the creeds of man has made room for those in the ranks to cling to what Harvey Cox calls "recently invented dogmas[89] What began with the teaching of signs and wonders not as spectacle, but of the revelation of a new era has become an obsession with predicting the future and reading the tea leaves of world events to signal the signs of the ends of the age.

The Assemblies of God was once an antagonist of the status quo and amongst her people today are the impassioned "super patriots" who have adopted nationalism as a religious creed. What once had the potential to be a radically inclusive spiritual fellowship where race and gender virtually disappeared has become today's predominantly white, middle- to upper-class adherents who are skeptical of what they view as radical feminism, multiculturalism fraught with issues of immigration, and the challenges of cultural change.

It is time to rekindle a discourse on history that is more telling about the present than it is about the past. When the Pentecostal movement broke forth and birthed the Assemblies of God, Americans were asking themselves

89. Cox, *Fire from Heaven*, 17.

who they were and who they wanted to be.[90] The rise of the Assemblies of God was not the accomplishment of the elite, but rather a gathering up of the poor and outcast, taking the despised things and seeing God glorified in them. Pentecostals did not prosper in the early twentieth century by blending into a cosmopolitan ethos. They succeeded by criticizing that ethos and suggesting alternatives.[91]

Fast-forward to the twenty-first century. While events like the Memphis Miracle—a 1994 convocation that assembled leaders from both white and black Pentecostal fellowships including the Church of God in Christ, the International Church of the Four-Square Gospel and the Assemblies of God specifically for the purpose of racial reconciliation—have tempered the issue of race among fellowships. Other contemporary voices have resisted women desiring a place in ministry and within the leadership of their church structures. The circular rhetoric of these conflicting voices is eerily similar to that which surrounded their foremothers.

## PREVIEW OF CHAPTERS

I present the following seven chapters to examine the history of women in Pentecostal ministry. First, in Chapter Two, I reconstruct the history of the Pentecostal movement and the distinct role of women within this history. In addition to the more widely accepted history, I include a discussion of arguments made by Darrin Rodgers, an Assemblies of God historian, who contends that within Scandinavian Pietism early pioneers on the Northern Plains had several encounters with the Pentecostal experience. This argument challenges the notion that Pentecostalism is a Southern import and includes a significant number of women who pioneered churches prior to and concurrent with the Azusa Street Revival. Many women who would later have significant influence in the formation and development of the Assemblies of God are more fully examined including Rachael Sizelove who first brought the news of the Los Angeles Revival to Springfield, Missouri, future home to the Assemblies of God World Headquarters; Lillie Corum, a cousin of Sizelove whose home served as the first Assemblies of God Church in Springfield; and Amanda Benedict whose year-long prayer and fasting (she drank only water and ate only bread) at the site of what is now Central Assembly of God and the adjoining Assemblies of God World Headquarters is credited with dedicating Springfield to the work of Pentecost.

90. Ibid., 32.
91. Ibid., 106.

In Chapter Three, I narrow my lens to the Assemblies of God as a specific example of the conflicting rhetoric surrounding women's roles in Pentecostal circles. I present an historical account of the formation of the Assemblies of God including the debate on the role of women in ministry at the first Hot Springs convention and the discourse of E. N. Bell, the first General Superintendent, on the issue of a woman's role in the new fellowship. I demonstrate that within these earliest documents and discourse, the rhetoric surrounding women in the Assemblies of God is established. Due to the number of women already engaged in Pentecostal ministry, women could not be simply ignored. Yet, I argue, a distinct rhetorical struggle emerges between doctrine and practice that solidifies within these very first discussions. In addition, the doctrine of the Assemblies of God, also known as The Sixteen Fundamental truths is examined. It is the theological foundation from which the Assemblies of God forms its rhetorical invention as a movement and continues to shape its distinctive doctrines including the initial physical evidence of speaking in tongues as an empowerment for service.

In Chapter Four, as the narrative moves from the formative era of the Assemblies of God and into years of sustained growth and influence. I argue that the Assemblies of God lost sight of its unique cultural and religious identity. Despite a radical beginning and a unique approach to theology, as the Assemblies of God grew and developed into an institution, strategic choices were made that sacrificed distinct elements of their unique history and ideology. These choices contributed to the tensions faced by women who desired a calling to church ministry and leadership. I examine how the idea of ministry in the Assemblies of God shifted from a prophetic position to a priestly function and as a result leaders issued a distinct call for greater male participation. I also analyze how continued centralization of power and institutionalization moved women away from the prominent role they had played during the early years of the movement. I survey shifts in the larger American culture including a stronger role for women in the workplace and the marketplace and the Assemblies of God's response to feminism. I engage previous sociological and theological scholars who argue that the Assemblies of God sacrificed its moment in time to be a catalyst for the changing role of women in the church and in American culture.

Women continued to create opportunities for service in ministry as a result of their spiritual empowerment through the experience of the baptism in the Holy Spirit. In response, the discourse on what role women could play continued to be a challenge for the leadership of the Assemblies of God. During these years of growth and influence, the challenge grew stronger as the secular world began to embrace a greater autonomy for women in the workplace and the marketplace. Despite a doctrinal stance that seems to provide carte blanche to women's leadership in the Assemblies of God, historical analysis reveals otherwise. Women in the Assemblies of God have engaged in a constant negotiation and renegotiation of their role.

In Chapter Five, my focus expands to examine the relationship of the Assemblies of God to the broader evangelical community. The issue of women in the Assemblies of God is symptomatic of greater issues at play in evangelical rhetoric. These issues include a lack of renunciation of past affiliations and historical patriarchy, a desire for greater cultural acceptance in the evangelical community, and the reaction to the secular women's movement, which was perceived as an assault on the family and traditional values. I survey how the Assemblies of God moved from the fringe of American evangelical culture to become a dominant fixture in the evangelical community and the largest denominational member of the National Association of Evangelicals. Given this shift in influence, it is also significant that challenges continue to be placed in the way of women's service in ministry both in the Assemblies of God specifically and in the evangelical community more broadly. The Assemblies of God might have had a greater influence in freeing women to serve in the ministry of the church, given the historical precedent set by women in the Pentecostal movement. However, the Assemblies of God has been molded and shaped by the standards of evangelical propriety regarding women's leadership rather than the other way around.

In Chapter Six, I focus on the most recent history of women in the Assemblies of God to the present. I continue to contend that women in Pentecostal ministry are central to the tradition's theological practice. I argue that changes in leadership, specifically George Wood's election to the office of General Superintendent of the Assemblies of God, signals a change in rhetorical practice with regard to the role of women in ministry. I also examine the implications of the adoption of a resolution at the 2007 General Council in Indianapolis, Indiana, to appoint one woman and one minister under the age of forty to the Executive Presbytery and how Wood's decision to include auditors in these meetings prior to the resolution taking effect in 2009 created a culture shift within the leadership of the Assemblies of God.

I chronicle the creation and implementation of the Network of Women Ministers, the first officially endorsed and funded department within the Assemblies of God organization to focus specifically on the support and promotion of women in all areas of the Assemblies of God. I have surveyed the rhetoric of this "network" and how they are engaging in discourse that will shape and reinforce the development of an entirely new generation of Assemblies of God churches and women serving in vocational ministry. I also note areas where weakness in the rhetoric still exists and the implications of these weaknesses in providing full acceptance of women as equal participants in ministry.

Finally, in Chapter Seven, I conclude with a summary of this history, its significance and implications for future research. I argue that the rhetorical invention of the Assemblies of God created a dynamic movement and a unique role for women to serve in places of ministry; however, it also brought equal frustration and disappointment to those who embraced their Pentecostal calling but were met with closed doors and insecurity from their male and even sometimes their female counterparts. However, I also argue that the renewed focus on women in the Assemblies of God is creating an opportunity for the development of a new rhetoric, which if the lessons of the past are learned well will create new spaces for women with more open doors and a renewed sense of calling and purpose not only in the Assemblies but across the Pentecostal movement.

## CONCLUSION

Early Pentecostal evangelists traveled from outpost to outpost by rail. Credential holders would apply for reduced clergy rates, which made constant travel more financially feasible. In the May 29, 1915, issue of the *Weekly Evangel*, a publication of the newly formed Assemblies of God, Executive Presbyter H. A. Goss instructed that women credentialed at any level domestically within the Assemblies of God, not apply for railroad clergy rates unless they receive a guaranteed salary. The Clergy Bureau would turn down their request and these women would lose the one-dollar application fee. Goss continues, "Let the women take notice of this, and trust God for full fare. This does not apply to men why [sic] are properly ordained nor to foreign women missionaries." [92]

Women are a defining force in the Pentecostal movement. The unique role that women have played and continue to play is one of both great mystery and great frustration. How women and the men that have supported their position have negotiated and renegotiated their opportunity for service makes for fascinating rhetorical, historical, and theological study. The rhetoric of these saints speaks not only to the Pentecostal movement or the Assemblies of God, but also mirrors the challenges facing the entire evangelical community. If the church is going to continue to play a prophetic role within the culture, it must understand and address the issues raised in this book.

92. Goss, "Notice to Women Missionaries," 2.

While Mae Eleanor Frey was never officially granted a credential from the Assemblies of God to pastor, she did hold a temporary pastorate in 1937 at age 72 before returning full time to evangelistic work. In 1944, J. Roswell Flower apologized to Mrs. Frey for suggesting that she should join the "superannuated" list of retired ministers.[93] Frey pointed out that she had enough engagements to keep her busy until 1948. "Mercy!" she cried, "Wait until I am dead, but not while I am alive."[94] At age 80 she was still contributing to the "aged minister's fund" from which she had every right to be benefiting. Flower responded to her yearly contribution by noting that his own mother who was similar in age could not have kept her pace.[95] Mae Eleanor Frey continued to preach the gospel until she retired from this life to her heavenly reward on December 4, 1954.[96]

Mae Eleanor Frey embraced the call of Howard Goss and trusted the Lord for full fare throughout her ministry career and was not sidelined by either the policy or the practice of the fellowship she revered. In one of her final letters to J. Roswell Flower she states, "It is wonderful to be alive in these days and being able to spread the gospel of good news. Pentecost is the grand message for these days of unrest, doubt, and fear."[97] This book is for Mae Eleanor Frey and the generations of women who have come after her who still believe that Pentecost is the grand message for these days of unrest, doubt and fear.

93. J. R. Flower to Mae Eleanor Frey, September 5, 1944.

94. Mae Eleanor Frey to J. R. Flower, September 11, 1944.

95. J. R. Flower to Mae Eleanor Frey, May 15, 1945; J. R. Flower to Mae Eleanor Frey, September 14, 1950.

96. M. E. Frey Deceased Ministers File.

97. Mae Eleanor Frey to J. Roswell Flower, August 28, 1950.

# 2

# The Touch Felt "Round the World"

## Pentecostal Rhetorical Invention
## and the Female Voice

*The promise of the Father has either been fulfilled, or has not. . . . "And it shall come to pass, after those days, that I will pour out my Spirit upon all flesh, and your sons and your daughters shall prophesy." And did one of that waiting company wait in vain; or did the cloven tongue of fire appear to all, and sit upon each waiting disciple, irrespective of sex? Surely this was that spoken of by the prophet Joel; and thus has the Holy Spirit expressly declared, through Peter. The dispensation of the Spirit was now entered upon. . . . Male and female were now one in Jesus Christ. The Spirit now descended alike on all. And they were all filled with the Holy Ghost, and began to speak as the Spirit gave utterance.*[1]

—Phoebe Palmer, journal entry, 1856

LATE INTO THE NIGHT on January 1, 1901, after sustained hours of prayer, Bible school student Agnes Ozman was suddenly overcome and began to speak in an unknown tongue. This language was neither her native tongue, nor a language she had been educated to speak. A student of former

1. Wheatley, *Life and Letters of Mrs. Phoebe Palmer*, 496–97.

40

Methodist pastor and teacher Charles Fox Parham, Ms. Ozman received the startling manifestation of the gift of tongues and in an instant became the first official Pentecostal of the twentieth century.[2]

According to J. Roswell Flower, founding secretary of the Assemblies of God, Ozman's experience was the "touch felt 'round the world."[3] What seems like an unlikely event to overshadow the entry of a new year and a new century, this seemingly insignificant experience triggered the formation of the world-wide Pentecostal movement: one of the most successful and fastest-growing religious movements in history.

To begin the story of the Pentecostal movement in this moment, however, would negate a complex history. Since the day of Pentecost recorded in the book of Acts, mysterious and mystical signs of Holy Spirit manifestations have been recorded. While some were lost to time and others dismissed as heresy, these outpourings of spiritual gifts created touch points that gave the modern Pentecostal movement voice. In addition to the mystical nature of what we now identify as Pentecostalism, another significant feature in the history of the person and work of the Holy Spirit on earth emerges: the role of women in receiving and sharing these gifts.

## The Significant Rhetoric of Pentecostal Women

Several historical and theological accounts record the history of the modern Pentecostal movement and many note the unique role women played in its formation and propagation. The scholarly conversation, however, lacks a deeper discussion of the constraints and opportunities that allowed women to create rhetorical space and walk freely in their newfound voice. As women stepped into this rhetorical space, the same arguments from Scripture that had been used to silence women could now be used to justify their speech. This twist is significant for a number of reasons. First, over the course of thousands of years, the church had perpetuated a belief that women had little or no role to play in the sharing of the gospel or leading religious congregations and movements. While women were welcomed into salvation, their roles were limited and their significance downplayed in the recorded history. Second, the adherents to the Pentecostal movement emerged as people who rejected what they believed to be a dead or dying religious culture and, therefore, set themselves apart from the practices of traditional Christian religion. Finally, the level of participation by women in both occupying and perpetuating the movement is continually noted in Pentecostal

2. Synan, *Century of the Holy Spirit*, 1.
3. Ibid.

histories and oral traditions, but the elements in this particular movement that created more rhetorical space for its female participants and more opportunities for their emergence as leaders and influencers of the movement have not been fully explored. Both the opportunities and constraints that women in the Pentecostal movement faced are inherently rhetorical and are rooted in the way people within the movement and the church used language and symbols to create and define their rhetorical space.

The known historical record supports the argument that women played a significant role in the formation of the Pentecostal movement. Female voices define Pentecostalism in a distinctive way, not by the number of women present or the leadership positions they held, but rather by the way their rhetorical presences transformed how the church communicates its message. They used the rhetoric of Pentecostal belief to persuade others to embrace the Pentecostal experience. Not only is their message a new paradigm of religious engagement, but also it creates rhetorical space for the female voice as a significant change in the religious landscape. The unique nature and significance of women's participation and leadership in the Pentecostal movement went beyond garnering women a seat at the table. It reconceptualized who God is and how we approach the work of the church in our culture. It quietly subverted centuries of religious identity and ideology. Historian Grant Wacker notes the disproportionate role of women in the early days of the movement while addressing the conflicting pressures faced by women from the movement's inception. Wacker contends that the question simply remains, "why?" The answer is found in the discourse of the movement itself, in the voices of women who participated in it, and in those who challenged their involvement. Language played a central role in shaping a place for women and forming a context in which people think about their role. What opportunities opened the door to feminine voices and what were the constraints that moved and closed these same doors? How did women engage and respond to these opportunities and constraints and what can we learn from them?

Wacker describes a period of powerful symbol formation that allowed Pentecostals to conceptualize their theology and practice their faith. Early Pentecostals set in motion ideas, practices, and institutions that lasted long after their own passing and created a system of rhetorical invention that continues to define discourse in American religion today. Pentecostals and their distinctive understanding of the human encounter with the divine included not only "primitivist" responses, defined as a desire to return to the fundamental or first things, but also a yearning to be guided only by God's Spirit in new ways. Pentecostal pragmatism also created space for those whom mainstream religious culture had not embraced as mouthpieces for spreading their message. Women used and were used by these symbols to engage and interpret Pentecostal theology, practice it authentically, and try to do proper justice to the symbolic as they argued for a place in public and religious life.

This chapter introduces and explains Kenneth Burke's concept of "scene" as an interpretive framework for the rhetoric of women in the Pentecostal movement and in the formation of the Assemblies of God. It engages the historical account of the Pentecostal movement by exploring its roots in Wesleyan theology and the influence of Susanna Wesley on her son's ministry philosophy and practice. Revivalist reform movements created a language of holiness, which empowered both men and women for religious service. The chapter also explores the influence of modernist epistemology and how the crisis of the American Civil War created opportunity for a new language of religious engagement. Finally, this chapter introduces the people and rhetorical forces that converged to unleash the Azusa Street Revival, launch Pentecostalism as a new religious force, and shift the religious landscape. Along the way, it highlights the narratives of several key women who, at each juncture in the development of the Pentecostal paradigm, defined and advocated for the unique rhetorical opportunities of women and navigated through the constraints that were equally as forceful as the movement itself.

## SETTING THE SYMBOLIC SCENE

To understand symbol formation and the ensuing rhetorical invention employed by Pentecostals and their power to create, shape, and reinforce ideas, attitudes and beliefs, we must first understand symbol in the Burkean sense. The symbol is a medium for exchanging ideas. It is anything that stands for or indicates something else. According to Zarefsky, symbols serve three purposes: they define a situation, they shape our response to the situation, and they make possible our interaction and communication with others.[4] Selecting symbols to indicate a situation helps define what that situation means. We make sense of the world by creating symbol systems that define and explain it. If rhetoric is the study of public persuasion, then it is also the study of how symbols influence people.

Zarefsky argues that rhetoric involves the selection of symbols that evoke support or opposition by virtue of prior experience and belief. Symbolic choices do not occur in a vacuum but are the result of perspectives and worldviews fashioned through our relationships and interactions. Zarefsky

---

4. Zarefsky, *President Johnson's War on Poverty*, 3.

also contends that symbol systems created by a community are constantly tested and modified through social interactions, and definitions that do not square with experience can be modified or rejected. Rhetoricians also must decide how to explain ambiguous situations so that they may be evidence for one's point of view rather than the opposite. A rhetorical perspective of history focuses on what happens to people and ideas in the process of persuasive transformation. To examine rhetorical history is to interpret, not just describe, how actors consciously viewed events.[5]

My aim is to examine the rhetorical history of the Pentecostal movement and interpret the complex relationships between its symbols and those of prior religious experience and belief. The symbol systems created by early Pentecostals were tested almost immediately through interaction and collision with centuries of established religious worldviews. How did early Pentecostals work through the conflict between prior religious understanding and the onslaught of new symbol systems that would define their movement? How did this conflict play out specifically with regard to women's roles? How did women encounter the Divine through this new religious worldview, and how did they view the events that led to their own persuasive transformation?

The complex theological and historical context from which Pentecostalism emerges provides the scene in which women form the basis of argument for their participation in this new movement. According to Kenneth Burke, arguments dominated by "scene" view the world as relatively permanent and deterministic. Persons functioning within a scene are constrained by its elements. Factors in the natural or social landscape limit their ability to act of their own volition: free will is supplanted largely by fate, thereby reducing action to motion.[6] Members in a community may explain their own behavior as motion because communal traditions or "laws," norms that they themselves have devised, control it but individuals who challenge the community behave more in terms of action or the willful violation of rules and boundaries. Preserving the integrity of the community becomes analogous to survival. Members of the community "instinctively" react to outside threats in order to maintain their scene as "impenetrable, eternally existent."[7] In examining the topography through the language employed and the relationships developed within the Pentecostal movement, we get a clearer picture of how the rhetorical drama, specifically the scene, was constructed. In other words, what

5. Ibid., 5–6.
6. Burke, *Grammar of Motives*.
7. Ibid., 131.

motives led to the interplay of language that created both opportunities and constraints for women to engage in the Pentecostal movement in ways previously off limits to them in religious life and practice?

## THE WESLEYAN ROOTS OF PENTECOSTALISM

Pentecostal historian William Menzies notes that Pentecostalism did not occur in a vacuum. Pentecostalism stands within the framework of orthodox Christianity while challenging believers everywhere to take a new and refocused look at the person and work of the Holy Spirit.[8] While nearly every Christian tradition acknowledges an outpouring of the Holy Spirit to Christ's followers in the days immediately following Christ's ascension and the presence of speaking in unknown languages on what has become known as the Day of Pentecost, most traditions believed this phenomenon applied only to the first-century church. The cessation of these unknown tongues and the signs and wonders that accompanied them has become widely accepted doctrine. Pentecostals take a considerably different view and argue not only that these manifestations of the Holy Spirit are present today but also that believers should actively seek them in their own lives and in corporate worship. Throughout the history of Christianity, many adherents have sought the gifts and power of the Holy Spirit, as evidenced in the second chapter of the book of Acts, which birthed the New Testament church. According to Pentecostal tradition, Scriptural evidence demonstrates that early Christian congregations also experienced the gifts of the Holy Spirit in their gatherings even after the day of Pentecost as described in Acts 2 (1 Cor 12 and 14).[9]

Modern Pentecostalism has several narratives regarding its origin. While the Pentecostal movement of the twentieth century began in the United States, much of its theology is rooted in earlier British perfectionist and charismatic movements. Historian and theologian Vinson Synan identifies the Methodist Holiness movement and the British Keswick "Higher Life" movement as those that prepared the way for what would later appear to be a spontaneous outpouring of the Holy Spirit in the United States.

Widely considered the grandfather of Pentecostal spirituality, John Wesley, an Anglican priest, experienced what he termed a "conversion" in 1738. Wesley's theology is contained in a series of journal entries, personal letters, and sermons written between 1735 and 1790. Methodism, as Wesley's teachings were called, was a new approach to Arminian theology as

8. Menzies, *Anointed to Serve*, 17.

9. McGee, *People of the Spirit*, 17.

well as a reaction against Calvinism that had dominated English social, religious, and political life.[10] From the beginning, Methodist theology placed
an emphasis on the conscious religious experience: believers could know
from a crisis experience of conversion that they were saved and such salvation was available to everyone.[11]

Wesley also advocated what he termed a "second blessing" or "entire
sanctification," an instant experience that he referred to as "Christian Perfection." In A Plain Account of Christian Perfection, Wesley urged his followers to seek a new spiritual dimension. This experience, as he described
it, was a sanctifying work of grace after conversion, which promised believers freedom from their moral natures that prompted sinful behavior.[12]
Wesley's heir apparent, John Fletcher, referred to this second blessing as
the "baptism in the Holy Spirit."[13] The Holiness Movement, both Wesleyan
and Reformed variations, adapted Wesley's view, providing a foundation
for the theology of Holy Spirit baptism, a distinguishing characteristic of
Pentecostal theology.[14]

This theology also began the formation of rhetorical invention that
provided a vernacular or a unique symbol system by which Pentecostals
could argue for their position and create a context for their existence. The
baptism in the Holy Spirit became the hallmark of Pentecostal theology
and while, over time, it evolved and developed from Wesley's viewpoint,
it remained at the core of what it means to be Pentecostal. Eventually, this
theology of sanctification and the manifestation of speaking in unknown
languages came to define Pentecostalism's return to the first things of the
Christian church with an emphasis on the provision of the Holy Spirit as
a means of empowerment for spiritual service. This restorationist understanding of sanctification and the Holy Spirit also influenced a rhetoric of
women's involvement and empowerment because a great and urgent work

10. Calvinism and Arminianism are two systems of theology that attempt to explain
the relationship between God's sovereignty and human responsibility in the matter of
salvation. Named for John Calvin (1509–1564) and Jacobus Arminius (1560–1609)
respectively, both positions can be summed up in five points: total depravity of humanity versus partial depravity, unconditional election versus conditional election, limited
atonement versus unlimited atonement, irresistible grace versus resistible grace, and
the perseverance of the saints versus conditional salvation with Calvinists believing the
former of each position and Arminians the latter. There are several mixes of the five
points of each and many adhere to some points but not to all in each theological system.
See also Synan, Holiness–Pentecostal Tradition, 2.

11. Ibid.

12. McGee, People of the Spirit, 17.

13. Synan, Century of the Holy Spirit, 15.

14. Tackett, "Embourgeoisement of the Assemblies of God," 34.

needed to be done to see others persuaded to turn to Christ for salvation. If believers are empowered for service through this gifting, then they have an obligation to spread the gospel of Jesus regardless of their gender.

## The Influence of Susanna Wesley

Wesley's theology and approach to ministry paved the way for the role women would play in the Methodist church well before the formation and growth of the Pentecostal movement. Susan C. Hyatt notes that the religious emancipation of womanhood began with John Wesley or rather, with his mother, Susanna.[15] Several scholars note that the greatest influence on Wesley's theology and his view of women in God's economy was his mother, whom they credit as the true founder of Methodism. A self-educated woman, Susanna Wesley established the format of Methodism through the writing of her family devotions. Instructed in theology by her father, Susanna believed that the activity of the Holy Spirit in the life of the believer was more authoritative than any dictate of the institutionalized church, and she imparted this belief to her children.

The mother of nineteen children, Susanna was determined that they would be educated and able to provide for themselves both spiritually and physically. Discouraged by her husband's failures and a lack of spiritual diversity in the church, Susanna set out to write her own biblical commentaries and meditations, which she used to educate her children. She held services in her home, which eventually attracted a public following, and nearly 200 people came each Sunday afternoon to hear Susanna Wesley teach.

While significant evidence exists of Susanna Wesley's influence on her son's theology, he was not always as bold in his interpretation of a woman's role. Early on in his ministry, Wesley emphasized the Apostle Paul's injunction against women's leadership and his call for women to keep silent in the church. He was also critical of the participation of Quaker women in their churches.[16] However, Wesley's paradigm of worship based on experience led to an expanded role for women. In small class meetings and larger public

15. Hyatt, "Spirit-Filled Women," 234.

16. Often overlooked, Quaker belief had a direct influence in many areas of Pentecostal thought. Gender equality typical to the Quakers characterized the Pentecostal revival. Men and women were equally responsible for their faith and the gifting of the Spirit was considered the qualifying factor for leadership activity and missions. No separate clerical class emerged. Countless Quaker women made a significant difference in equipping women for leadership in the Pentecostal movement and other social movements of the nineteenth and twentieth centuries. See also Hyatt, "Spirit-Filled Women," 235.

meetings Wesley allowed women to pray, testify, read sermons, and eventually extemporaneously exegete and apply biblical texts. Wesley did not identify such actions as preaching and was careful to avoid the term.[17]

In 1748, Wesley wrote to a fellow minister that although Paul allowed women to labor with him, it could not have been in ways that were contrary to Paul's previous injunctions. Wesley questioned whether prophesying was really preaching (an issue that would come up again with early Pentecostals). However, in 1761, Wesley assures a woman named Sarah Crosby that it was acceptable for her to read the notes from a commentary or a previous sermon before she spoke a few words publicly. He later advised her to "intermix" her own short exhortations in her prayers, but to keep away from preaching by never citing scriptural text. She should also speak for only a short period of time and avoid identifying services as prayer meetings.[18]

By 1777, Wesley no longer distinguished between preaching and other forms of exhortation. When asked about women in Scripture who had received "extraordinary calls" that allowed them to preach, Wesley used this same language and stated that he had been persuaded that the strength of the Methodist cause rests on it. Obviously, Paul had made exceptions, and so if Methodist women's hearts were also "strangely warmed" by the Spirit as was his own, then they were permitted to preach. When challenged on why he allowed women to preach, Wesley replied, "Because God owns them in the saving of souls, and who am I to withstand God."[19]

Wesley's theology profoundly changed the landscape of protestant religion in Europe and even more so in the United States. For the first time, a specific rhetoric on the person and work of the Holy Spirit emerges and explains why this "warmed heart" experience is important to the believer. Wesley also makes a centuries-old break with the church universal in his approach to women. While Wesley begins with the same justifications for women's silence as were used throughout church history and are often still seen today, he could not reconcile his own experience and understanding with this perception. Eventually, the experience overtakes both theology and history, and the semantic differences between *prophecy* and *preaching* become negated by the greater need to spread the gospel. This same line of argumentation will be used later by Pentecostals. While their previous religious understanding would not have allowed for women to have a role in Christian ministry, their experience provides evidence otherwise. Experiential understanding creates

17. Roebuck, "From Extraordinary Call to Spirit Baptism," 247.

18. Ibid.

19. Hyatt, "Spirit-Filled Women," 236.

the opportunity for women's involvement and challenges the constraints of previous theological practices.

## Methodism in the United States

The spread of Methodism in the United States was swift. Circuit riders penetrated the new American frontier preaching a religion of fire and brimstone and establishing the camp meeting as a regular and institutionalized part of American religious life. According to Synan, those who attended such camp meetings generally expected their religious experiences to be as vivid as the frontier around them.[20]

This radical revivalism, despite constant critique and criticism, persisted because it was a phenomenally successful means of recruitment. The purpose of this phenomenon was not to find new avenues of exegesis or theological insight, but rather to save souls by any means possible. Historian Nathan O. Hatch notes that these circuit riders were "professional organizers" whose themes were repentance, salvation by faith, and the witness of the Spirit. Formal education among circuit preachers was scarce, and for followers of Wesley, and later Francis Asbury (1785–1816), the explicit goal was to use the lay minister to create a movement of the people. The circuit rider ministered to people regardless of gender, class, race, ethnic group, or ecclesial tradition. Much of Wesley's formality gave way to what Hatch refers to as the "roaring extemporaneous ethos of the camp meeting."[21] The promotion of the lay minister proved a defining element for early Pentecostals. "Every man or woman," even those who had not been bred or educated to be the mouthpiece of God, common everyday people, and often the lowest of society, were anointed to serve. Similarly, the emphasis on zealous evangelism became a hallmark of the latter Pentecostal movement, and from this radical revival culture, Pentecostals developed a sustained discourse.

An additional challenge to the religious rhetoric of the revivalist culture and its emerging theology is that it wholeheartedly embraced the epistemological assumptions of modern thought. As George Marsden has noted, American Protestantism during the eighteenth and nineteenth centuries embraced "Scottish Common Sense Realism," which encouraged both "democratic" and "anti-elitist" notions that people "can know the real world directly and that "[t]the common sense of mankind, whether of the man behind the plow or the man behind the desk was the surest guide to truth."[22]

20. Synan, *Holiness–Pentecostal Tradition*, 9–14.
21. Hatch, *Democratization of American Christianity*, 55.
22. Marsden, *Fundamentalism and American Culture*, 14–15.

Mark Noll has referred to these assumptions as part of an influential "didactic Enlightenment" or "Scottish Enlightenment" that attracted Protestant educators and ministers with a particular fervency in the late eighteenth and early nineteenth centuries.[23] This intellectual framework effectively made evangelical Protestantism "dynamically powerful in the early history of the United States," but it fostered a "weak intellectual legacy" that produced "dysfunctional and anti-intellectual responses to the social, intellectual, and theological challenges" facing the nation and the church.[24]

Revivalism opened up rhetorical "space" for more egalitarian participation. No greater example exists of the democratic spreading of the gospel than the inclusion of women in the process. The impact of women's participation in evangelism on the church or the culture were a minor consideration. The message must be spread. Early lack of engagement with what women's participation would mean and how the church would change meant that later reaction was swift and strong to maintain the stasis of the religious scene and constrain women's rhetorical presence. This delayed reaction eventually created a rhetorical tension between the method and the message of revivalism.

## CHARLES FINNEY AND REVIVALIST REFORM

Inspired by the hope of a "Christian" America (not the perceived secular culture that had taken hold in the fledging country), the "holiness crusade" of the Methodists gained a tremendous following. Revivalists such as Charles Grandison Finney (1792–1875) argued for Christian perfection or sanctification by exercising free will and cultivating right intentions. They insisted that sin and holiness could not exist in the same person.[25] Finney increasingly used the language of the "baptism in the Holy Spirit" as the means of entering into entire sanctification and proposed the possibility of receiving subsequent "fresh" receptions of the Holy Spirit.

Finney's "Oberlin Perfectionism" emerged during his time at Oberlin College in Ohio and differed somewhat from traditional Wesleyanism. Finney and Oberlin theologians such as Asa Mahan argued that the only thing that stood in the way of the revival was the church's failure to exercise its spiritual duty and call congregants to repent of individual sin and the corporate sin of American society.[26]

23. Noll, *Scandal of the Evangelical Mind*, 84–85.
24. Ibid., 105–7.
25. Synan, *Holiness–Pentecostal Tradition*, 15.
26. Tackett, "Embourgeoisement of the Assemblies of God," 36.

While Finney believed in personal piety and revivalism, he also advocated social reform as a means of national repentance. Failure of the church to urge social reform hindered revival.[27] These reforms included compassion for the poor, the egalitarian relationship of women and men, and the emancipation of the African-American slave.

## Reform and the Influence of Women

Finney and Mahan also helped to establish Oberlin College as the first co-educational college in the world for the purpose of advancing Finney's blending of revival and reform. Mahan (who would later participate in the Keswick movement with Hannah Whitall Smith) was also a strong advocate for increased education and social roles for women. The most controversial of Finney's new measures regarded the practice of allowing women to pray out loud and testify in mixed company. He suggested that the epitaph for his gravestone to read, "The first man, in the history of the race, who conducted women, in connection with members of the opposite sex, through a full course of liberal education, and conferred upon her the high degrees that had hitherto been exclusive prerogative of men."[28] Educating women allowed them to obtain a level of credibility beyond their role in the home and to participate more fully in society and its reformation.

Over time, several women participated in the ministry of Charles Finney. These women shared their conversion experiences in mixed-gender meetings and were often met with supportive audiences. They also visited houses of prostitution and women's prisons, distributed tracts, and formed societies for the promotion of benevolence, missions, and education. This taste of responsibility may have influenced some women's appetites for greater autonomy not only in the church but also in society.[29] The link between social reform and personal spirituality created an opportunity for women to engage in public life and would, over time, develop opportunities for women to take leadership roles in church and culture.

## The Perfecting of American Life

By 1840, perfectionism was becoming a theme in American social, intellectual, and religious life. From these perfectionist teachings, many reform

---

27. Ibid.
28. Hyatt, "Spirit-Filled Women," 237.
29. Roebuck, "From Extraordinary Call to Spirit Baptism," 251.

movements emerged to "perfect" American social life including women's suffrage, the abolition movement, anti-masonry, and various temperance campaigns.[30] This attitude of reform is particularly important as it creates an environment that examines the culture for more than just the obvious sin of rejecting salvation offered through Jesus Christ. Reformers viewed many established cultural norms as sinful. Allowing women to speak publicly or elevating the status of African-Americans to a position of citizen was, to them, not just cultural reform but an eradication of sinful behavior. The religious establishment had long defended sidelining women and oppressing slaves. This shift toward advocacy called not only the culture but also the church itself into question.

The dominant role that religion had played in American culture and its use of Scripture and church doctrine to justify social norms, including the subjugation of women and the perpetuation of slavery, increased the church's culpability in such social "sins." The evangelical church in America had embraced an Enlightenment approach to Scripture and perpetuated the status quo. Revivalist movements such as Finney's were not completely immune to this philosophy, but their "common-sense" approach to biblical mandates became a rallying cry to challenge the culture and see repentance as a means of social as well as spiritual change. Pentecostals would not only reject and be rejected by the secular culture in the United States but they would also encounter the same rejection from the more mainline religious establishment. Pentecostalism emerged as a movement to restore the church and to be the "voice crying out into the wilderness" to prepare the way of the Lord to a country that they believed had essentially lost its way. However, they would also be caught in the dysfunctional web that had been weaved rhetorically throughout this period of church history. The same common-sense understanding of Scripture that justified both an abolitionist and a pro-slavery position would also substantiate a position that subjugated women to men especially within the hierarchy of the church while at the same time encouraging their participation in newfound religious revivalism. For every opportunity that reform seemed to create, an equal and often stronger constraint accompanied it fueled by an epistemological approach to biblical interpretation and its resulting rhetoric.

The religious revivals and their attendant push for social reforms, however, were not unique to the United States. The events were mirrored in Europe and the ensuing European revival movements and teachings came back across the Atlantic to intermingle with the revivalist culture of the American West.

30. Synan, *Holiness–Pentecostal Tradition*, 17.

## *The Keswick Movement and American Holiness*

The Holiness emphasis found expression in various offshoots of the revivalist movement in the United States and in England. An example of it can be found in the Keswick "Higher Life" conferences in England and subsequent Northfield Conferences conducted by Dwight L. Moody (1837–1899) in Massachusetts.

Begun in 1875 as a counterpart to the American holiness movement, the Keswick summer conferences were led by Hannah Whitall Smith (1832–1911) and her husband, Robert. A Quaker woman from Philadelphia, Hannah Whitall Smith was active as both a religious and a social reformer. She served as the first Superintendent of the Evangelistic Department of the Women's Christian Temperance Union, and along with Dr. Katherine Bushnell, she organized the evangelistic arm to create a campaign for the advancement of social purity. A close ally of Susan B. Anthony, Whitall Smith also worked diligently to see women achieve the right to vote and receive full citizenship in the United States.

Hannah Whitall Smith, like Finney and Mahan, defended her social activism by way of the gospel. She noted that women were made free by the working out of the principles of Christ who had declared that there was neither male nor female in Him.[31] Like her friend and mentor, Susan B. Anthony, Whitall Smith prayed fervently for something to shock or startle women in the United States into a state of self-respect. What lay in front of her both in doctrine and in practice may very well have been the answer to her prayers.

## *Empowerment for Service*

The Smiths were the first to introduce what would become a point of great doctrinal contention within the movement. The new Keswick emphasis displaced the concept of the second blessing as an eradication of the sinful nature in favor of the baptism of the Holy Spirit as an empowerment for service. This shift proved deeply influential in the development of Pentecostal doctrine, and it eventually became the cornerstone of defense for women's involvement in ministry. If the baptism was for both men and women and it was a sign of empowerment, then it was not the women themselves who were seeking after a position of authority; instead, it was the Holy Spirit providing justification for their work. The rhetoric of Spirit empowerment

---

31. Hyatt, "Spirit-Filled Women," 240–41.

created a significant opportunity for women's participation and leadership, creating lasting consequences for the Pentecostal movement.

Advocates of Spirit empowerment portrayed it not so much as a cleansing experience or a state of perfection, but more as a state of being anointed by the Holy Spirit. Out of this shift, a rift began to emerge amongst these teachers and the more traditional holiness teachers in the United States. Dwight L. Moody, R.A. Torrey, dean of the Bible Institute of Los Angeles (now Biola University), A.J. Gordon, founder of Gordon College, A.B. Simpson, founder of the Christian and Missionary Alliance, and other evangelists and teachers embraced the Keswick version of the second blessing as empowerment. Torrey wrote, "The Baptism with the Spirit is not intended to make us happy . . . not even primarily for the purpose of cleansing from sin, but for the purpose of empowering for service."[32] This change from "cleansing" to "empowerment" was later used fervently by supporters of women's leadership roles. If the Holy Spirit could and would baptize women, then they were empowered for spiritual service in spite of their cultural or social position.

### The Empowerment of D. L. Moody

Perhaps no one person was more influential in spreading this new doctrine of Holy Spirit empowerment than Dwight L. Moody. Already a famous and powerful minister and evangelist, Moody was influenced to seek a more powerful experience of the Holy Spirit by two women from his Chicago church who prayed for him constantly to receive this new "baptism." While Moody resisted at first, he eventually asked these two women to pray for him specifically for this purpose. During a prayer meeting in 1871, Moody reported being filled with the Holy Spirit in a sudden and dramatic way, claiming his soul was "bathed in the divine" and the room "seemed ablaze with God."

Following this experience, Moody began to conduct conferences like his Keswick counterparts. The annual Higher Life Conference in Northfield, Massachusetts, began in 1880 and attracted thousands of people who came to seek their own "personal Pentecost." Moody also turned his attention to higher education, founding the Moody Bible Institute in 1889. Moody's doctrine continued to be taught there well past his death in 1899. According to Synan, Moody's passing signaled a milestone in the tradition that emphasized a subsequent work of the Holy Spirit after conversion. The notion of a personal Pentecostal experience was no longer bizarre or fringe teaching. It

32. McGee, *People of the Spirit*, 18.

was becoming widely accepted in American and British religious life as an attainable experience for modern times.[33]

The shift to interpret the second blessing as empowerment also opened the door for women to engage in service. Women like Hannah Whitall Smith were not simply looking to reform the lives of others, but because of this gospel they were themselves transformed. This message liberated women and gave them an opportunity to be a part of the service. If the Holy Spirit provided empowerment for service and women were receiving the Holy Spirit, then they too must be available to serve. As mainstream as the teaching on empowerment for service would become so too would the mindset that this empowerment was not limited to men, but was also available to and expected of women.

The theological foundations established by Wesley and extended through the work of Finney, Moody, and the Smiths were critical to setting up the theological underpinnings of Pentecostalism. Their emphasis on experience and the transition of their theology from personal redemption to empowerment for service altered the rhetorical landscape to allow a role for those previously exempted from religious service including the undereducated, minorities, and women. These shifts were not simply ideological or merely semantic; instead, they were practically applied in the lives and ministries of real people. With each contribution and every struggle to work out their faith in the midst of cultural norms and challenges, these figures provided the theological foundation and the practical application that proved vital to how Pentecostal women later argued for their own rhetorical space and meaningful contributions.

Theological change paralleled social change and the faith/practice dynamic was put to a significant test. The American Civil War not only challenged and reshaped the political and cultural landscape in the United States, but it also challenged the religious landscape and created an environment that ushered in a season of great crisis.

## "COMMON-SENSE" BIBLICAL INTERPRETATION AND NATIONAL CRISIS

Corresponding to the burgeoning "holiness" movement, a social movement to eradicate the practice of slavery was also growing. Many new converts to "sanctified" Christianity came to believe that slavery was a danger to both society and the church and that it should be abolished. Division over the issue threatened the young holiness movement. Like the impending

33. Synan, *Century of the Holy Spirit*, 30.

division that led to Civil War, northern and southern factions of the church felt the tensions inherent in the issue of slavery. The influence of "modernist" epistemology manifested itself in the rhetoric surrounding the war and the religious as well as political drama that ensued. The emphasis on literal, "common-sense" understandings of biblical truth and interpretation led directly to and reinforced a painful and irreconcilable impasse concerning how to arrive at a biblical position on the question of slavery. As a result, many Protestant denominations were torn apart and the broader cultural authority of the Bible and religious faith were both tarnished.[34]

According to Noll, the cultural authority of the Bible was at this time "one of the fundamental supports of American civilization" and the truth and authority of Scripture was best interpreted by the common sense of ordinary people.[35] Evangelical discourse had grown powerful, authoritative, and mobilizing, and evangelicals believed that "they had the power within themselves to discover the true meaning of sacred texts, the power to see things in general as they really were, the power to act effectively against those in the wrong and the power to choose righteously when faced by moral dilemmas."[36] The result was a "first-order theological crisis" that divided the faithful in public discourse where pro-slavery advocates solidified their arguments with Scripture and anti-slavery attempts to argue beyond prooftexts appeared weak. Noll notes that the impending war was about defining the Union, legitimizing slavery, and the limits of states' rights, but more significantly, it was a religious battle over how to interpret the Bible and how to promote moral norms in public life.[37] This divide removed any possibility of finding common ground concerning the role of Scripture on the question of slavery and cast the issue as a referendum on the future of "Christian civilization." Both sides polarized the differences that tore long-established denominations apart, including the Baptists and Methodists, and hastened the call to arms as the only means to resolve the impasse. This discourse, on both sides, permanently undermined religious prestige and cultural authority, and according to Noll, profoundly delayed any meaningful public engagement with the underlying issues of race that has had longstanding consequences in evangelical discourse.

Mark Steiner argues that the discursive drama that surrounded the Civil War and the modernist epistemology that fueled it had religious consequences, in addition to its political and social consequences. He notes that

34. Steiner, "Liability of the Enlightenment," 295–98.

35. Noll, *Civil War as a Theological Crisis*, 22.

36. Ibid., 25.

37. Noll, *God and Race in American Politics*, 14.

Noll has suggested that the centrality of Protestant religion to American political life before and during the Civil War meant that the irresolvable conflict over the biblical witness on slavery functioned to magnify the social and regional differences of the period and to give those differences a profoundly moral—and even religious—charge. It also obscured the differences between the issue of slavery and the issue of race and further naturalized racial prejudice that would simmer below the surface of American culture for nearly another century.[38]

While the issue of race dominates the history of this period, the impact was equally as severe on other social challenges, specifically the role women played in the church and within the greater American culture. The interaction of pietism, revivalism, and "modernist epistemology" functioned powerfully to open up rhetorical space for women, but ironically, these same features—particularly "modernist epistemology"—would also figure prominently in efforts to constrain these spaces. The battle over how to (and in turn, who gets to) interpret the Bible and how to promote moral norms or a change in these norms is significant to this study as it challenges us to examine further how we think and work through our justifications for long-held beliefs and practices. Much of the institutionalized church was being torn apart during this period and in the midst of this dysfunction, the groundwork was laid for a whole new paradigm to approach the work of the church. How this new movement would approach this convergence of change would have a profound impact on women.

## The Parallels of Language about
## Women and the Slave

I would argue that the evangelical discourse of this period had a profound effect on women. While on one hand, women began to find their public voice in ways that had not been seen in the fledgling nation, the same modernist epistemology that fueled the slave debate would have serious consequences for the perception of women's roles in the culture and especially within the church. The abolition movement provided a vehicle for women's public discourse, and the arguments used in favor of freeing the slave were often linked to the plight of women as another marginalized segment of society. The public speaking skills of those women who were bold enough to defy their culture and sometimes even the law to preach and debate on the issue of slavery were strengthened. However, as with the challenge to predestined roles based on

38. Steiner, "Liability of the Enlightenment" 295–98.

skin color, the challenge to predestined roles based on gender was obscured by the conflict over the nature and interpretation of Scripture.

## THE MINISTRY OF PHOEBE PALMER

One of the most dominant female religious voices in the United States during this time was Phoebe Palmer. Along with her husband, Dr. Walter Palmer, Phoebe had embraced holiness theology through the persuasion of her sister, Sarah A. Langford. Sarah had begun holding "Tuesday Meetings for the Promotion of Holiness" in her parlor in 1835. By 1839, Phoebe had become the leader of the "Tuesday Meetings." In this same year, the first periodical of the holiness movement *The Guide to Christian Perfection* or *The Guide to Holiness* was published. The Palmers purchased and published *The Guide* in 1865 and it would eventually boast a circulation of 30,000.[39] Through a growing evangelistic work and her writings and publications, Phoebe Palmer's work was unprecedented.

Phoebe Palmer's influence was far reaching in both the holiness and later Pentecostal movements.[40] While Phoebe Palmer was at first reluctant to minister, she was greatly influenced by Wesley's language of an extraordinary call and the modernist epistemology, which Noll describes as the implicit trust that the Bible was a plain book whose authoritative deliverances could be apprehended by anyone who simply opened its covers and read. Noll cites an invocation by Palmer from an 1865 article in *The Guide* in which Palmer states, "The Bible is a wonderfully simple book; and, if you had taken the naked Word of God as . . . your counsel, instead of taking the opinions of men in regard to that Word, you might have been a more enlightened, simple, happy and useful Christian."[41] Clearly shaped by this epistemological approach and her culture, Palmer begins with the "simplicity" of Scripture, but her experience with the Holy Spirit solidified her doctrine and shaped her understanding of a woman's role in ministry.

### The Promise of the Father

In her now-famous justification for women's roles, *The Promise of the Father*, Palmer lays out this position and begins to popularize the use of what

39. Synan, *Holiness–Pentecostal Tradition*, 17–18.

40. McGee, *People of the Spirit*, 27–29; Synan, *Holiness–Pentecostal Tradition*, 17–18; Hyatt, "Spirit-Filled Women," 239–40; Everts and Schutte Baird, "Phoebe Palmer," 269; and Roebuck, "From Extraordinary Call to Spirit Baptism," 245.

41. Palmer, "Witness of the Spirit," 137, as quoted in Noll, *Civil War*, 20.

would become Pentecostal language to justify the public role of women in the church. Her argument is the first to link the account of Pentecost in Acts 2 where both genders are receivers of the baptism in the Holy Spirit to the doctrine of empowerment for service in women as well as men. Despite opposition, Palmer recognized the need for women and called the church to acknowledge Joel's prophecy regarding prophesying daughters.[42] She also develops a sophisticated understanding of what a prophetic call to ministry involves and uses it to reinterpret other passages of Scripture that appear to restrict the ministry of women.[43]

Palmer began her argument with a focus on the women present on the day of Pentecost. She declared that their willingness to be obedient to Christ's command to gather and their subsequent endowment of the Spirit was evidence of God's designs for women's public ministry. Palmer asked if it was good enough for the first church to empower women, why was it not good enough for the church today? Her answer: things had indeed changed since the first century church and that the church was weakened as a result. In Palmer's view, churches that restricted the ministry of women disabled themselves, as if cutting of a limb intended for the sole purpose of spreading the gospel message to the whole world. Palmer argued, "If the Spirit of prophecy fell upon God's daughters, alike as upon his sons in that day, and they spoke in the midst of that assembled multitude, as the Spirit gave utterance, on what authority do the angels of the churches restrain the use of that gift now?"[44]

From here, Palmer launched into a point-by-point refutation of the so-called "problem passages," which seem to restrict women's ministry participation (1Cor 14:34–35 and 1 Tim 2:12). While on face value these passages may seem to limit women, they conflict with other Scriptures authored by the Apostle Paul that appear to endorse women's ministry. Palmer argued for historical context and proper understanding of the entirety of the Pauline letter, "What serious errors in faith and practice," she wrote, "have resulted from taking isolated passages dissevered from their proper connections to sustain a favorite theory!"[45]

When placing these "problem" passages against those in Rom 16 and Acts 18:26 where Paul praises Palmer's namesake, the Deaconess Phoebe and Priscilla, the leader of a house church who taught the Christian faith to a man, named Apollos, she concludes that there is no sound biblical warrant

42. Palmer, *Promise of the Father*, 14–23.

43. Everts and Schutte Baird, "Phoebe Palmer," 269.

44. Palmer, *Promise of the Father*, 70.

45. Ibid., 49–51.

for the restriction of women's ministry. It is only, according to Palmer, the "Man of Sin" and ignorance that have influenced the church.

Finally, Phoebe Palmer argued that the church is simply inconsistent in its teachings and practice. If women were to truly be silent in the church, then they should not be able to participate in any form of public worship whatsoever. Palmer wrote, "If the apostle intended to enjoin silence in an absolute sense, then our Episcopalian friends trespass against this prohibition at every church service, in calling out the responses of women in company with men in their beautiful church liturgy, and when they repeat our Lord's Prayer in concert with their brethren. And thus do they trespass against this prohibition every time they break silence and unite in holy song in the church of God of any or every denomination."[46]

The rhetoric of Phoebe Palmer is not inconsistent with the rhetoric of women seeking to justify their calling today. It is important to note again that women in antebellum America were still barred from public speaking, much less preaching and Palmer's very public defense of women's rhetoric and ministry is striking given the social constraints of her day. While the social mores might have changed, it seems the battle lines of argument over the issue have not. These same Scriptures are being used to limit women's roles and those who advocate for women's roles use similar lines of argumentation to Palmer's to refute them. The long standing consequences of this "didactic" Enlightenment approach continue to resonate through to the present day. While Phoebe Palmer clearly embraced the epistemology, she does begin to engage in a rather thoughtful approach to her position, but the opportunities she sees in the Scriptures do not adequately answer the constraints to any satisfaction of those whose "common-sense" views the Scriptures differently. Despite this impasse, Palmer uses her newfound influence to create her own opportunity by taking every invitation offered to her while always walking a tightrope of cultural limitation.

## Women's Participation Demanded

As a result of her writing and teachings in the "Tuesday Meetings," Palmer was asked by her Pastor to teach classes in her local church and as more opportunities to speak about her sanctification came her way, she began to gain more confidence. She believed that each invitation to speak was providential and while still unsure of her own worth, she could not deny that she felt that extraordinary call that Wesley had spoken of in his own life. Over time her certainty grew and her doctrine demanded that all sanctified

46. Ibid., 56.

women publicly share the good news of the gospel. This increased interest in sanctification provided the church an opportunity to correct a wrong that had been propagated for centuries.

Phoebe Palmer is a vital player in the holiness and later Pentecostal movements, but she was not a radical reformer. While she argued fervently for a woman's place in the church, she worked fully in the context of her culture with regard to her place in her home and her family. For Phoebe Palmer, this call of ministry was not a justification for women to abandon their roles as wives and mothers. As her evangelistic work began to grow, Dr. Palmer left his medical practice for six months each year so they could minister together around the United States, Canada and Great Britain. Mrs. Palmer never referred to herself as a preacher and in any situation where her authority might be in question, she was careful to follow protocol. She often gave her message following a local minister and her husband worked alongside her in praying, reading Scripture, and giving the final call for salvation.

Phoebe Palmer's prophetic understanding of ministry highlights the nature of scriptural interpretation that was advocated by Finney and Mahan. Scripture is meant to be interpreted by Scripture and not presented in isolated instances, and historical context is vital. Her approach to ministry is not an affront to centuries of scriptural understanding, but rather an empowered approach. Women who speak in this context are instruments of the divine. Therefore women who engage in ministry are radically dependent on the Holy Spirit, and if either women or the church loses this spiritual fervor, the ministry of women will go into decline.

The rhetorical situation that Phoebe Palmer created for women in public and religious speaking is important to note, not simply because she is a female leader. Palmer manages to present one of the most sustained public arguments for a woman's role using culturally accepted terms while building on the contextual theological arguments of Scripture. She represents what traditional conservative Christians revere as the cultural sphere for a woman, while articulating a place for herself and her sisters using the very same biblical interpretive approach her male counterparts were using to argue against the sin of slavery. Palmer was careful to leave the symbolic understanding of a woman's place in relation to her husband untouched, and yet build upon accepted theological interpretations to quietly subvert the accepted understanding of leadership. This theme was consistent amongst women such as Susanna Wesley, Hannah Whitall Smith, and Phoebe Palmer. Theirs was never a stance for taking leadership by asserting their right to lead, but rather they managed a symbolic shift in the rhetoric of emancipation, which provided opportunity for them to present a God-ordained message. By meeting the arguments the church had presented against them and answering them with Scripture as well as the prevailing doctrine of their day, these women changed the language of leadership to include women. Rather than focusing their rhetoric on their right to be empowered as women in God's economy, they created a rhetoric that focused on Spirit empowerment that was apart from them personally or their desires and which they were commanded to obey if they were truly living out the Christian life. The Holy Spirit freed them from the bondage of silence and commanded that they preach the gospel to every nation not unlike their male counterparts endowed with the same power.

The coming Pentecostal movement would create a proving ground for Palmer's theology and practice. The emphasis on the experience of the Spirit brought the permission to speak or prophesy further into the realm of women, but greater understanding of women's roles stayed relatively unchanged until the Spirit was once again poured out on prophesying sons and daughters.

## CIVIL WAR DEPRESSION AND THE HOPE OF REVIVAL

The religious awakening that had been growing in the United States began to wane. As the nation drifted into war, American thought became more political and secular. The dispute over slavery moved from a theological and political discussion to a military contest. The perfection sought by so many through the double blessing of conversion and sanctification had failed to avert the messiness of war.

Several scholars and historians note that the years surrounding the Civil War were framed by a moral depression.[47] While the nation was looking for optimism following the war, the moral climate tended to dampen any positive outlook for many Christians. The credibility of established Protestant religion had been shattered. According to Noll, these children of the Enlightenment were also children of God and in this situation, the "clarity about the workings of divine providence posed a particular problem because God appeared to be acting so strikingly at odds with himself."[48]

While this period of reconstruction and rapid industrialization is often framed as a "Gilded Age" in American history, several issues including the excesses of capitalism and the pre-welfare-state-corrective led to a decline in a post-millennial belief system and opened the door for the pre-millennial

47. Synan, *Holiness–Pentecostal Tradition*; McGee, *People of the Spirit*; and Blumhofer, *Restoring the Faith*.

48. Noll, *Civil War*, 75.

dispensationalism that was championed by leaders such as Moody, Torrey and Scofield and remains a hallmark of evangelical thought today.

The hope and optimism of spiritual blessing amongst the faithful dimmed, and a more pessimistic outlook flourished among evangelicals. Rather than a period of prosperity and tranquility, the forecast took on an apocalyptic nature and a prophetic tone. As time was ticking away to the end of the age, according to this perspective, Christians had little time to evangelize and spread the news of the soon return of Christ. In the dark days following the war, the impoverished states of the former Confederacy turned to religion for comfort and became a hotbed of religious activity, which would lay foundations for further development of a distinct rhetoric that would define the Pentecostal movement. The political and social attitude had become dim and the institutionalized church had lost the credibility needed to provide the answers and hope people were looking for to heal the wounds of war and economic strife. Yet, people still began to look to something greater than themselves or their institutions to provide a sense of relief for their pain and to give them hope that the coming age was going to be one of renewal. The religious rhetoric that dominated war time was no longer sufficient, and people began to search for a new language to express the hope and healing only God could provide. Religious publications teemed with news of the evangelistic efforts, and leaders in the Methodist church called for a return to Wesleyan principles as an answer to the postwar crisis. In the North, a renewed emphasis on the camp meeting resulted in an entirely new holiness crusade. Convergence of the focus on evangelism and the return of the camp meeting provided an ideal environment for spreading the revival message and a new voice to share the good news: the female voice.[49]

## Approaching a New Century

As the twentieth century dawned and industrialization swept the nation, significant progress was made in science, technology, and religious thought. Unbridled hope in the ability of human achievement spawned a paradigm based in the unlimited potential for discovery and invention. Aspiration to eliminate every misery of humankind marked the attitude of the new age. Yet, these years of great progress were also marked by great despair. Gary McGee notes that under the veneer of popular piety, the corruption and greed of government officials and industry became more and more widespread. Industrialization and immigration contributed to a rapid

49. Synan, *Holiness–Pentecostal Tradition*, 23; McGee, *People of the Spirit*, 21.

urbanization of the country. Rural migration to these new cities of industry swelled, and newly freed African-Americans, as well as Asian, European and other immigrants existed in conditions that bordered on the exigencies of pre-war slavery.[50] These rural migrants and ethnically diverse immigrants collected in the ghettos of developing cities that were unprepared for their arrival. Great financial panic brought distress in both 1873 and 1893. The gulf between the very rich and the extremely poor seemed to widen, and social issues such as alcoholism were on the rise. In spite of this period of struggle, Menzies notes, church membership was on the rise giving the impression of a thriving spiritual nation.[51]

Menzies argues, however, that the powerful revivals of the early nineteenth century, which encouraged a vital religious experience, were exchanged for a more "cultural-religion" in which prevailing social values became identified with Christianity. What developed was a mood of self-satisfaction and optimism, which resulted in spiritual complacency in many churches across the land.[52] The scientific establishment dominated by the theory of Darwinism, the growth of Modernism and higher criticism, and the rise of the social gospel all considerably impacted the church. Revivalism came under heavy critique as being antiquated and out of touch with the new ways of religious and social thought.[53] As a result of this perceived attack on more conservative theological ideals and what was viewed as an alarming trend in American religion, two parallel and sometimes overlapping movements began to gain attention: the Holiness revival and Fundamentalist dispensationalism.

## A Revival of Holiness

The revival of religious activity in both the North and the South brought a connection to holiness themes including salvation, healing, personal holiness, and the soon return of Christ. Many holiness believers and teachers referred to this collection of ideas as the "Four-fold Gospel": Jesus as Savior, Sanctifier (or "Baptizer" in the Holy Spirit), Healer, and soon-coming King. Everyone who sought for it could receive "full salvation" in body and soul; they could be cleansed from sin, healed of any sickness, empowered

---

50. McGee, *People of the Spirit*, 20.

51. Menzies, *Anointed to Serve*, 18.

52. Ibid., 19.

53. Synan, *Holiness–Pentecostal Tradition*, 23; Menzies, *Anointed to Serve*, 20–21.

for service, and ready for the Lord's return in the "last days" according to Acts 2:17–21.[54]

Blumhofer writes that the post-war holiness movement, with its stress on religious experience and the work of the Holy Spirit, influenced churches both inside and outside of the Wesleyan tradition and began to spawn countless independent churches. In addition, the movement created a sense of meaning for African-Americans, who were struggling to chart their course in a post-slavery America, as well as for women who yearned to give "public verbal expression to their faith."[55]

The holiness movement provided three important biblical themes that strengthened a woman's right to public influence. First, the biblical admonition of neither male nor female in Christ was championed. In 1891 William B. Godbey wrote, "It is the God-given right, blood-bought privilege, and bounden [sic] duty of the women, as well as the men to preach the Gospel."

Second, redemption became an argument for biblical equality. If women were under the curse as a result of the fall, then by virtue of redemption, the curse associated with that event [women's subordination] is broken by the work of Jesus Christ. Finally, the third theme is one of Pentecost. Based on Joel 2:28 and Acts 2:17–18, Scripture points to the outpouring of the Holy Spirit on men and women alike, empowering both equally for gospel ministry.[56]

## The Rise of Fundamentalist Dispensationalism

A close relative of the renewed holiness movement, dispensationalism finds its origins as a modern movement in the British sect, the Plymouth Brethren. John Nelson Darby (1800–1882), the chief advocate of dispensationalism preached all over the United States, but it was his Bible studies with concerned church leaders that gained considerable public attention. Darby divided history into seven time periods or "dispensations." In this division, he insisted that events detailed in biblical history were about to begin ushering in the seventh and final dispensation that would begin with the secret rapture or sudden removal of the church from the world. Claiming that the return of Christ is always imminent, he stressed that the responsibility of the believer is to be always ready and to engage in militant evangelism to make the world ready.[57] These Bible studies eventually became known as

---

54. McGee, *People of the Spirit*, 25.

55. Blumhofer, *Restoring the Faith*, 29.

56. Hyatt, "Spirit-Filled Women," 238.

57. Blumhofer, *Restoring the Faith*, 16.

the Niagara Bible Conference, met for nearly fifteen years, and influenced such leaders at W. J. Erdman and A. J. Gordon as well as C. I. Scofield, whose Scofield Bible exerted great influence in spreading dispensationalism throughout the country.[58] While Scofield's influence dominated for nearly fifty years, many argued about Darby's view of the dispensations and the rapture and making Christ's return their focused conviction. This emphasis on the "blessed hope" was frequently noted as the crux of what truly transformed lives. The "blessed hope," according to Blumhofer, radically reordered priorities. Personal holiness replaced striving for worldly success, ambition, or recognition.[59]

Many of these same leaders were also involved in several prophecy conferences across the United States. According to historian Gary McGee, these conferences warned the faithful that the time for evangelism was nearing expiration and judgment was looming. Only a heaven-sent revival could stop the destructive force of humanity. [60] Darby's influence, a dominant force from 1897–1901 according to Menzies, is easily recognized because of the emphasis on Bible study and prophecy.

The second ingredient in the emerging Fundamentalist movement was the Princeton Theology. This stream of thought, developed by A. A. Hodge at Princeton Seminary, embodied in its tenets the core of the Fundamentalist platform: the rational defense of the faith, verbal inspiration of the Bible, and the inerrancy of Scripture.

Although strong Fundamentalist sympathy existed amongst early Pentecostals, the two movements never fully blended in part because later Fundamentalist leaders, such as William Jennings Bryan and Bob Jones, came to the table with a decidedly Calvinist theology, and Pentecostals, who would emerge equally Arminian in their theology, were unwilling to align themselves too closely with the movement.

The emphases on dispensationalism and Fundamentalism not only created an opening for Pentecostalism, but also played a significant role in the arguments for and against women's involvement. The focus on the end times and soon return of the Messiah meant that there was work to be done and people needed to do that work. If the harvest is ready and the laborers are few, then everyone has a role to play—both male and female—if the world was to be evangelized before the Second Coming. However, Fundamentalism's doctrine of inerrancy challenged the uses of context in scriptural interpretation and looked only to the written word for enlightenment. The

---

58. Menzies, *Anointed to Serve*, 24.

59. Blumhofer, *Restoring the Faith*, 16–17.

60. McGee, *People of the Spirit*, 25.

so-called "problem passages" such as those in 1 Corinthians and 2 Timothy that admonish women's silence and rebuke them from teaching men, when read as they are written, appear to provide no place for the female voice in the spreading of the gospel. As one door of justification for a woman's place opened, the constraints of the age seemed to immediately shut those same opportunities down.

While the onslaught of war and reconstruction had settled some issues of national consciousness, a great struggle for social significance in the life of the former slave and the call to greater equality for women remained. The Civil War serves as a significant turning point in American religious culture, and if the build-up of revival that had begun prior to the war was going to re-emerge in the age of Reconstruction, then the role of women in the public square and more specifically within the church was going to be addressed. The symbol formation that occurred during this time period grew significant and the voice of women emerged strong. A return to the emphasis on revival and divine healing, which had dominated the culture prior to the Civil War, provided women with a revived message and a revived platform.

## The National Holiness Association

While the holiness movement had been a predominant force prior to the Civil War, internal struggles and the onslaught of the war, particularly in Southern churches, left the movement dampened. However, within the ranks, a conviction developed that a holiness revival like that which had swept the country in 1858 would once again make things right. Many believed that the only way that the religious pendulum would swing back was through the return of the pre-war camp meeting revival.

In 1867, at a camp meeting in Vineland, New Jersey, the National Association for the Promotion of Holiness came into being and the modern holiness crusade began.[61] By 1883, a total of fifty-two "national" camp meetings were held, including once in 1860 which recorded 20,000 people in attendance. It appeared that the Methodist church would once again be the chief holiness sect in the nation. This was not to be, however, and before long the holiness message found itself unwelcome amongst the more mainstream Methodist congregations. Those in favor of holiness teachings became less loyal to the church and those loyal to the church became less loyal to the doctrine of holiness. Gradually, adherents were less and less welcomed. Between 1893 and 1907, nearly 25 separate holiness

---

61. Menzies, *Anointed to Serve*, 25; Synan, *Holiness–Pentecostal Tradition*, 25–26.

denominations came into existence. Some of the more notable denominations to form during this time included the Church of the Nazarene, the Church of God (Cleveland, Tennessee), The Pentecostal Holiness Church, and the Church of God in Christ.

## Bi-Racial, Interdenominational and Led by a Woman

While the holiness movement was rejected by the predominantly white Methodist church, it found particular success in black Methodist churches. The African Methodist Episcopal Church (AME), founded in 1787 had always held to the Wesleyan teachings of entire sanctification, and the late 1870's found them firmly in the holiness camp. A leading voice in this movement was Amanda Berry Smith, a freed slave, who received the second blessing after having attended meetings held by fellow evangelist Phoebe Palmer at her Tuesday meetings for the promotion of holiness. Eventually leading evangelistic meetings throughout Great Britain, Africa, and India, Amanda Smith's ministry was eagerly received by whites as well as blacks. Her 1893 autobiography helped to spread the holiness movement across many denominational, theological, and national boundaries.[62] Smith's leadership is also significant as it was a rarity for women in the African-American church to achieve any level of public acclaim. For her to have crossed both her own cultural boundaries as well as those within the white community sets her apart as key figure in the growth of the holiness movement.

In June 1877, under the leadership of George C. Whitefield, an interdenominational "Holiness Conference" brought together speakers from Methodist, Presbyterian, and Baptist churches. These meetings were bi-racial, interdenominational, and supportive of women's spiritual leadership. Slowly and subtly, space was created for women to both participate in the religious sphere and serve in positions of leadership. The issue of women was not a dominant theme; however, the opportunity for women to have a voice was setting an important cultural and theological precedent for Pentecostal women who would emerge with much greater fanfare and attention.

## The Gospel of Healing

While the holiness movement is primarily defined by its evangelistic efforts, a second theme emerged as a defining characteristic of the movement. The "gospel of healing" became a major theme for several influential holiness

62. Synan, *Holiness–Pentecostal Tradition*, 28.

leaders and pioneered the healing crusades that Pentecostals would later imitate. Women also found a home among holiness leaders who championed healing as a central theme and were frequent participants in healing meetings. As with the manifestation of speaking in tongues, divine healing is an experiential act in which women can engage both as a participant and as a practitioner. A tenet of the emerging four-fold gospel of Pentecostal belief, divine healing provided an opportunity for women to serve as a conduit of God's power and to testify to miraculous occurrences being made manifest at holiness meetings. A. J. Gordon maintained that like forgiveness of sins, healing was available to anyone who was willing to ask. He believed, as did others, that the final dispensation of the Spirit was to increase knowledge of Christ, the healer.

Like Gordon, A. B. Simpson made the gospel of healing a central focus and an organizing principle of the organization he founded, the Christian and Missionary Alliance. While Gordon's views came from his writings, Simpson's were rooted in his experience. including a healing from heart ailments early in his ministry. Blumhofer notes that several of Simpson's colleagues feared Simpson's insistence on healing as they felt it would lead to advocacy of other spiritual gifts. They argued that if one expected healing for the sick, then the gift of tongues must be included. Simpson dismissed their claims and argued that tongues had only ceased in the early church because they were abused for vain display, but that these gifts would be returned if the Church would claim them for the diffusion of the Gospel.[63]

If Gordon was the academic and Simpson was the pastor in his approach, John Alexander Dowie was the flamboyant and outspoken salesman.[64] Dowie built a nationwide reputation and following around his assertion that God had restored the gift of healing to the church through his ministry. In 1893, he arrived in Chicago and opened a mission opposite Buffalo Bill Cody's exhibit at the Chicago World's Fair.[65]

Dowie not only believed that the gift of healing marked the beginning of the end times restoration of spiritual gifts, he emphatically rejected all medicines and medical professionals and publicly criticized his contemporaries who preached healing but still engaged in these humanly contrived means of treatment.[66] Over the course of the next decade, he would open several "healing homes" where the sick could come to be prayed for on a consistent basis. On New Year's Eve, 1899, he announced the purchase of

---

63. Blumhofer, *Restoring the Faith*, 20–21.

64. McGee, *People of the Spirit*, 38.

65. McGee, *People of the Spirit*, 39; Blumhofer, *Restoring the Faith*, 22.

66. Blumhofer, *Restoring the Faith*, 22.

farm land on the shores of Lake Michigan where he would build, in his plans, a model Christian community. Zion City's economic, social, and spiritual regulations reflected a blend of biblical, utopian, and modern concepts that was well-designed for future growth. Streets and landmarks boasted Old Testament names and omitted saloons, gambling halls, theaters or dance halls, hospitals, doctors, or apostate churches.[67] He provided opportunity for women and African-Americans to serve in public roles in his organization alongside white men and many of his followers would later identify with Pentecostalism.[68]

Dowie's flamboyant advocacy of divine healing was clearly on the fringe, and his inclusion of women and African-Americans in the leadership of his organization further contributed to his negative notoriety. However eccentric and seemingly odd healers like Dowie presented themselves, their arguments for an emphasis on healing would provide another open door through which women would find their voice and also find these same arguments used in an effort to silence them.

Like the emphasis on evangelism, divine healing would become a central purpose in the Pentecostal movement. The link between divine healing and other spiritual manifestations such as tongues is also significant. Each of these emphases would eventually be pulled together to form the gospel of Pentecostalism (Jesus Christ as Savior, Baptizer in the Holy Spirit, Healer, and Soon-coming King), which would define the movement. The inclusion of women in each aspect of the four-fold message as both receivers of this gospel as well as full participants in extending the message to others is a significant shift from prior religious practice. The opportunities for their participation were intentional and represented in the flesh a significant shift in how religion was practiced.

### Maria Woodworth-Etter and Trance Evangelism

If one person, one woman, personifies the late nineteenth-century emphasis on evangelism and healing, it is Maria Woodworth-Etter (1844–1924). Often precluded from traditional public ministry and discouraged by her husband, Woodworth-Etter joined a local Quaker meeting where she found both spiritual and emotional support. Among the Quakers she prayed for empowerment for service and claimed to have been "filled with the Holy Ghost and fire and a power that never left."[69] Satisfied that she had

67. McGee, *People of the Spirit*, 40.

68. McGee, *People of the Spirit*, 41; Blumhofer, *Restoring the Faith*, 23.

69. Blumhofer, *Restoring the Faith*, 24.

the spiritual energy she needed, Woodworth-Etter began to preach and achieved considerable notoriety.

In her meetings, she highlighted the need for salvation, but her fame spread when people in her services began falling to the ground and went into what appeared to be a trance. She considered this behavior evidence of the Holy Spirit's baptism. Although critics labeled her the "trance evangelist," this phenomenon was hardly new in American revival circles.[70] She eventually widened her message and began to pray for the sick on the assumption that all who had a sufficient faith would be healed. Anyone who failed to be healed was responsible for that failure through either a lack of faith or a harboring of sin.[71]

She began to travel coast to coast in tent meetings with seating for eight thousand, preaching a message that offered room both for the emotions and for spiritual "victories," which included physical healing. Her theology would eventually resemble A. B. Simpson's, and she would play a pivotal and controversial role in the Pentecostal proclamation of healing.[72] Having been dismissed from several previous denominations with which she was affiliated, Woodworth-Etter would identify with the Pentecostal movement in 1912. Until her death in 1924, her "radical strategy" of ministry helped form the framework for later Pentecostal evangelism.[73]

Despite the constant rejection by established religious communities and by her own husband, Woodworth-Etter continued to do the work she believed she had been called and empowered to conduct. From itinerant laypersons moving from camp meeting to camp meeting to the shifting theology of sanctification and the focus on divine healing, Maria Woodworth-Etter embodied the totality of the opportunities created by these unique and significant shifts in religious practice. The lack of organization or structure in the movement also created opportunity for women like Woodworth-Etter to engage in ministry work. In every denomination where structure existed, constraints became evident almost immediately. These opportunities and constraints would continue to co-exist in the Pentecostal movement and like Maria Woodworth-Etter, Pentecostal women would also have to navigate an increasingly complicated landscape of theological empowerment in constant conflict with structural development.

70. McGee, *People of the Spirit*, 42.

71. Blumhofer, *Restoring the Faith*, 24.

72. McGee, *People of the Spirit*, 42–43; Blumhofer, *Restoring the Faith*, 24.

73. McGee, *People of the Spirit*, 42; Blumhofer, *Restoring the Faith*, 24.

## The Person and Work of the Holy Spirit

Like evangelism and divine healing, a growing interest in the person and work of the Holy Spirit formed the fervor from which Pentecostalism emerged. While premillenialists, many of whom believe that Christ will return to earth and remove his believers before reigning on earth for a thousand years, longed for personal holiness and an empowerment for service, advocates of healing searched for other gifts of the Spirit. Others looked for a "higher" or deeper life filled with more spirituality. Each of these fueled interests in what Blumhofer calls "a Holy Spirit who is neither abstract nor remote but constantly and personally active."[74]

This renewed interest in the Holy Spirit found expression in many segments of Protestant religion both liberal and conservative. These organizations and movements were not mutually exclusive and overlapped in teaching, personalities, and in personal piety. According to Blumhofer, they sang the same gospel songs, revered the same heroes and heroines of the faith, coveted intense religious experiences, subscribed to the same religious periodicals and read the same devotional literature. Despite their united response to modernity and a shared spirituality, it is important to note the various streams that represented separate contexts. They each offer a sense of the different emphases that "informed a growing popular radical evangelical fascination with the person and work of the Holy Spirit."[75]

In this focused view of the person and work of the Holy Spirit the defining feature of Pentecostal theology would burst forth. As noted in the controversy within the ministry of men like A. B. Simpson, renewed interest in the gifts and manifestations of the Holy Spirit inevitably would lead to an interest in the gift of speaking in tongues. While none denied the outpouring of tongues and fire in the first Pentecost as described in the second chapter of Acts, many were skeptical of a new Pentecost to be revealed in their time.

Nearly every Pentecostal historian and theologian credits Charles Fox Parham as the person responsible for introducing the practice of tongues speaking as a stated doctrine. It was Parham who first singled out "glossalalia" or speaking in tongues as the initial physical evidence of having received the baptism in the Holy Spirit. He taught that this experience should be a part of normal Christian worship rather than a bizarre by-product of religious emotionalism.[76]

74. Blumhofer, *Restoring the Faith*, 24–25.

75. Ibid., 25.

76. Synan, *Holiness–Pentecostal Tradition*, 89.

## THE MINISTRY OF CHARLES FOX PARHAM

Charles Fox Parham (1873–1929) faced lifelong struggles with various physical ailments and impairments. Parham sought refuge in the Christian faith because of its promise of hope for a better day. He entered college in Kansas to prepare for Methodist ministry, but was again struck with illness. In Parham's personal religious world, every event and subsequent decision was charged with spiritual significance. His approach to his own health fit this pattern.[77] Parham concluded this illness was due to a rebellious spirit and as a result he sought God earnestly for healing, promising to dedicate his life to the Gospel ministry if he was spared. Although he claimed instant healing, full recovery took time. His health restored, Parham set out into full-time ministry at the age of 19.

Deeply influenced by Wesleyan-holiness theology and teachings on divine healing and dogged by conflict with church officials, Parham left the Methodist faith and set out on his own. As a result, Parham's theology came from many sources. He traveled to Chicago to hear John Alexander Dowie, and on to Nyack, New York, to meet with A. B. Simpson, and then on to Maine to investigate the teachings of Frank Sandford, form where he went on to spend a one-month campaign in Winnipeg, Canada.[78] It was with Sandford that Parham's doctrinal beliefs were renewed again after hearing the story of African missionary Jennie Glassey. Glassey, a student of Sandford's, claimed to speak miraculously in an African dialect proving that she was called to be a missionary in Africa. Glassey's testimony helped Parham distinguish between the second experience of sanctification and the third experience of empowerment for service. In Parham's logic, the Holy Spirit would baptize believers giving them the gift of tongues or an unlearned human language for world evangelism.[79] This tongue-speech provided evidence for the third blessing that had previously been missing from his prior holiness and Wesleyan teachings.

Like many of his contemporaries, Parham believed that "the Apostolic Faith" or "true biblical Christianity" could not be practiced in traditional settings. Rather than establish a permanent church, Parham conducted his work as an itinerant evangelist and was a frequent guest at the homes of those he was ministering to at the time. A true "man of the people," Parham would discuss his religious beliefs with his host families in a practice that

---

77. Blumhofer, *Restoring the Faith*, 44.

78. Synan, *Holiness–Pentecostal Tradition*, 90.

79. McGee, *People of the Spirit*, 54.

was apparently common and welcomed.[80] Often in these discussions, Parham would find himself at odds with others in attendance, but used these "debates" as a means of refining his ever-growing theology. Once again, however, Parham would find himself in a dramatic moment with spiritual significance when both he and a young son took ill and two family members died under mysterious circumstances. This tragedy prompted Parham to seek out a more permanent base of operations and to once again alter his approach to his faith. Renouncing all medical intervention, Parham claimed that the power of God to sanctify the body from disease was as powerful as the ability to sanctify the soul from sin.[81]

## The Manifestation of Tongues

In 1900, Parham moved his wife Sarah and their family to Topeka, Kansas. There he established the Bethel Bible School in an elaborate, unfinished mansion known locally as "Stone's Folly." Parham felt strongly that something beyond the experience of sanctification was available, and perhaps this charismatic "baptism in the Holy Spirit" was what would be needed to meet the challenges of a new century.[82]

Parham began to lead his students at Bethel through a study of the major tenets of holiness theology including sanctification and divine healing. As their study approached the second chapter of the book of Acts, Parham encouraged his students to study the events that transpired on the day of Pentecost in Jerusalem including the act of speaking in other tongues. He shared with them his belief that anyone who seeks to receive this same "gift" would speak in an unlearned language for the purpose of missionary preaching.

As Parham prepared to leave the school for a meeting in Kansas City, he implored his students to study their Bibles and identify scriptural evidence for the receiving of the baptism of the Holy Spirit. Upon his return and to his astonishment, the students had come to agreement that speaking with other tongues was all the evidence they would need. The pattern of Spirit baptisms in Acts chapters 2, 10, and 19 established tongues as the biblical evidence along with Mark 16:17–18, which states, "They will speak in new tongues."

Convinced that this conclusion was proper interpretation of Scripture, Parham called his students to join him in conducting a watch-night service

80. Blumhofer, Restoring the Faith, 46.

81. Ibid., 47.

82. Synan, Holiness–Pentecostal Tradition, 90.

on December 31, 1900, which would continue through the night and into the New Year. Around eleven that evening, a student named Agnes Ozman requested Parham to lay his hands on her and pray that she be baptized with the Holy Spirit with the evidence of speaking in tongues. Shortly after midnight, it was reported that Ozman began to speak in another language and a halo or glow began to surround her face.[83]

While this event is widely regarded as the beginning of the modern Pentecostal movement in America, several discrepancies between the accounts of Parham and Ozman have emerged. According to Blumhofer, Parham's claim of consensus about the evidence of tongues is inadequate. Ozman herself, even after her tongues experience, did not consider tongues the only evidence given to those who received the baptism, nor did she expect the Holy Spirit to manifest himself to others as had allegedly happened with her.[84] This event is also not the only time that tongues-speech was recorded in the United States.[85] It is however, the first time that we see the manifestation of tongues specifically linked with the language of the Baptism of the Holy Spirit and presented as the initial physical evidence of this outpouring. This argument of initial physical evidence would come to define the doctrine within the Assemblies of God as a distinctive element that differentiated them from other Pentecostal and Charismatic movements.

In addition to establishing a pattern of doctrine, Ozman's experience also signaled a fulfillment of the Prophet Joel's proclamation that the Holy Spirit would be poured out on all humanity and both men and women would prophesy. The fact that a woman was the first person to be baptized in the Holy Spirit in this manner did not go unnoticed and created other opportunities for women to participate in the new manifestation of religious practice.

Within several days of the Ozman experience, more than a dozen others had spoken in tongues including Parham who reported that his newly equipped "apostles" had spoken in several foreign tongues including French, Chinese, Swedish, and Italian.[86] News of the events spread quickly. Local and regional media, interpreters and language experts as well as government officials converged on the school to investigate the

83. Synan, *Holiness–Pentecostal Tradition*, 91; McGee, *People of the Spirit*, 55.

84. Blumhofer, *Restoring the Faith*, 51.

85. See also Rodgers, *Northern Harvest*. Rodgers argues that prior to the events in Topeka, the manifestation of foreign tongues was a common occurrence amongst Scandinavian pietists who had settled on the Northern plains. Many of these people would later identify with the Pentecostal movement and specifically with the Assemblies of God.

86. McGee, *People of the Spirit*, 55.

new phenomenon. One report noted that it was doubtful that anything in recent years had awakened such interest and excitement or mystified the people more than these events.[87]

Parham immediately began teaching that missionaries no longer needed to feel compelled to study foreign languages to preach on the mission field. One only needed to be baptized with the Holy Spirit to preach to the native population in languages not known to the preacher.

In Parham's work, the connection between the rhetoric of empowerment for service is coupled with a foreign language being given as a means of taking the gospel to foreign lands. This claim becomes especially important for women in the Pentecostal movement because in it their legitimacy on the foreign mission field is established. Their qualifications for serving overseas were met with the provision of a language to communicate, empowered by the Holy Spirit to share the gospel. The addition of what appeared to be legitimate languages was one more confirmation of a woman's ability to serve.

While women missionaries faced many of the same rhetorical challenges as their domestic sisters, they achieved a greater sense of clarity in their service because a man may not have been available with the gift of that foreign language to serve. Until a suitable male leader could be found, single women operated overseas with much more freedom than their counterparts in the States.

Parham's message, however, was not nearly as successful as he had hoped it would become. Stung by criticism and a series of setbacks including the death of his young son and the sale of Stone's Folly from underneath him, Parham was wounded deeply but would not be deterred. After attempting to revive the Bible school in Kansas City only to again face failure, Parham traveled to the popular resort community of El Dorado Springs, Missouri, where the therapeutic quality of the water supply was thought to provide healing. There he prayed for Mary Arthur, and her dramatic healing of one eye and other ailments again drew immediate attention to Parham's ministry. The response was astonishing as Parham began a series of meetings in Arthur's home town of Galena, Kansas. The meetings recorded over eight hundred converts, a thousand healings, and several hundred baptized in the Holy Spirit with other tongues. Parham's Apostolic Faith movement had once again found new life.[88]

87. Synan, *Holiness–Pentecostal Tradition*, 92.

88. McGee, *People of the Spirit*, 56–57.

## The Education of William Seymour

Eventually, at the request of friends, Parham established his ministry and a new Bible school in Houston, Texas. Among those influenced by Parham's ministry in Houston were several African-Americans who had great interest in the holiness movement. One was Lucy Farrow, who, at one time, had worked as a domestic for the Parham's and Neely Terry from Los Angeles who worshiped at a holiness mission in the city. Another would be William J. Seymour who, along with Farrow, was well known in Houston's holiness missions.

Despite his frequent denials, Parham's worldview nurtured racist tendencies and, combined with the racial mores of the Deep South, tensions often surfaced.[89] Nonetheless, many African-Americans attended Parham's meetings. Farrow arranged with Parham for Seymour to attend the Bible school, but the law would not allow for a black student to be schooled alongside white students in the same classroom. It quickly became apparent to Parham that Seymour possessed a great desire to attend classes and a great thirst for learning. This zeal to be educated in the study of the Gospel overcame even Jim Crow. Parham permitted Seymour to sit in the hallway (other accounts record that he sat behind a curtain) to receive his lessons.[90] For several months, Seymour heard the new Pentecostal theology from Parham and took every opportunity afforded to him to preach this new message.

While Parham had intended to send Seymour to preach "to those of his own color" in Texas, a different opportunity changed the course of Seymour's life and impacted the entire Pentecostal movement.[91] After hearing Seymour preach, Neely Terry returned home to Los Angeles where expectancy of a revival intensified as believers heard and read about events occurring in the South as well as overseas in Wales. Terry belonged to a holiness group led by Julia W. Hutchins, and she implored Hutchins to call Seymour to Los Angeles. Seymour accepted the invitation, and with a train ticket paid for by Parham, he arrived in February of 1906 to take on a ministry that would far exceed his wildest imagination.[92]

What was about to take place in Los Angeles would challenge assumptions about not only religious theology and expression, but also call into question preconceived notions about race, class, and gender in the church. Most of the influential voices in the holiness and Pentecostal movement

89. Blumhofer, *Assemblies of God*, 89.

90. Blumhofer, *Restoring the Faith*, 55; McGee, *People of the Spirit*, 58; Synan, *Holiness–Pentecostal Tradition*, 93.

91. Blumhofer, *Restoring the Faith*, 55.

92. McGee, *People of the Spirit*, 58–59; Synan, *Holiness–Pentecostal Tradition*, 95.

up to this point had been educated, white males who carried an ethos of religious grooming and an already established level of influence. William Seymour in contrast was the very embodiment of the collective history of the holiness/Pentecostal movement. If the challenges of race and class could be overcome by a dramatic move of the Holy Spirit, gender may also cease to be a constraint.

## THE AZUSA STREET REVIVAL

Upon his arrival in Los Angeles early in 1906, William Seymour took over the pastorate at Julia Hutchins's Holiness Church and preached his very first sermon on the text of Acts 2:4. In it he proclaimed that speaking in tongues was the biblical evidence of receiving the Holy Spirit, although he had not yet received the gift. He also immediately encountered resistance. Hutchins and others in leadership in the Southern California Holiness Association rejected this message as contrary to true holiness teaching. Returning to the church for the following service, Seymour found the doors padlocked shut and his theology unwelcome there.

While Julia Hutchins may not have appreciated Seymour's viewpoint on this third blessing, many of her church members did. Homeless and penniless but undaunted, Seymour was invited to stay at the home of Richard Asbery, located at 214 North Bonnie Brae Street. At this point, Asbery was skeptical of Seymour and did not accept his new teachings, but he allowed him to hold meetings and preach in his living room. For several days, the small group held prayer services until April 9, 1906, when Seymour and seven others fell to the floor and began to speak in tongues.[93]

Word of this event traveled quickly in both white and black communities. For several nights, crowds gathered on the porch, including what remained of Julia Hutchins's church and several other holiness congregations. In the services that followed, the music was raucous and demonstrations of tongues were so pronounced that onlookers began to gather in the streets to view the events. Eventually the crowds became so large that the front porch collapsed.[94]

Shortly thereafter, Seymour rented a former African Methodist Episcopal Church turned livery stable and tenement house at 312 Azusa Street. Blumhofer notes that while little to look at, the new building was just what would suit Seymour's needs. The distance from residential areas assured

93. Synan, *Holiness–Pentecostal Tradition*, 96.
94. McGee, *People of the Spirit*, 59.

freedom from noise complaints, and its simplicity made the setting more conducive to the informality and spontaneity these worshipers coveted.[95]

No sooner had Seymour begun preaching than a monumental revival broke out with nearly 350 people filling the building and scores more being forced out onto the lawn. The meetings at the Apostolic Faith Mission quickly caught the attention of the media, which only increased curiosity. Enthusiastic worship opened the services with singing followed by testimonies of healing and other "victories" and prayer for the sick. Altar calls for those seeking salvation and Spirit baptism followed lengthy times of preaching, moments of silence, shouted praises to God, and some reports of persons falling "under the power" marked the order of the services. With all the media attention and participants traveling around to bear witness to their experience, word of the revival spread quickly across North America and Europe. William Seymour and congregant Clara Lum produced the *Apostolic Faith*, a newspaper that chronicled the events, from September 1906 to May 1908. The first run was five thousand copies and by 1907 the pressrun reached forty thousand.[96] Nothing seemed to be able to quell the growing revival from spreading, including the great San Francisco earthquake. Participants viewed the destruction as a sign from God that judgment was at hand and their efforts were needed now more than ever.

In the meetings at Azusa Street, racial, gender, and class discrimination were absent. African-Americans, Asian-Americans, Caucasians, and Jews, both men and women from every income level attended side by side to hear William Seymour preach. Frank Bartleman, a participant in the meetings and the person most noted for having kept journals and notes about the event proclaimed, "The color line was washed away in the blood."[97] While over time, the majority in attendance at the Azusa Street events would be Caucasian and lower- to middle-class Americans, the fact that race, gender, and class blended so easily would play a defining role and have a significant impact in the characterization and growth of the Pentecostal movement.

More than mixed worship caught the attention of the media and church leaders. While it was difficult enough to imagine the races worshiping together, the greatest amount of controversy exploded over the intermixing of race and gender. White men were being prayed over by black women. Men of color were laying hands on white women and leading them to the baptism experience. Uneducated washer women were providing Christian

95. Blumhofer, *Restoring the Faith*, 56.

96. McGee, *People of the Spirit*, 60.

97. Synan, *Holiness–Pentecostal Tradition*, 99; McGee, *People of the Spirit*, 62.

teaching to the learned and the cultural elite.[98] The impact of women, both black and white, during the revival and in the years that followed, is as defining and groundbreaking as the doctrine.

## The Women of Azusa Street

While the events at Azusa Street would define and give them a voice, several of the women who would march on to the world's stage at Azusa did not come there as novices. Historian and theologian Estrelda Alexander notes, they had experience in ministry as pastors and evangelists throughout the country.[99] Anna Hall, Mabel Smith, Lucy Farrow, and Neely Teery had all been acquainted with Parham's work in Houston, and they had come to Los Angeles already having experienced speaking in tongues.

Unfortunately, we still do not know a great deal about most of the women who were a part of the revival or who may have gone out and begun ministry work as a result of their experience. Surviving documents and personal journals reveal a commanding presence of female participation and leadership in various areas of the work in Los Angeles. Many of these women remain virtually nameless, with only "Mrs." and the name of her husband listed as a reference, or at best the title of "Sister" or "Mother" before a last name to indicate the presence of a female. However, as a result of renewed interest in Pentecostal history and the 100th anniversary of the Azusa Street revival, this challenge is beginning to be corrected. Many names have surfaced in several historical accounts and in the discovery of more primary documents. Yet, even among these gleanings, details are missing about who these women were prior to Azusa Street or what may have become of them, but what is known is striking.

Women at the Azusa Street Mission were preachers and teachers. They led the congregation in worship and handled many of the administrative responsibilities, including examining potential missionaries and evangelists for ordination. These women provided both spiritual and organizational oversight to bring a sense of order and purpose to the growing

---

98. Alexander, *Women of Azusa Street*, 37.

99. Significantly, Alexander's work does something that no other historical account of the Azusa Street revival or the Pentecostal movement accomplishes. While others devote a chapter or passage to women, Alexander has conducted a specific and biographical history on a significant number of influential women from the revival. She has gained access to primary source material and personal information about who these women were and the roles they played in the Pentecostal movement that has previously been ignored or left out. I am deeply in debt to her scholarship and her insight into the role of women in the Pentecostal movement.

body of believers. In the beginning, six of the twelve elders at the mission were women: Jennie Evans (Moore) Seymour, May Evans, Phoebe Sergeant, Ophelia Wiley, Clara Lum, and Florence Crawford. Upon the death of William Seymour, his wife, Jennie took the helm of the mission and continued to lead for eleven years until her own death.[100]

Several more women became evangelists and missionaries who took the Pentecostal message from Azusa throughout the world. Daisy Batman, May Evans, Ardella Meade, Lillian Garr and Rosa de Lopez joined their husbands in ministry teams. Lucy Farrow and Julia Hutchins, who first rejected Seymour's message, but then were later converted and became ardent Pentecostals joined larger missionary organizations. Others like Ivy Campbell, Mabel Smith, Lucy Leatherman, and Rachel Sizelove went out as single missionaries and evangelists and dedicated their entire lives to the work of the Gospel.[101] While most organized denominations had not begun to ordain women or allow them in the pulpit, these women claimed for themselves ordination by God and created opportunity for ministry.[102] What the larger society had not been able to accomplish with regard to the liberation of women, these women, empowered by the Spirit, carved out for themselves.

The role of women at the Azusa Street Mission was not without its challenges even among those who participated and led the revival. Female leadership would eventually cause a break between Florence Crawford and William Seymour that would lead Crawford to leave Los Angeles and begin her own denominational work in Portland, Oregon. While Crawford had gained respect as a leader and overseer within Seymour's ministry, subtle changes over time seemed to limit the level that she would ultimately be able to attain. While she does not directly conjecture, Estrelda Alexander notes two scenarios regarding changes in the structure at the Azusa Street Mission that eventually led to the departure of Florence Crawford, Clara Lum, and the entire mailing list for the Apostolic Faith publication.

First, Alexander notes that in developing a doctrinal statement for the mission, Seymour made distinct roles for men and women.[103] Women were allowed to minister and to lead in the worship, but baptism and ordination were to only be conducted by men. The ranks of elder and bishop also seemed to be restricted to men as Seymour created a liturgy for the ordaining of leaders. Yet, Seymour also created a system of leadership assumption that

100. Alexander, *Women of Azusa Street*, 12.

101. Some of these women were single, never married women and others went out without their husbands.

102. Ibid., 38.

103. Ibid., 66.

paved a direct path for the woman who would become his wife, Jennie Evans Seymour, to assume the leadership of the mission upon his death.

Quite possibly, the issue of Jennie Seymour may have played a greater role than any doctrinal statement in the breach with Crawford and Lum. Clearly, Clara Lum was instrumental in helping Seymour create a periodical for the mission and recorded most of Seymour's sermons in shorthand; less clear is the exact extent of their personal relationship. Estrelda Alexander speculates that Seymour and Lum may have had a deeper relationship than what appears on the surface and that they entertained the idea of marriage.[104] However, when William Seymour consulted his friend, C. H. Mason, founder of the Church of God in Christ, Mason cautioned Seymour against such a relationship. For the first time, race may have been a problem within the leadership at Azusa Street because Lum was a white woman. Mason believed an inter-racial relationship would cause too much trouble for the mission and destroy the work there.

Shortly after William Seymour married Jennie Evans Moore, Clara Lum left her work at the mission. Lum never married. Alexander notes that this departure may also have been the final issue between Florence Crawford and Seymour, as she left the mission permanently thereafter as well. Jennie Seymour was be the only woman who continued as a member of the board at the mission.[105]

Several of these women would have a significant influence on the formation of the Assemblies of God, either through direct involvement or as a matter of influence over those who would go on to found the fellowship. Others would become charter members of the organization and continue to minister and influence for the first time as a part of an organized church.

Farrow, who first introduced Seymour to Parham would also have an influence over a founding father of the Assemblies of God. Within a few months of coming to Azusa Street, Farrow left to embark on a preaching campaign. At a meeting in Texas she again joined up with Parham and served on the ministry team at one of his meetings. In the audience that evening was Howard Goss, who would prove instrumental in spreading the Pentecostal message throughout the Midwest and in founding the Assemblies of God. Goss had initially rejected the idea of the initial evidence of tongues, but Farrow's sermon convinced him of the truth of this doctrine. He went forward in this service to have Farrow pray for him, and as she laid her hands on him, he notes that the Spirit of God struck him like a bolt of lightning. Goss's wife Ethel, who was also in this service reported

104. Ibid., 52–53.
105. Ibid., 67.

about Farrow: "Although colored [sic], she was received as a messenger of the Lord to us, even in the deep south of Texas."[106]

Like Farrow, Lucy Leatherman would also play an influential role in life of a future leader in the Assemblies of God. One of the most educated women involved with the revival, Leatherman also traveled the farthest and most often to spread the message of Pentecostalism. While best known for her work in Arabic cultures and other remote areas where women were severely limited in their status, mobility, and influence, she also had a deep passion for ministry in the United States. She especially became concerned about New York City. After one visit, Leatherman contacted Parham and asked him to send someone to New York City. As a result of Leatherman's efforts in the city, Parham sent another woman, Marie Burgess, to New York to plant a church there. Burgess would become an incredibly important figure in the Pentecostal movement and specifically the Assemblies of God with the founding of Glad Tidings Tabernacle. Her influence and ministry would produce the largest Pentecostal congregation on the East Coast and the largest missionary budget in the missions-minded Assemblies of God.[107]

Ivey Glenshaw Campbell holds two distinctions among the women from Azusa Street. She was the first white woman to speak in tongues at the revival, and she was largely responsible for spreading the Pentecostal message through Ohio and Pennsylvania. A seamstress by profession, it was her holiness background and her contacts with other women in her work that led her to the Azusa Street mission. She returned to her home state of Ohio upon being issued "missionary" credentials by William Seymour and began to hold several revival meetings beginning in her home town of East Liverpool.[108] Her meetings were very successful and attracted many people including church leaders from other Pentecostal gatherings. In June 1907 she would join a camp meeting in Alliance, Ohio, which had a major impact on the Pentecostal message moving into the Northeast. More than 700 people attended this meeting including J. Roswell Flower, who would go on to become the founding editor of *The Pentecostal Evangel* and founding member of the Assemblies of God. Campbell would also align herself with the fledging Assemblies, but her ministry would be short-lived. It is reported that her health was quite fragile and she returned to California where she lived with the Seymour's and Farrow above the Azusa Street Mission. She died there in 1918 at the age of 44.[109]

106. Ibid.

107. Ibid., 71, 74.

108. McGee, *People of the Spirit*, 66–67.

109. Alexander, *Women of Azusa Street*, 148.

In the case of each of these women, the Pentecostal paradigm provided the opportunity for them to engage in ministry and to create for themselves an open door to serve as a minister. Very rarely did established churches, denominations, or other institutions provide these opportunities. When institutions would not provide the credentials necessary for them to minister, women claimed ordination for themselves through the Pentecostal message. They used the very words, language, and symbols that legitimized Pentecostalism to legitimize their own service. These women created their own space when society could not or would not create space for them. When these women presented the message they believed they were empowered to give, they could be accepted regardless of physical, theological, or cultural constraints, which on the surface seemed insurmountable.

Despite this acceptance in the moment, opportunity often swiftly met with constraint. Few of these constraints were directly related to Pentecostal theology or rhetoric. Yet, where constraints were in place, women still found means to engage in influence with or without an official title or the backing of an institution. Even when their names were not recorded for posterity or the details of their work were lost to the history books, the fingerprints of women's involvement in spreading the Pentecostal message are evident. One of the purposes of this study is to offer a corrective to the historical record and to give voice to the impact that women had in creating and perpetuating one of the most successful religious movements in history. By reinserting the narrative of women's leadership into the historical record, a more complete picture of the uniqueness of the Pentecostal movement and its transformational paradigm become more clear and powerful.

## The Sparkling Fountain

Through their rhetorically sanctioned, willing defiance of conventional wisdom and religious tradition, each of these women played a key role in bringing future leaders into the Pentecostal paradigm. One of these women, Rachel Sizelove, received a vision that would transform not only individuals, but an entire city, Springfield, Missouri. Within a few short years, Springfield, Missouri would become the home of the world-wide headquarters of the Assemblies of God.

By the time Rachel Harper Sizelove arrived at the Azusa Street Mission, she was already accustomed to life as a full-time minister. Shortly after her conversion, Rachel noted that she felt the Lord laid it upon her heart to "go and get sinners saved." So she did. Along with her husband, Joseph, Sizelove had spent much of her adult life as a circuit-riding evangelist of the Free Methodist Church. At the time of the revival, the Sizeloves were still living in a Free Methodist colony near Los Angeles.[110] While at first they regarded the events at Azusa with curiosity, the Sizeloves would soon experience the Pentecostal outpouring for themselves. Sizelove was one of the first women licensed by the Azusa Street Mission when her Methodist church rejected what they considered fanaticism making it impossible for her to continue serving as a circuit rider.[111]

In May of 1907, she left California to carry the message of Pentecost to her sister's home in Springfield, Missouri. While traveling to Missouri, Sizelove met another woman from the Azusa mission who was traveling east to embark on a ship for Africa. The two women struck up a quick friendship and spent the remainder of their journey holding services and spreading the Pentecostal message to anyone and everyone on the train with them.[112]

According to Sizelove's own account, she arrived at the home of her sister, Lillie Corum on Division Street in Springfield where the Holy Spirit gave her a message in tongues, which confirmed to her that this is where she was to hold meetings.[113] Lillie was the first person to receive the gift of tongues at these "cottage" meetings. Corum records in her notes that people were very interested in what they were experiencing and word traveled quickly of these events. She also notes that people were skeptical and searched their Bibles and said that if it was truly of God then it would stand.[114] The evidence proved irrefutable, and as Sizelove traveled back and forth between Missouri and California, the gathering grew.

In April 1911, Corum and Amanda Benedict received permission to erect a tent on the corner of Campbell and Calhoun Streets in which to hold their meetings. At that spot, Benedict carved out her own contributions to the city that would become the headquarters of the Assemblies of God. After receiving her own personal Pentecost, Benedict often found herself up entire nights praying for the city of Springfield. Eventually, in Benedict's account, God gave her a vision of storm clouds attempting to roll over the city. For a year, she ate nothing but bread and water, and she stayed in the tent erected for the Pentecostal meetings to pray for victory over these dark powers. [115]

110. Ibid., 170.

111. Alexander, *Women of Azusa Street*, 173; See also a tract by Rachel Sizelove entitled, "Sparkling Fountain for the Whole Earth" reprinted from *Word and Work*, 1, 11, 12.

112. Alexander, *Women of Azusa Street*, 173–74; See also Sizelove, "Sparkling Fountain," 1, 11, 12.

113. See also Sizelove, "Sparkling Fountain," 1, 11, 12.

114. Typed notes by Lillian (Lillie) Corum dated 1920–21.

115. Booze, "Amanda Benedict Prayed," 13.

According to Corum, Benedict was well educated and should be preaching the gospel, but her place of ministry was to be a person of intercessory prayer. "Never had I met a person who prayed as she prayed, fasting from food, and from sleep praying all night" stated Corum in her personal notes, "yet looking bright and happy in the morning."[116]

In 1913, Sizelove returned to Springfield to a "good sized assembly of baptized saints." In a tract, which was reprinted from an article published in 1934 in *Word and Work*, one of many periodicals published for an audience who identified with Pentecostalism and often used as an evangelistic tool, Sizelove records a vision she received in the bedroom of her sister's home. She states she was carried away in the Spirit and a sparkling fountain appeared before her in the heart of the city of Springfield. This spring would flow toward the East, the West, the North and the South until the whole land was "deluged with living water."[117] By November of that same year, Rachel formally organized the congregation that had formed and installed her sister, Lillie, as its pastor. This small group would become the first Assemblies of God congregation, Central Assembly of God in Springfield, Missouri, located at the site of the tent first erected by Corum and Benedict. Adjacent to Central Assembly now sits the worldwide headquarters of the Assemblies of God.

Historians do not note, nor does Sizelove indicate in her own writings whether she sensed the importance of the events that she participated in. In her typed, but unpublished biography, she does not hold either the Azusa revival or her vision of Springfield as important events in her own spiritual journey, devoting only six pages to the revival and not mentioning the vision of the fountain.[118] However, Sizelove would later develop a greater appreciation for the historic events that had occurred in her life and would write the aforementioned article about her vision in the Pentecostal periodical.[119]

Several important and defining issues resulted from the events at Azusa Street and the uniquely diverse group of men and women who participated in the revival. The revival carried on for three and a half years, and in that time, the doctrine and identity of the Pentecostal movement was solidified. The Azusa event is the catalyst that moved tongue-speech from

---

116. Typed notes by Lillian (Lillie) Corum dated 1920–21.

117. See also Sizelove, "Sparkling Fountain," 1, 11, 12.

118. Alexander, *Women of Azusa Street*, 176–78.

119. Prior to her death in 1941, Rachel Sizelove made another priceless contribution to the Pentecostal legacy of the Azusa revival in individual issues of *The Apostolic Faith*, which she had collected and saved and eventually donated to be preserved.

a random event sprinkled through history to a fully defined doctrine.[120] While Parham turned his back on William Seymour and the events at Azusa upon visiting the revival services, his insistence on tongues as the necessary, biblical evidence of the Holy Spirit's baptism eventually created a division within the holiness ranks and created the Pentecostal movement. Pentecostals had settled on a single incontrovertible and repeatable kind of evidence so that they no longer needed to be able to "prove" that they had received the experience.[121] Seymour's success both in numbers and in breeching the cultural divide may simply have been too much for Parham, but Pentecostalism would succeed and would do what the holiness movement had been unable to do as a movement.

## THE SCENE IS SET

The formation of the Pentecostal movement has many narratives, like a fabric weaved together with many individual threads. These various threads on their own do not seem significant, but put together, they form a pattern that set the stage for a dramatic reconception of God and the person and work of the Holy Spirit. Throughout this history, women played a significant role and greatly influenced the movement. From the family devotionals of Susana Wesley, which helped to form her sons' burgeoning theology, to the visions and fasts of women like Rachel Sizelove and Amanda Benedict, which transformed the Queen City of the Missouri Ozarks into the leadership and educational hub of the largest and fastest-growing Pentecostal denomination in the world, the actions of these women on their own may not seem noteworthy, but placed together and in the context of the development of Pentecostal theology, their participation and willingness to challenge the conventional wisdom of their day created a revolutionary place for women.

Women were seriously constrained by the prevailing scene of religious tradition. The church and its traditions were challenged by the presence of the female voice and responded naturally to this perceived threat by "circling the wagons" in an attempt to maintain the integrity of the community. However, the presence of the feminine was not the only challenge the church was experiencing within its ranks, and as the Pentecostal paradigm began to push away at these constraints, women claimed for themselves the opportunity to burst the borders of religious tradition and take their message to the people. However, the prevailing rhetoric contained in thousands of years of historical church practice would not be silenced so quickly, and

120. Synan, *Holiness–Pentecostal Tradition*, 111–12.

121. Ibid., 112.

women would continue to have to find their voice and navigate the delicate waters between the opportunity of their empowerment for service and the constraints laid out by those they sought to serve.

For most of these women, their participation and influence was not about women's rights. Their concern was not feminism or overcoming oppression. What they were called to do, they needed to do quickly and without hesitation. Estrelda Alexander notes that these women came looking for power and they found it.[122] They were not after human power but rather power to carve out rhetorical space where they could speak Good News into the unknown with unknown tongues. Rhetoric for healing and deliverance from life's maladies was their desire. They sought the power to withstand the culture, those who would mock and scorn, and the power to speak truth to power when the church rejected them.

The history of the Pentecostal movement as well as its broad and somewhat colorful development from the streams of Wesleyan holiness, Quaker piety, and radical evangelicalism is also a history of symbol formation, which defines the movement itself and advocates for its contribution to the religious landscape. This symbol formation shapes a rhetorical space for women, often made by women, to establish their legitimacy as part of the fabric of Pentecostal culture.

While Phoebe Palmer never held an official position with a membership card or credential papers to acknowledge her right to speak, she defied the culture and defied religious history to speak anyway and present one of the more sustained, unrivaled arguments for women's leadership. Women like Palmer, Hannah Whitall Smith and Lucy Farrow were not looking to be icons of feminist power, just the opposite in fact. These women had bottled up inside of them a passion to see the message of Jesus communicated. That goal was the heart of their rhetoric. Legitimization of their right to engage in this rhetoric was an added blessing, but legitimization was not their intention or purpose in choosing to speak publicly or to open their homes and lives to those who would come to hear them teach and preach.

As the Pentecostal movement became more established, the questions of doctrine become an area of great contention. The vernacular of Holy Spirit Baptism, empowerment for service, and prophecy versus preaching/teaching were debated and refined. As a result of this organization and what some might term institutionalization, the issue of women continued to play a role, only this time as matter of official record. Votes will be taken about creating opportunity for women or engaging constraints on them.

---

122. Alexander, *Women of Azusa Street*, 180.

The formation of the Assemblies of God saw increased rhetorical invention in which the four-fold gospel became as much about work as it was about the business of saving souls. The question of who could engage in this work and with what freedoms and limitations was a primary development and would come to define the Assemblies of God as a key player in the debate over women's leadership within the church.

# 3

# Women Welcome?

## Discursive Tension and the Formation
## of the Assemblies of God

*Men have hypocritically objected to women making them-
selves conspicuous in pulpit work. . . . [These women] did
not push themselves to the front, God pulled them there.
They did not take this ministry on themselves, God put it
on them.*

—A. G. Jeffries in the *Weekly Evangel*, 1916

*Sometimes it is risky for women to venture into ministries
where a man's voice is expected to be heard. But those who
value the message, realizing its eternal dimensions, accept
their assignment in obedience to God. They verbalize what
God's Word says and what He has done in their lives.*

—Sandra G. Clopine in the *Pentecostal Evangel*, 1994

IN *ANOINTED TO SERVE*, Menzies notes that it would not be accurate to
give complete credit for the entire story of the spread of Pentecostalism to
the revival at Azusa Street in Los Angeles. Yet, without question it was the
"Great Revival" that was the most significant instrument in the launching of

a coordinated movement.[1] Several other revivals erupted around the world concurrently with the event in Los Angeles and immediately after not only within the United States but also across the globe. Little evidence of visible links among the events exists, but certainly some reports credit the testimony of others with inspiring a yearning for a spiritual renewal that seemed to sweep the earth.

In the United States, the newly forming Pentecostal message spread quickly and often resulted in the formation of independent congregations. While Parham's view of doctrine (i.e., salvation by grace, sanctification as a second work distinct from salvation, and baptism in the Holy Spirit for empowerment as a third experience, divine healing and the imminent return of Christ) seemed to dominate, and as the revival spread, believers naturally came from diverse backgrounds and brought with them various challenges to the fledgling movement.[2]

Women embraced the new movement and were as eager as men to spread the Pentecostal message. The influence of women such as Phoebe Palmer played a significant role in the rise of the feminine voice throughout the growth of holiness expression, and the way in which women participated and led at Azusa Street was nothing short of precedent setting. As the years passed, opportunities for women diminished within the Apostolic Faith Mission in Los Angeles apart from Jennie Seymour. Yet many women were uninhibited. Several struck out on their own as evangelists and missionaries while some even began their own churches and denominations. Some who went out from Azusa Street would become significant players in the years to come as the movement spread, grew, and organized.

Women were not simply present at the birth of the movement; they engaged in discourse, which carved out a distinct rhetorical space and created a unique opportunity for their participation and leadership. When the constraints of culture and historical religious ideology stepped up to challenge their place and position, women who believed they were empowered by the Holy Spirit found opportunities to serve despite the constraints placed upon them. The discrepancies between the opportunities presented to and created by women and the challenges placed before them by cultural context and religious ideology are revealed in rhetoric. The historical, cultural, and theological context in which the Pentecostal movement progressed contributes to this talk and permeates the formation of ideology and practice that creates dissonance and tension both within the fellowship and without. The

---

1. Menzies, *Anointed to Serve*, 60.
2. McGee, *People of the Spirit*, 72.

relationship between the church and women is distinct and how Pentecostals have talked about this relationship is even more distinct.

One way of understanding this relationship is to narrow the focus from the broader history of the Pentecostal movement to the formation of the Assemblies of God, the largest and arguably the most successful, organization with the Pentecostal tradition. The early years of the fellowship defined the doctrine and theology of women's ministry rhetoric and shaped future dynamics that continue to challenge women's callings to the present day. Adopting William Durham's "finished work" theology and embracing the view that the baptism in the Holy Spirit is an empowerment for service separated the Assemblies of God from other Pentecostal and holiness organizations. These unique doctrinal choices that gave birth to the Assemblies of God also created and restricted women's rhetorical space within the movement, including issues surrounding the definition "elder" (pastor), licensure and ordination, and the roles of women serving stateside versus those serving overseas.

In these early years, women's participation in the Assemblies of God was a doctrinal distinctive rivaled only by the doctrine of initial physical evidence. The very justifications for the existence of Pentecostalism in the prophecy of the Prophet Joel and first evidenced on the Day of Pentecost in Acts 2 establishes biblical precedent not only for the movement itself but also for the inclusion of women to participate fully in the work of leading the church and advancing the gospel message.

Yet, what was so ground-breaking was not simply the advocacy for the participation of women, but the doctrinal argument of empowerment to serve regardless of gender. By this time, most Methodist churches had rejected the Wesleyan view of the baptism in the Holy Spirit all together and many holiness churches that had broken away from the mainstream Methodist church continued to embrace the Wesleyan theology that focused on sanctification as second work of the Holy Spirit following salvation. The baptism in the Holy Spirit was a sign or evidence of a sanctifying work of grace following conversion meant to perfect the Christian and eradicate their sinful nature. The Keswick emphasis embraced by leaders such as D. L. Moody on Holy Spirit empowerment displaced this concept and focused on the manifestations of the Holy Spirit as an anointing for service. The idea that if the Holy Spirit experience, which early adherents argued as evidence for a new Pentecost, was also an empowerment for service, then the empowerment of women was natural evolution because women could also receive this experience.

As with these doctrinal choices, so too the symbolic choices of early leaders shape the rhetorical history of women in the Assemblies of God.

These rhetorical choices defined the opportunities available to women and the discourse surrounding them that ultimately led to dissonance rather than harmony.

The known historical record supports the argument that despite several challenges, women played a unique and significant role in the Pentecostal movement and in the formation and growth of the Assemblies of God. The evidence of this argument is found in the discourse of the Assemblies of God, its early leaders and its participants. Language loomed large in the formation and shaping of a place for women and in the context of how others viewed their participation and leadership. Women who embraced the Assemblies of God as their ecclesiastical home and who sought to share its message with others faced opportunities and constraints that were inherently rhetorical, symbolic, and rooted in discourse.

The symbols used in the Assemblies of God shaped a response to the roles women played and in turn defined what these roles mean. Significantly, these symbols influenced those who were advocates of women's participation and those who were not, and their rhetoric resulted in tension. The level of women's participation cannot be denied, yet it seems that the very same rhetoric that set the Assemblies of God apart, including a rejection of traditional religious culture, is the very rhetoric used to perpetuate and promote women's silence.

The scene in the rhetorical drama that extended from the early Pentecostal movement came to have meaning for the Assemblies of God and for women. According to Burke, those who function within a scene are constrained by the elements of the scene. To build on Burke's ideas regarding scene, behavior by those in the Assemblies of God is controlled by "norms" that members of the community themselves devised and those who challenge the boundaries become a threat to the survival of the organization. The integrity of the community is challenged and it becomes almost instinctual for members of the community to react to these challenges. Members of the community seek to limit or even eliminate those who challenge the boundaries so that they can maintain their vision of what the scene is and how they function within it.

What motives led to the interplay of language, which created both opportunities and constraints for women to participate in the Assemblies of God in ways previously limited to them in religious life and practice? The clues lie in the rhetorical history of the Assemblies of God throughout its formative years (1914–1935) both chronologically and biographically. The historical, theological and cultural roots that created the Assemblies of God and the actors, both men and women, who shaped the rhetoric of the Assemblies of God, are key with regard to understanding women's roles. The symbolic choices employed by the early founders and participants in the Assemblies of God set the linguistic boundaries for who could engage in this work and with what freedoms and limitations. The debate over where these boundary lines lie is also a key aspect of the development of the Assemblies of God and would come to define it as a major player in the debate over women's leadership within the church.

## CONFLICT AND CONTROVERSY

One of the greatest challenges to women in ministry in the Assemblies of God has been the conflict between women's institutional authority and cultural authority. Institutional authority can be defined as any "official" authority within an organization. In the case of the Pentecostal movement and later the Assemblies of God, this institutional authority includes issuing credentials, ordination, and using the term Elder or Pastor to refer to the position held. Cultural authority, on the other hand, refers to participation in activities within the movement, which for women means such as activities as playing a musical instrument, teaching children, and preparing meals for gatherings. Cultural authority might also allow women to speak publicly outside of any official capacity including things like public prayer, reading Scripture, and participating in evangelistic campaigns. Blumhofer concludes that institutional authority has been restricted since the Assemblies of God's founding, but cultural authority women engaged in "sometimes obscured the restrictions."[3] For example, the call and the anointing on a person's life were far more valued by ministers and congregations than any card or piece of paper. However, the challenges to women's institutional authority have often impacted their cultural authority.

### Culture and Theological Conflict

As Pentecostalism spread, believers from Wesleyan-Holiness backgrounds were often natural converts, but so were Baptists, Presbyterians and many others who witnessed the revival spirit for themselves and were baptized in the Holy Spirit. With more and more theological diversity making up the growing movement, disputes were a natural outcrop of the rapid development and lack of centralized teachings resulting from the revivals. While some credentials were offered from the Azusa Street Mission and other fledgling organizations, those spreading the Gospel lacked coherent

---

3. Blumhofer, *Restoring the Faith*, 174.

credibility and a consistent message. Historian Gary McGee outlines three disputes that characterized much of the early tension within the movement. The first dispute revolved around the value of the book of Acts for building doctrine. McGee states that how one thought about this book naturally had an effect on their doctrine of speaking in tongues as the initial physical evidence of the Baptism in the Holy Spirit.[4]

Because many from the earlier holiness movement had used the terminology of the Baptism in the Holy Spirit, newly minted Pentecostals found themselves dismayed when many rejected their teachings. One of the most vehement in opposition to the new emphasis on tongues was Alma White, who claimed to be the first American woman ordained a Bishop. White led a holiness group called the Pillar of Fire and it seemed she held not only a theological opposition to Pentecostalism but also a personal grudge. White's estranged husband, a former Methodist minister whom she had displaced in the pulpit, was a quick convert to Pentecostal theology and practice. Claiming the tongues emphasis was a work of Satan to distract people from God's end-time promises to them, White wrote numerous articles and spoke out publicly against the movement and its growing population.[5]

While others did not go as far as White, by 1907, other holiness teachers were publicly rejecting the movement's distinction that tongues was the initial physical evidence of the Holy Spirit's baptism. Early on, as the movement grew, leaders such as A. B. Simpson of the Christian and Missionary Alliance and Keswick teacher Arthur T. Pierson as well as Moody Bible Institute President and heir apparent to D. L. Moody, Reuben A. Torrey had strongly affirmed the obligation of Christians to seek a greater revelation from the Holy Spirit. Each of these men believed that tongues could be expected in the last days. However, the perceived focus on seeking manifestations rather than seeking God created a sense of excess that these leaders were not able to reconcile.

## Durham's Finished Work Theology

In addition to the matter of tongues, a dispute arose over the nature of sanctification, which, unlike the previous issue, did stem from differing denominational backgrounds. Participants who came from a Reformed tradition where sanctification occurred first at conversion then progressed over time challenged the Wesleyan-Holiness thought that sanctification was both instantaneous and complete. This controversy reached its peak in 1910.

4. McGee, *People of the Spirit*, 72.
5. Blumhofer, *Assemblies of God*, 181.

William H. Durham of the North Avenue Mission in Chicago, more than anyone, challenged the holiness doctrine of a second work of grace taught by Parham, William Seymour and others within the movement. A former Baptist, Durham heard of the events at Azusa Street and was impressed by the experiences of acquaintances that had traveled there to take part in the revival. Seeking his own experience, he traveled to the Apostolic Faith Mission and received the Baptism in the Holy Spirit for himself in March 1907.[6]

Durham then returned to Chicago and to his congregation where he vowed to never again preach the traditional holiness message of sanctification. Several of his parishioners had also experienced a Pentecostal outpouring, and Durham's work in Chicago became a center for Pentecostal teaching in the Midwest. Durham also began to publish a paper he called *The Pentecostal Testimony* in which he could spread the message of Pentecost to friends and family outside of Chicago. Several important figures in the Pentecostal movement also spent time in Durham's congregation: A. H. Argue of Winnipeg, Manitoba, in Canada; E. N. Bell, the first Chairman of the Assemblies of God; and Aimee Semple McPherson, arguably the most famous female Pentecostal minister and denomination founder of the International Church of the Four-Square Gospel.

Despite the success of the Chicago mission and Durham's own experience, he continued to struggle with the issue of sanctification. After careful study, Durham argued that a complete transformation in the heart of the sinner takes place at conversion, which is the gift of salvation in its complete power. Using 1 Cor 15:22 regarding the resurrection of believers, Durham concluded, "The simple truth is that a sinner is identified with Adam. A believer is identified with Jesus Christ. No man is identified with Adam the first and Adam the second at the same time."[7] In his assessment, grace at conversion finds perfection only through continued growth.

At a Pentecostal convention in 1910, Durham would preach a sermon titled, "The Finished Work of Calvary" in which he would discredit the Wesleyan view of sanctification as a second definite work of grace and set off a fire storm of controversy throughout the Pentecostal and holiness ranks. Menzies quotes a portion of Durham's sermon in his 1971 account of events, which led to the eventual formation of the Assemblies of God and which would later adopt Durham's doctrine. Durham argued that as he began to write against the Wesleyan view that it takes two works of grace to save and cleanse a believer, it became clear to him that when one is converted (or

6. McGee, *People of the Spirit*, 83.

7. Ibid., 84.

born again), he/she cannot be outwardly cleansed while the heart remains with enmity against God. He denied that God does not deal with the nature of sin at the moment of conversion. Salvation could not have taken place if the heart of the person remained "unclean." Durham continued that salvation was a complete change of heart and a change in the very nature of the being and that the old nature, which was sinful and depraved, and the very thing that was condemned is "crucified with Christ."[8]

Opposition to Durham's view mounted swiftly. He was forced to resign from his church in Chicago and was later turned away by William Seymour in Los Angeles. However, Durham won over Frank Bartleman, whose writings and journals chronicled the Azusa events. With Bartleman's help, Durham began a new congregation in Los Angeles, but the controversy grew more and more bitter.

Durham would not live to see his profound impact on the Pentecostal movement. While differences between Reformed and Wesleyan views of sanctification remained fuzzy for many on the grassroots level, Durham's theological position would draw a large segment of emerging leaders closer to a Reformed theology. According to McGee, only those holiness Pentecostal bodies in the Southeast and the Apostolic Faith associations of Parham and Florence Crawford would preserve the Wesleyan view.[9] This shift would be profound for women who sought to participate in the leading of others to Pentecostalism. The finished work theology and the emphasis on Holy Spirit's outpouring as empowerment for service cleared further ground for the argument in favor of women's participation in ministry. Whereas traditional holiness teaching had focused on the Baptism of the Holy Spirit as a means of personal cleansing and perfection, the shift in theology demanded a response from the believer to serve in the spreading of the Pentecostal message. Few disagreed that women could receive salvation as well as participate in the manifestations associated with the Baptism in the Holy Spirit. In Durham's view, salvation was complete and instantaneous, and the "old man" (or woman) had escaped condemnation. The infilling of the Holy Spirit, then, was a sign of empowerment and a means of authority to share the gospel of Jesus Christ with others. These were radical shifts both in terms of theology and ministry. Women embraced this shift and their newfound freedom to exercise authority in religious and public life in ways previously restricted to their male counterparts.

Another controversy, on the nature of the Godhead, was also brewing among the splintering Pentecostal groups, but it would not fully develop for

8. Menzies, *Anointed to Serve*, 75.

9. McGee, *People of the Spirit*, 85.

some time. Smaller divisions also threatened to become larger problems as the movement spread and teachings became more and more distant from those of any organized doctrine and leaders like Parham, Seymour, and Durham. According to Blumhofer, many were troubled by strange teachings and perceived excesses. Some Pentecostals concluded that if they were to realize their potential and a full-scale end-times renewal, then adherents needed to step up and take responsibility for the direction of the movement. This handful of leaders began to explore the advantages and disadvantages of cooperating in a loosely structured network that would "preserve their autonomy but also provide a forum for consideration of mutual concerns."[10]

## THE CALL TO ORGANIZE

Some of these leaders had already begun to network loosely. For example, Howard Goss and several other former associates of Parham's Apostolic Faith fellowship gained permission from C. H. Mason of the Church of God in Christ to ordain white ministers in the mostly black organization and issued credentials to them under the name "Church of God in Christ and in unity with the Apostolic Faith Movement." Other organizations from Alabama and Mississippi soon aligned themselves with Goss who was headquartered in Arkansas. However, the vague nature of their associations prompted them to believe that a bolder move toward cooperation was necessary.

Eudorus N. Bell, a former Southern Baptist turned Pentecostal preacher and publisher of a periodical called *Word and Witness*, agreed to publish the formal call for a gathering of those with Pentecostal ties who desired to see a more established formation of doctrine and unity. Bell called this gathering the "General Convention of Pentecostal Saints and Churches of God in Christ." Signed by Bell, Goss, Mack M. Pinson, Arch P. Collins, and Daniel C. O. Opperman, the call ran in the December 20, 1913, edition and twice more in February and March 1914.[11] Laymen and ministers were included in the invitation, which was specifically directed to churches that called themselves Pentecostal or Apostolic Faith Assemblies and Church of God in Christ who desired unity in purpose. Specifically, the call noted that it was only for those who believed in the baptism in the Holy Spirit with supernatural signs that followed. It also noted that the meeting was not for contentious or divisive persons.[12]

10. Blumhofer, *Restoring the Faith*, 116.

11. McGee, *People of the Spirit*, 111.

12. *Word and Witness*, December 20, 1913, 1.

Following the call to gather, five subjects were put forth to be considered and constituted the reason for organizing: First to be addressed were issues over doctrinal teaching so that greater unity be established to avoid division and false teaching. Second, organizers desired to conserve the work going forward both domestically and overseas and deal with how to fund these missions. Third, they proposed to understand what was needed in the foreign field so that the funding for missionaries was adequate to their living needs and to avoid wasteful spending. The fourth area of discussion focused on the chartering of churches and creating a legal standing for them to be recognized and protected by the laws of the land with all the rights and benefits afforded to official institutions. The final issue to be addressed was the establishment of a Bible training school. This new training school would educate ministers and missionaries on conducting a ministry work, and establish what leaders termed a "literary department for our people."[13]

These men did not intend to create a denomination, nor did they expect any longevity in terms of official organization. The hope was to conserve what they viewed as the core Pentecostal message and preserve a history and identity during the brief time leading up to Christ's return. The call received a storm of criticism, and even some of those who issued the call wondered if they would be ostracized for participating in an organizing meeting. Several dire predictions were issued over the idea of trying to organize a movement of the Holy Spirit and leveled criticisms that anyone who tried would lose their power with God and their influence over men.[14] Goss, however, tried to calm these fears when he remarked, "From the Book of Acts, as well as from our own experiences, I was led to see that even Spirit-filled people needed some restraint. Just as a good horse still needs a harness to produce worthwhile results, the movement needed a legal form of written cooperative fellowship."[15]

On April 2, 1914, a group of both male and female "workers" and "saints" convened in the Grand Opera House on Central Avenue in Hot Springs, Arkansas. This location was already very familiar to many in the movement as home to a thriving Pentecostal congregation led by Goss. Maria Woodworth-Etter, the famous healing Evangelist, had conducted several weeks of meetings in the Opera House and drew substantial crowds.[16]

While most of those in attendance at the conference were from the Midwest, twenty states were represented as were several foreign missions.

13. Ibid.

14. Blumhofer, *Restoring the Faith*, 116.

15. Goss, *Winds of God*, as cited in McGee, *People of the Spirit*, 111.

16. Blumhofer, *Restoring the Faith*, 117.

The exact attendance is unclear, but estimates suggest anywhere from 200 to 300 people attended over the course of the gathering. Cavaness notes that, according to J. Roswell Flower, recording secretary, only sixty-eight registered as delegates, but a report in the *Word and Witness* claims that 120 ministers signed the list as delegates. The only extant list has 110 names recorded of which twenty-two (20 percent) were women.[17]

Because of the suspicion and tension surrounding the meeting, no business was conducted for three days. These three days were devoted specifically to preaching, prayer, fellowship and an impromptu parade through the streets of Hot Springs. On April 6 they began to conduct business. A "Declaration of Independence" was drafted as were several resolutions. According to Blumhofer, the group adopted the term General Council, which was taken from a reference in Acts chapter fifteen to the Council at Jerusalem. This term had been previously used by some holiness groups as a designation for association meetings. Bell was appointed the Chairman and a young evangelist from Indiana, J. Roswell Flower, as secretary. The first order of business following these appointments was to limit the voting rights to men. Given the history of Pentecostalism up to this point and the theological shifts that seemed to empower women (and the significant number of women present at the meeting), this first decision stands out. One would assume that it would have been obvious that women who could affirm the anointing of the Holy Spirit would be allowed to participate in the decision-making right alongside their men; instead, the issue of cultural versus institutional authority manifested itself as an official distinction. This immediate and significant constraint placed on the women present lay the foundation for ambiguous and often conflicting views on women that would emerge from the new fellowship. While the culture may have embraced women's participation in the reception of the Pentecostal experience, there were clear limits to what the community was willing to accept with regard to women's full participation in the institutional authority of the church. Significantly, no indication exists that the women present opposed this decision or that discussion ensued on the matter.[18] From the outset, women's opportunities are constrained despite a theological stance and daily practice that should have indicated greater opportunity for women. The challenge, then, is in understanding why.

17. Cavaness, "Biographical Study," 104.

18. There is nothing in the official meetings of the first General Council that any discussion was held on the matter or that the vote was or was not unanimous. It simply states in the minutes that "on motion it was adopted that all male Ministers and Delegates be eligible to vote." See also General Council of the Assemblies of God, General Council Minutes, 1914, 2.

After this first decision, a conference committee comprised of delegates from each attending state was assigned to frame the Preamble and Resolution of Constitution. Blumhofer notes that the document was specifically designed to dispel any hesitations about centralization and creed. It declared that the participants were part of a "General Assembly of God (which is God's organism)." It also disavowed any sectarian intensions as an organization to legislate, form laws or articles of faith, or exercise "unscriptural jurisdiction" over members.[19]

Despite what Blumhofer calls its cumbersome language, the preamble was welcomed with shouts of praise and quickly passed unanimously, and the group incorporated as the General Council of the Assemblies of God.[20] A full constitution and bylaws would not be established until 1927, so this jumble of disjointed thoughts and ideas served as a guiding principle for cooperation amongst a growing constituency. One very important concept established through this preamble is the idea of "voluntary cooperation among churches" rather than a centralized governmental structure seen in many other religious denominations. The ideology and authority structure of a "fellowship of like-minded believers" rather than denominationalism existed from the very beginning of the Assemblies of God and would become a hallmark of the Assemblies for both good and bad throughout its history.[21] This structural decision is important to note as it is one of the challenges to reform and other matters of institutional change within the Assemblies of God. For example, while General Superintendents may believe that more women need to be serving in positions of pastoral ministry, the national office does not have the authority to issue a decree or require its churches to hire women, place them on church boards, etc. While the fellowship's position on issues like the role of women can be stated directly and published in official documents, voluntary cooperation and the authority of the local church supersedes this ideology. Although this stance is one of the unique aspects of governance of the Assemblies of God, it is also one of the great roadblocks to correcting teaching and practice that may be contrary to what the national body states the organization believes or acts upon.

Incorporation also provided many benefits to those who associated with the new General Council. Of particular interest to ministers was the ability to qualify for a clergy discount on the railways. At a time when many could not afford long-distance travel, this discount would aid evangelists and other itinerant workers in their ministries. It would also serve as an area

19. Blumhofer, *Restoring the Faith*, 118–19.

20. Blumhofer, *Assemblies of God*, 203.

21. McGee, *People of the Spirit*, 114.

of controversy regarding women who associated with the General Council as their status with the organization determined their qualifications for the ministerial travel discount.

The assembly also agreed to create an advisory board that would be known as the Executive Presbytery. The delegates settled on twelve members to represent the twelve disciples of Jesus and charged them with distributing funds to missionaries, overseeing publications, serving as corporate legal custodians as well as planning and providing continuity between conferences of the General Council.[22] In addition to the five issues, addressed in the original call, the first General Council dealt with only two other issues, both of which would prove to have longstanding significance: women in ministry and divorce/remarriage.

## THE RIGHTS AND OFFICES OF WOMEN

According to several historians, the discussion regarding women in ministry bears the unmistakable imprint of E. N. Bell, and much of the polity of the early years of the Assemblies of God was undoubtedly influenced by his training and service as a Baptist minister in the American South, particularly his position on the role of women in ministry.[23] Bell contended that women could be promoted to every area of ministry, except where they might be placed in authority over men. He argued that in his reading of the biblical narrative, he found no evidence that a woman had ever pastored a church: "No woman has been known to have been appointed by the Lord as an elder or an apostle, or to any position where ruling with authority is inferred."[24]

While women could be ordained as missionaries, Bell insisted that women "take up some regular and systematic work for the Lord under the proper oversight of some good brother whom God has placed in charge of the work."[25] For Bell, this directive was not based on a belief in inferiority. Rather, the purpose of this position was to be helpful to women and "alleviate women from heavy responsibility."[26] The only exception, as Bell viewed

22. Ibid., 116.

23. Ironically, while Blumhofer, McGee, and Cavaness all make reference to Bell's positions, William Menzies makes no mention of the actions regarding women in his chapter on the birth of the Assemblies of God. He also fails to note that women even attended this early council or those that closely followed. Cavaness is the first to point this out in her work on Assemblies of God Missionaries.

24. Bell, "Women Elders," 2.

25. Bell, "Some Complaints," 2.

26. Tackett, "Embourgeoisement of the Assemblies of God," 270.

it, occurred when a man was not available to fulfill the responsibilities of the pastorate and even then, a woman's service was temporary. "If men fail God and don't take care of his flock in any place, and God does actually raise up a capable woman and make her do it for Him to their good and His glory, then we had better let God alone."[27]

The issue of institutional authority is a sticking point on the argument of women's leadership. However, the latter arguments by Bell seem to contradict his logic. He argues that he can find no biblical precedent for women in institutional leadership, but he claims God *could* grant her that authority (assuming no man is available), in which case one should not question God. The theological position of Bell and other Pentecostal leaders that the Baptism in the Holy Spirit with supernatural evidences such as tongues is the indicative sign of God's anointing and empowering for service would seem to indicate that no additional proof of authority is needed. While this position continues to be a line of argumentation used by those who oppose women's leadership, Bell took his position further. He granted little room for women to serve as deacons. He acknowledged only some biblical evidence for deaconesses, such as the example of Phoebe (Rom 16:1-2). He also acknowledged the word for "deaconess" was literally translated as "servant." However, this admission clearly made him uncomfortable. Bell stated, "So it is perfectly scriptural to have deaconesses in our churches where we have sisters qualified and capable for this office."[28] This concession was in no way an acknowledgement of equality; rather, he believed that women should serve only in this capacity if they are surrounded by plenty of male deacons. One was not a substitute for the other. Bell wrote,

It would be scriptural to have deaconesses in a church where there are plenty of deacons, as they are not substitutes one for the other, only mutual helpers in the service of the church and of Christ. Look up in ancient church history of the work of each. By common consent she might do the work of deacons until you can get a deacon to do it, but this would not make her the scriptural deacon. She is only a deaconess.[29]

Bell fervently argued that this form of polity was actually most friendly to women. In an editorial called "We Fellowship All" that included a heading entitled "Women Welcome," he stated,

No such thing has ever been done. We know of no Movement where women of ability and filled with the Holy Ghost, have been more highly honored or given as much freedom than

27. Bell, "Questions and Answers," 8.

28. Ibid., 9.

29. Ibid.

among us. She is given the right to be ordained, to preach, witness, give advice, act, as an evangelist, missionary, etc. The only
thing not thrown unscripturally upon her weak shoulders is the
making of her a Ruling Elder.[30]

Again, Bell's own rhetoric is contradictory by first acknowledging that
the Pentecostal movement is at the forefront of promoting women in ministry positions, but then immediately turning around and using language
that limits what positions they may hold; all packaged in the framework
of kindness to his female counterparts by not placing too heavy a burden
upon them. He never states that the Scripture rightly divides these offices,
but rather he implies it is a protection mechanism against requiring too
much of the weaker vessel. In each instance where Bell notes the opportunities that Pentecostalism inherently provides women, he immediately
places a constraint upon their ability to operate in these opportunities
through his discourse.

Bell's positions were an acceptable compromise between those who
would "silence the women totally" and those who would give authority to
women "which God has given to men." Bell continued, "There are some
things under normal conditions that God does not require of women and
which the Scriptures, neither by New Testament example nor by precept
make the regular duty of women to do and one of this is to be the Ruling
Elder in the Church of Christ."[31]

While the word "elder" is never clearly defined in these early accounts, General Superintendent George O. Wood and Assemblies of God
theologian Zenas Bicket both equate the term specifically to the position
of pastor and/or the administrator of the holy ordinances of the church.[32]
Wood states that the ban on eldership for women was also a ban on ordination and specifically the role of pastor. However, the challenge to the
fledgling Assemblies, according to Wood, is the number of women who
were already ordained and those who performed these functions anyway
regardless of the official prohibition by the Council.[33] This definition is
particularly challenging for women today who are looking both for a biblical mandate for their service as well as a historical mandate within their
fellowship. The question of "why" is never answered. Theologically, opportunity has been made by way of the Baptism in the Holy Spirit. Women
were sent out to do the work along with their male counterparts; however,

30. Bell, "We Fellowship All," 2.
31. Ibid.
32. Wood, "Exploring Why We Think," 2; Bicket, "Dealing with the Questions," 81.
33. Wood, "Exploring Why We Think," 2.

when organization of the fellowship comes about, these issues are not directly addressed. Rather than address the contradictions within their own rhetoric, these leaders resorted to the parsing of words and the semantic use of terms like "elder" or "pastor" to shift the discourse away from practices that were already occurring.

Bell simply would not address the contradiction within the Assemblies of God between women pastoring churches they had pioneered versus women pastoring churches that had been previously established by men. He specifically indicated his intention to squelch further discussion on the subject at upcoming Council meetings stating "If Jesus tarries and he is present at the next General Council[,] he [Chairman Bell] will oppose any further discussion of women's rights. We have other things more important to do which ought not to be neglected by wasting time beating the bushes around about small and non-essential matters."[34] Clearly, Bell did not consider women's activities in the movement a significant issue and appeared to be annoyed that the Council addressed it at all.

At the first General Council, the men present voted a resolution that affirmed Bell's position and the official minutes of the meetings and published reports of the gathering indicate that the women present did not dissent. The council instructed women to "be in subjection" and not "usurp the authority over the man." The council authorized licenses for female evangelists and missionaries while explicitly preventing them from serving in pastoral positions or in administrative offices where they would be in authority over men.

The original "Rights and Offices of Women" resolution acknowledges the mighty hand of God on the women for proclamation and prophecy, while at the same time relegating them to subjection and placing them firmly in the position of "helper" to their male counterparts. The resolution also recognizes a woman's right to be ordained, not as an "elder" as it had been defined (or not) by the council, but rather as evangelists and foreign missionaries.

In approving this resolution, the General Council ruled that women had no ability in missions or evangelism to administer any of the ordinances of the church including the right to conduct marriage and funeral services, to lead congregants in the celebration of the Eucharist (or communion), or to baptize converts in water. Later, in 1914, in response to a request from missionaries Hattie Hacker and Jennie Kirkland, women missionaries serving overseas were permitted to administer "baptism, marriage, burial of the dead

34. Bell, "We Fellowship All," 2.

and the Lord's Supper when a man was not available for the purpose."[35] This privilege was to be exercised only in cases of emergency and was carefully restricted to women serving overseas. Women evangelists who served in the United States would not be granted the same privilege until 1922.[36]

Cavaness notes that this ambiguity—of accepting women on one hand and denying them a vote and congregational leadership on the other—set a tone and a pattern of discourse for official attitudes toward women ministering that would affect the fellowship from this point on. I contend that this inherent contradiction immediately creates rhetorical dissonance for those who support women's ministry service. While women may not have openly objected to the resolution, they did not have a vote, which may have contributed to their lack of opposition. Early historical accounts of the Council leave women out entirely and do not mention them as delegates or even their presence at the meeting. The fact that no opposition is recorded does not prove simple concession among the women present. The movement's decision concerning women does not appear to have been intended to conclusively settle the issue within the movement. Pentecostals did not set out to change the culture regarding women's engagement. The empowerment of women became a defining aspect of Pentecostalism because women embraced the theology and resulting empowerment of the Baptism in the Holy Spirit and were compelled to share their newfound power with others. This opportunity is what defined their place and not the artificial constraints of human choice. Pentecostal women did not need an official document for them to serve, and they simply would not go away.

While Chairman Bell may have desired to restrict discussion on the matter further, the issue was clearly not resolved. Despite the limitations of polity established by the fellowship, women continued to pioneer the work of the Assemblies of God and subsequent meetings of the General Council were forced to confront this reality.

The Executive Presbytery called a second Council session later in November 1914. The official list of ministers had grown dramatically by this time to 531 credentialed ministers who represented 35 states, Canada and 11 additional countries. Of these, 150 were women, which was nearly one-third of the ministry body.[37] The very first resolution presented addressed the status of "Lady" delegates, who were determined by the Council to be

35. General Council of the Assemblies of God, Executive Presbytery Minutes, 1914, 23.

36. General Council of the Assemblies of God, Executive Presbytery Minutes, 1922.

37. General Council of the Assemblies of God, General Council Minutes, 1914, 13–16.

"advisors" but not voting members. These women advisors were to be mature believers who would cooperate fully with the fellowship and, as such, should be extended the same advisory status in their local districts.

Cavaness presumes that, since the women referred to were not only mature believers but also, in many cases, credential holders, the resolution only gave them token recognition. The following September, in 1915, the *Word and Witness* periodical published a special call inviting "the sisters to be present and take part in the deliberations" because "the brethren need their presence and their prayerful assistance."[38] The 1915 Council meeting minutes note that "On motion, the sisters attending the Council, who are mature believers and in co-operative fellowship with our testimony were requested to register as advisory members of the General Council."[39] Cavaness notes a significant change included with the ministerial list issued with the certified minutes: a statement that affirms that all ministers named in the list were authorized to perform marriage ceremonies, administer the ordinances of the church, bury the dead and perform any other function of the regular ministry of the Gospel in accordance to the laws and customs of the State in which the minister resided. This ministry list included the names of approximately 89 women who were serving in some sort of missions or evangelistic position. An exact number is hard to discern because of duplicate names, names with only initials, and others listed as "Mrs." along with the name of their husband. In addition, the list specifically states that it does not include licensed ministers or home missionaries.

Over the course of the next two years, little is mentioned about women other than B. F. Lawrence's 1916 report of seventy men and women ministers "in hearty cooperation" with Southern Missouri. Beginning in 1917, a new controversy (the third major controversy as outlined by Gary McGee) would emerge within the fellowship that would overshadow the discussion on women.

### Proof of a Calling and a Rhetorical Bind

The controversy, which would come to be known as the "Jesus Only" movement, centered on the proper way to baptize the believer in water. Some argued that baptism should be done only in the name of Jesus while others maintained validity in baptizing in the name of the Father, the Son, and the Holy Spirit. This challenge over baptism and the nature of the Godhead caused nearly a fourth of the ministers and missionaries within the newly

38. "General Council Meets in St. Louis," 1.

39. General Council of the Assemblies of God, General Council Minutes, 1915, 3.

formed Assemblies to leave. The debate forced the adoption of what would be termed the Statement of Fundamental Truths, which outlined sixteen theological principles that would guide the doctrine of the Assemblies as it moved forward. Quickly adopted, the Statement of Fundamental Truths has changed very little since the time of its first ratification.

In light of the adoption of the statement of faith, the Executive Presbytery issued new credentials to its ministry body. Once again, the Council was forced to deal with the issue of women's roles. The official minutes note the controversy: "Some time was spent in discussing the question of whether sisters present should be requested to vote, but it was finally decided to leave them on the same basis as in former councils, namely as advisory members, with the privilege of participating in all discussions."[40] This statement is not without irony as at that same council, Elizabeth Sisson, a respected evangelist gave the keynote address entitled "The Building of the Body of Christ."

The 1917 General Council did bring some organizational changes to the fellowship including the appointment of Laura Radford to the Missionary Nominating Committee, which had significant responsibilities. Another significant committee, the Foreign Missions Committee, also elected members, including two missionaries, one of whom was Susan C. Easton, the only woman who has ever served as a full-fledged member of that body. However, after serving only a year, this committee's responsibilities were transferred back to the Executive Presbytery, and Easton returned to her missionary appointment in China. The only other woman to have served was Eleanor Bowie, a former missionary and then Dean of Women at Central Bible Institute, who was appointed eighteen years after Radford in 1935. It is unclear how long she served, but she is named only as an auxiliary member.

In addition to these committee changes, the process and authority of ordination also changed. The Council in 1917 recommended that all candidates for ordination be proven license holders (those holding official credentials issued by the District Councils) prior to their ordination. While local churches could still administer the ordination, it was the districts that had the official authority to examine those who were licensed and ordain at their choosing. In their seminal analysis of the Assemblies of God, Charles Barfoot and Gerald Sheppard cite the negative consequences of this action for female ministers:

> Over time it would become increasingly difficult for a woman to move out of the "licensed" and into the "ordained" category of ministry. The socio-religious function of preaching was shifting

40. General Council of the Assemblies of God, General Council Minutes, 1917, 9.

from a prophetic to a priestly performance. With the centralization of ecclesiastical authority . . . in addition to being "called,"
one now had to be "proven."[41]

Previously, the calling and anointing of the Holy Spirit by means of
Spirit baptism was enough to provide opportunity for ministry service.
Now, as the Assemblies of God became more organized and centralized in
its authority structure, official documentation including testing and inter-
viewing were necessary to prove one's capability and calling. The establishment of a "professional clergy" created an additional constraint on women's
service and again emphasized the differences between women's institutional
and cultural authority. The discourse of what it meant to be called and empowered for "official" service to the fellowship changed and along with it,
opportunities for women were limited.

Constraint increased in 1918 when a discussion again took place regarding the terms "deacon" and "elder." According to the official minutes, former
Chairman Bell "proved" that an elder is equal to a bishop, not a deacon and
concluded that "the preachers were the elders." The question of women serving in any of these positions is eerily absent from the discussion.

The definition of terms remained an issue long after Bell's "proof."
Some members defined "elder" only as denominational or district-level
leadership, while others held it synonymous with senior pastors, and others
specifically excluded women even as deaconesses. The debate over the symbolic choice of these terms is significant. Early Pentecostal leaders were in
a rhetorical bind. The same Scripture that justified their own existence also
affirmed women's participation. Their doctrine on the Baptism in the Holy
Spirit, which distinguishes them from most religious movements including their relatives in the Methodist and Holiness camps, does not exclude
women from experiencing the anointing and empowerment for ministry.
Therefore, they are left with a handful of Scriptures which seem to prevent
women from leadership and public speaking and to support their own
cultural biases on women's positions in leadership. The lack of self-critique
combined with these theological and cultural challenges leaves them to
make specific rhetorical choices in order to create a definition by which they
justify their own work while maintaining the cultural status quo without
entirely alienating a significant portion of their membership.

In an analysis of the Assemblies of God ministerial roster from 1918,
21 percent of the Assemblies of God ministers were women. Sixty-four
percent of the home missionaries were women. Two-thirds of those who
stated they were pioneering churches were women. Single women made up

41. Barfoot and Sheppard, "Prophetic vs. Priestly Religion," 10.

over one third of the Assemblies of God foreign missionaries increasing their numbers from 10 of 27 in 1914 to 95 of 250 in 1925.[42] Most probably, many of the women listed as home missionaries may have actually served as pastors in their foreign congregations although their official title with the Assemblies would have remained "missionary." In addition, an undetermined, but impressive number of Assemblies of God churches were begun by female evangelists and several congregations that could not afford male pastors often accepted the services of women.[43]

While women served in a variety of positions before and after these early General Council gatherings set official policy for women and while many believers recognized women's authority to serve in practice if not in policy, the challenge seemed to be in the wisdom of women serving alone. In a 1913 article in the *Word and Witness* publication, an unnamed missionary expressed open concern about women missionaries who served alone. "It seems to me unwise and not according to the word for women to go out alone."[44]

This viewpoint would surface several times over the formative years of the Assemblies of God and still manifests itself today in the way single women are treated in their credentialing process and in the appointment (or lack thereof) of women to local church boards and District leadership positions. The theological argument for women's ministry was not based upon the Acts 2 account, as so many had used in defense of both the existence of Pentecostalism and empowerment for service. Rather, it was Paul's declaration in the book of Galatians that as children of Christ, distinctions are not to be made between men and women. The minutes of the General Council seem to confirm this scriptural distinction. "That in the matter of salvation, the lines of sex are blotted out."[45] However, in 1 Tim 2:11–15, women were not to serve in positions of authority over men. The Council reaffirms this position when it stated that women were "to be helpers in the Gospel."[46] So, while women could preach and prophesy as evangelists and missionaries, they could not serve as elders. By choosing these words and defining them as such, they were able to reconcile, for a time, the obvious contradiction of their own arguments.

42. McGee, "This Gospel," 91.

43. Blumhofer, *Restoring the Faith*, 121.

44. "As Viewed by a Missionary," *Word and Witness*, November 13, 1913, 1.

45. General Council of the Assemblies of God, Combined General Council Minutes, 1914, 7.

46. Ibid., 7.

At the 1919 General Council, three women were ordained, but Chairman John Welch explained again that voting privileges were reserved for male ministers and male delegates. These newly ordained women had "proven" themselves worthy of ordination, but were still second-class when it came to voting on matters of doctrine, policy and leadership. Cavaness states, "Obviously the resolutions having to do with women's status were voted on only by the men, too!"[47]

The ambiguity regarding a woman's position within the Assemblies was also complicated in more tangible ways. Women could serve as evangelists and were credentialed as such, but even in this capacity, their position would be restricted. Evangelistic work often requires extensive travel, and much of the travel in these days was conducted by train. Credential holders in the United States could apply for reduced rates, and that had been part of the rationale behind the early attempts at organization prior to 1914. The railways' clergy bureaus were no longer recognizing women as ministers who did not serve in the same capacities as men. Women who applied for these clergy rail fares were turned down. In a notice published in the May 29, 1915, issue of the *Weekly Evangel*, Goss requested that women home missionaries or evangelists who held credentials with the Assemblies of God not apply for these clergy rates unless they received a guaranteed salary. Goss states, "Let the women take notice of this, and trust God for full fare. This does not apply to men why [sic] are properly ordained nor to foreign women missionaries."[48]

By 1922, the Assemblies of God ruled once again on the issue of railway fare as the clergy bureaus further resisted recognizing any woman minister because of the lack of authorization to pastor or administer church ordinances. While the Executive Presbytery objected to this decision because women were authorized to perform these tasks when necessary, they were forced to rephrase their credentialing statements, as the bureau stated that without such an exception clause, women would not be recognized.

The new credentials issued to women were accompanied by a letter to women ministers informing them of how they were to respond to the clergy bureaus. The letter states that women were not "to do these things [administer ordinances or serve as a pastor] in the future any more than in the past. They will be expected to do such things only when ordained men are not present . . . or when such real emergency makes it necessary. . . . Yet,

47. Cavaness, "Biographical Study," 112.

48. Goss, "Notice to Women Missionaries," 2.

from now on they [women ministers] may answer honestly that they are authorized to marry people, administer the ordinances, etc."[49]

To satisfy the clergy bureaus further, an annual questionnaire was developed by the General Council to strengthen their case that women were really acting as ministers. While men and women were required to fill out the questionnaires, women were asked numerous gender-specific questions. "Are you single or married?" "How much time is given to household duties?" "Do you actually expound the Word the same as do men?" "Do you receive separate offerings [from a husband for married women] for your own services?"[50] While the Executive Presbytery had to recognize that women were serving in official ministry, they were clearly struggling with the egalitarian nature of Pentecostal ministry and how to recognize women within it.

### Flapper Evangelism

The debate over women in ministry also continued to play out in the pages of Assemblies of God publications and those being published by independent Pentecostal groups. Women were asserting themselves more and more in society and the suffrage movement, which was so intrinsically linked with the Quaker church and in the early days of the holiness movement, eventually led to the passage of the 19th Amendment to the United States Constitution, granting women full citizenship and the right to vote. With changes in societal rights, women began to express themselves and their newfound equality in fashion, politics, and religion.

Frank Bartleman, the former journalist convert from the Azusa Street Revival who had embraced William Durham and eventually joined the ranks of the Assemblies of God, wrote frequently in Assemblies of God publications and was unconvinced that the women's movement was the appropriate direction for Pentecostals. Bartleman argued that the promotion of women ministers had made them [Pentecostals] "effeminate" and that men's "fleshly attraction to the opposite sex"[51] had overcome their ability to think critically about this issue. While men might be attracted to short hair, short skirts and painted faces, God was not going to change the order of creation by elevating women to a place of equality. In an article entitled "Flapper Evangelism:

49. Credential Committee, "Dear Sister."
50. "Dear Brother Minister in the Lord."
51. Bartleman, "Flapper Evangelism," 2.

Fashion's Fools Headed for Hell," Bartleman conceded, "Women have their place in ministry, but not in the position they are grasping at today."[52]

While Bartleman comes on a bit strong, other preachers and missionaries also complained about Christian women who were luring men into sin with their newfound freedoms of dress and who were bowing to the god of fashion and should not be allowed on the platforms of churches. Miss N. Moomau, a missionary to Shanghai, published the rhetorical question: "Is it not a shame that young women in low-necked blouses and short skirts . . . are permitted to appear on the platform which should be sacred, and allowed to lead in public worship?[53] Neither Moomau nor Bartleman, like others who admonished women, addresses or critiques changing men's fashions nor men's responses to women's attire, but like the annual clergy questionnaire, only address their outrage toward women.

Few in the Assemblies of God were convinced that these new social mores were healthy, yet the General Council responded positively to the national suffrage of women.[54] The same year that women in the United States were granted the right to vote and Aimee Semple McPherson preached in the General Council meetings each afternoon, ordained women including missionaries, evangelists, and states-side pastors of churches finally received voting rights in the 1920 General Council. The resolution that passed acknowledged favor in granting women a larger share of responsibility and privilege within the Assemblies of God. It also called for the restrictions against the voting rights of women to be removed from the Minutes and records of the Council and that women be given equal status to their "brethren" in voting upon all issues and questions before the Council as well as the right to speak openly and freely from the floor.[55]

While it would seem that the debate had shifted to more cultural constraints such as hair length, the cut of blouses, or the wearing of pants, rather than the theological constraints of Paul's admonishment that women be silent in the church, the Assemblies of God was forced to continue confronting the role of women. Apparently, the Assemblies could no longer justify preventing women a vote in their Councils when the law of the land allowed women to vote on matters of temporal concern. It could be argued that this shift in voting rights should have made a significant impact on how women's leadership was viewed, but again the discourse employed by those who defined the terms of the debate proved challenging.

52. Ibid.

53. Moomau, "Cleansing of the Temple," 6.

54. Tackett, "Embourgeoisement of the Assemblies of God."

55. General Council of the Assemblies of God, General Council Minutes 1920, 48.

When the combined 1914–1920 minutes of the previous General Councils were published, the section "Rights and Offices of Women" had been edited as was supposed to happen per the resolution in 1920. However, it was edited without comment or additional Council action. The original minutes declare that women could be "ordained, not as elders, but as Evangelists and Missionaries after being duly approved, according to the Scriptures." The new wording stated, "ordained, not as elders, but as evangelists, after being duly approved, according to Scriptures; and that they serve as assistant pastors, missionaries, or as evangelists."[56] While some minor language was adjusted, nothing in practice changed. Women still served as pastors as well as in the categories mentioned.[57]

At the 1921 General Council, evangelist Roxie Hughes Alford was the Friday evening speaker. While her husband served as a full-time minister in Dallas, Texas, Roxie had a very successful ministry of her own—preaching 235 times that year alone. Women had now earned the right to vote at Council meetings, but their preaching was largely limited. Roxie Alford was the last woman to preach an evening service at General Council for nearly 60 years.[58] This situation again highlights the complexities of the choices made by those in power positions. The numbers of women serving amongst the ranks of the Assemblies continue to grow during these years and while adjustments were made back and forth on their status within the organization, few women were promoted even within the opportunities presented to them on a national level.

In 1922, a form letter was sent to women by the Credentialing Committee that attempted to clarify their position with the Assemblies of God as well as again clarify to the Clergy Bureau that they were fully ordained. The bureau wanted ordination papers to be more specific about the duties of women serving in the Assemblies. The letter was to be kept in an envelope with the credential and not to go out of the woman's possession. New credentials were issued to "ordained women who are actually preaching the Word just the same as ordained men do."[59]

This letter followed action by the Executive Presbytery in their July 1922 meeting:

> While not encouraging women to be pastors, to marry people, and to administer the ordinances of Baptism and the Lord's

56. General Council of the Assemblies of God, Combined Minutes of the General Council, 1914–1920, 9.

57. Cavaness, "Biographical Study," 113.

58. Ibid.

59. Credential Committee, "Dear Sister."

Supper, it has nevertheless been understood all along that they could so these things when some circumstances made it necessary for them to do so. It is not intended to encourage the women to do these things in the future any more than in the past. They will be expected to do such things only when ordained men are not present to do them. Or when some such real emergency makes it necessary for them to do so. Yet from now on they may answer honestly when they are authorized to marry people, administer the ordinances, etc. Be careful not to boast over having this authority . . . if . . . you should let trouble arise, this might compel the Executive Presbytery to recall the new forms.[60]

Despite all the advances and opportunities created for women as a result of changes in the secular culture, once again, the leadership of the Assemblies of God assumes a position that reinforces the dissonance created by their own rhetorical dichotomy. Moreover, by their continued failure to self-critique their own position on women in conjunction with the inherent discrimination with which they apply their theological and cultural standards, these early leaders are able to absolve themselves of responsibility for taking a clear position of religious revolution. What women were doing in the Assemblies of God was a radical departure from any other firmly established religious denomination at the time. Pentecostal theology provided the open door, but the further removed the Assemblies became from their own radical birth, the more closely aligned with the status quo they actually became. As a result, Pentecostal women were empowered by changes in the secular culture rather than in the mandate they received of the Holy Spirit. The Pentecostal tradition missed the opportunity for both cultural revolution and spiritual revival that would have had a greater impact and more far-reaching implications for women in America.

According to Howard Kenyon, the new credentials were for women "who were fully qualified preachers, who gave their full time to the ministry, who had appointments to preach separately from their husbands, and who gave the main message from the Word at these services, whether their husbands were present or not."[61] Women also had to take up separate collections. In the annual ministers' questionnaire, they had to report the amount of time they spent on household duties. This stipulation, as well as the others, was not asked on the questionnaire for their male counterparts, many of whom were these women's husbands.

60. General Council of the Assemblies of God, Executive Presbytery Minutes, 1922.

61. Kenyon, "Analysis of Ethical Issues," 200–201.

Women had overcome several challenges to their ministerial authority, including the privilege of railroad passage at the clergy rate and the right to vote openly at General Council, but it is clear that the desire of the Council was for more men to assume ministry positions both at home and on the mission field. J. Roswell Flower, now serving as the Missionary Treasurer, wrote, "The crying need on every mission field is for men. Young women have volunteered in far greater numbers than men for pioneering in China, India, and Africa and South America."[62] He called for men to go to specific places where "consecrated Pentecostal" woman had struggled to open mission stations stating that "even if the women still have to do pioneer work they need men to come in and occupy the stations." Flower was approving exactly what the missionary woman was lamenting: "We women give our lives in pioneer work for the opening of these mission stations, and then when things go easy we turn them over to the men to manage them."[63]

Flower went so far in this article to describe another missionary agency that had so many more women missionaries than they could use that they began restricting their schools to only male volunteers. This was somewhat of a veiled threat, as the newly opened Central Bible Institute received both men and women. The message seemed clear: male students were preferred. These statements also seem to discount the successful work women were doing when he stated, "This is not the only field that is suffering for the want of men."[64] While the work of women missionaries had been supported since the inception of the Assemblies of God, this office of ministry was unable to avoid the controversy over what constituted female leadership. After a decade of sending women overseas in an official capacity and having them pioneer the work in unknown locations without the "protections" that a male could have offered them, the rhetorical stance of Assemblies of God leaders now changes significantly and speaks of the dangers of women's service or the obvious lack of male willingness to "do the dirty work." This complaint is accompanied by the request that men now move in and take over so as to relieve the women of overwhelming responsibility. The stunning inconsistencies in the rhetorical stance of these leaders creates an obvious tension for women desiring to serve in these capacities, but the overwhelming lack of self-critical examination and outright hypocrisy in undermining the contribution these women made would lead to a significant decline in the number of women serving overseas and domestically in the years to come. The number of men suddenly called to these foreign fields did not rise significantly;

62. Flower, "Men Wanted," 12.
63. Cavaness, "Biographical Study," 115.
64. Flower, "Men Wanted," 12.

instead, women were less willing to do the work only to be replaced once the mission had been established.

Again in 1925, the General Council meeting brought changes to the Assemblies of God Constitution and Bylaws regarding the female pastorate. Under Chairman W. T. Gaston, the Executive Presbytery laid out "The Interpretation of the Constitutional Agreements and Essential Resolutions." In Article VIII, Section 1, Women: "Equal rights of franchise are granted to women who qualify as members in the Council Fellowship. They shall have the right to vote on matters of common interest in the local assemblies, in the District Council and in the General Council." Section 2, Ordination of Women: "Women may be ordained in any degree except eldership and be licensed to preach as provided for men." The Scripture references and reasoning of former documents was taken out. This wording was carried over to the Constitution and Bylaws Article 5, Section 1.[65]

The year 1925 was also significant for women serving as foreign missionaries. The Missionary Department became the first separate department of the fellowship. Over 65 percent of the missionary force was women. Etta Calhoun, one of the most noted women in Assemblies of God missionary culture who never actually served as a missionary (caring for her invalid mother prevented her from serving overseas), organized the first Women's Missionary Council (WMC) in Houston, Texas. Her work with the Women's Christian Temperance Union (WCTU) trained and proved her leadership gifts. The WMC would have a profound impact on Assemblies of God missions for decades. According to McGee, the number of ordained women in the Assemblies had started to decline, and "their status was unfortunately complicated by restrictions and hesitations," but many women found a home in leading prayer groups and providing practical support for missionaries. The WMC "established a clear identity for them in the denomination, although not in the ranks of the clergy."[66]

The adoption of the 1927 version of the Assemblies of God Constitution and Bylaws signals the end of the formative years of the fellowship. The "cooperative fellowship" moved toward a more institutionalized and authoritarian framework. The new constitution provided the Assemblies of God with more formal structure and again affected the procedures for credentialing. This change in procedure would influence women's ordination well into the 1930s. E.S. Williams, elected General Superintendent in 1929, was even more conservative on his position regarding women's ministry

65. General Council of the Assemblies of God, General Council Minutes, 1927, 16.

66. McGee, *This Gospel Shall Be Preached*, 81–85.

service. Once again acknowledging a woman's right to minister, he asserted that this could only be conducted under the headship of a man.

Women played a significant part in the growth of Pentecostalism and in the building of the Assemblies of God. Women were not simply present at the birth of the movement, but engaged in discourse that carved out a distinct rhetorical space and created a unique opportunity for their participation and leadership. When the constraints of culture and historical religious ideology stepped up to challenge their place and position, women who believed they were empowered by the Holy Spirit and not by human means found the opportunities to continue to serve despite the constraints placed upon them. The discrepancies between the opportunities presented to and created by women and the challenges placed before them by cultural context and religious ideology are profoundly rhetorical. They are rooted in how people engage discursively. The historical, cultural, and theological context in which the Pentecostal movement emerged contributes to this controversy and permeates the formation of ideology and practice that creates dissonance and tension both within the fellowship and to the outside observer.

The early years of the fellowship defined the doctrine and theology of women's ministry rhetoric and shaped the future dynamics that continue to challenge women's callings to the present day. The adoption of William Durham's "finished work" theology and the embracing of the view that the baptism in the Holy Spirit is an empowerment for service separate the Assemblies of God from other Pentecostal and holiness organizations. These unique doctrinal choices that gave birth to the Assemblies of God both created and restricted a woman's rhetorical space within the movement including the definition of "elder" (pastor), licensure and ordination, and the status of women stateside versus those who served overseas. As with these doctrinal choices, so too would the symbolic choice of early leaders shape the rhetorical history of women in the Assemblies of God. These rhetorical choices set the tone for how women were established and the discourse that would ultimately lead to dissonance rather than unity on the issue of women in the fellowship.

In the early years, women in ministry in the Assemblies of God was a doctrinal distinctive rivaled only by the doctrine of initial physical evidence. Within the discourse that formed the Assemblies of God, the opportunities for women should have far exceeded mere participation. The very justifications for the existence of Pentecostalism in the prophecy of the Prophet Joel and first evidenced in the Day of Pentecost in Acts chapter 2 establishes biblical precedent not only for the movement itself but for the inclusion of women to participate fully in the work of leading the church and advancing the gospel message.

The known historical record shows that despite several challenges, women played a unique and significant part in the Pentecostal movement and in the formation and growth of the Assemblies of God. The evidence of this argument is found in the discourse of the Assemblies of God, its early leaders and its participants. Language played a central part in the formation and shaping of a role for women and in the context of how others viewed their participation and leadership. Women who embraced the Assemblies of God as their ecclesiastical home and who sought to share its message with others faced opportunities and constraints. These opportunities and constraints are inherently rhetorical, symbolic in nature, and rooted in discourse.

I have focused on the symbols that define the role of women in the Assemblies of God, how these symbols shape a response to the roles women play and in turn define what these roles means. The significance of this book is in how these symbols influenced those who were advocates of women's participation and those who were not and the tension that resulted from their rhetoric. The level of women's participation cannot be denied, yet it seems that the very same rhetoric that set the Assemblies of God apart, including a rejection of traditional religious culture, is the very rhetoric that was used to perpetuate and promote women's silence.

I have centered my analysis on how the scene in the rhetorical drama was extended from the early Pentecostal movement and what it means for the Assemblies of God and for women. Through this analysis, we have seen that, as Burke asserts, those who functioned within this scene are regarded as being seriously constrained by the elements of the scene. Building on Burke, the behavior by those in the Assemblies of God is controlled by "norms" of credentialing that members of the community themselves devised and those women who challenge the boundaries became a threat to the survival of the organization. The integrity of the community was challenged and it became almost instinctual for members of the community to react to these challenges. Members of the community sought to limit or even eliminate those who challenged the boundaries in order to maintain their vision of the scene and how they function within it. This perceived threat had to be constrained by the call for more men to apply for positions of leadership.

In examining the rhetorical topography through the detailed description of the language employed and the relationships developed within the fledgling Assemblies of God, we have seen a clearer picture of how the rhetorical drama, specifically the scene, was constructed and what it means for the Assemblies of God and for its women. The symbolic choices employed by the early founders and participants in the Assemblies of God profoundly affected rhetorical invention and set the boundaries for who could engage in this work and with what freedoms and limitations. The debate over where these boundary lines are located is also a key aspect of the development of the Assemblies of God and would come to define it as a key player in the debate over women's leadership within the church.

While women had significantly developed and pioneered the work of the Pentecostal movement and the Assemblies of God, at every turn, their right to serve was challenged. Theologically and culturally each of these challenges were often addressed and yet, the significant impact on the women who served was made in the symbolic choices communicated in and through their leaders. They wanted to be known as the religious section of society that did more for women than any other up to that point, yet at every turn male leaders placed constraints on just how far women could proceed in carrying out the empowerment bestowed upon them at their personal Pentecost. And yet, when met with these constraints, the women who were called and empowered created their own rhetorical space and seized opportunities for service. While official numbers dwindled and names disappeared from the ministerial rolls, women in the Assemblies of God continued to speak their message of good news and did not go quietly into the night. For them, obedience to the call of God seemed more significant than the policies and procedures of man.

# 4

# The Female Voice

## Prophetic vs. Priestly Dissonance

*As the Holy Ghost takes sway and control, women rise in place, position and power. . . . In these days of promise, these "latter days," there is an overturning, an awakening, an enlargement of vision. Women under the anointing and imbuing of the Holy Ghost is to be a great factor in the . . . work of these latter days. . . . Every woman should receive and honor the Holy Ghost, as He is the Great Emancipator, and the blessed Equalizer, and as He controls, He brings in the equality of the sexes, the brotherhood of man, the sisterhood of woman, the unity of the race, His own Motherhood, the brotherhood of Jesus and the Fatherhood of God.*[1]

—Stephen Merritt, *Midnight Cry*, 1916

WHILE MERRITT'S THOUGHTS MAY have been the perspective of many in the early days of the movement and the promise that Pentecostalism offered women, it was certainly not met with great adulation. Rather, the discussion of women in the "priestly" functions of the church began to create fissures in the movement almost immediately.

Despite a lack of desire to continue debating about women in the growing movement, and in the Assemblies of God specifically, women

1. Merritt, "Women," 5.

would not go away quietly. For the first time in Church history, women had a scriptural and doctrinal basis for their inclusion in the ministry of the church. This justification was rooted in the very Scriptures and doctrine that gave rise to the very existence of Pentecostalism. Some people did not simply challenge women's roles in ministry on cultural or domestic grounds, rather they challenged the very nature of women's intellect. The argument began to be made that women were unable to serve effectively because they did not possess the intellectual capacity required to fully engage in ministry positions. To take the matter further, the argument was presented that this lack of intellect was by divine design from the moment of creation; God had simply made women less capable than men intellectually.

Warren Fay Corothers, a Methodist-turned-Pentecostal from Texas who briefly served as an Assemblies of God executive, was a leading voice on limiting women's involvement. In a book on church government published in 1909, he alleged that a divine sanction for male leadership was found in creation: as man was exclusively created in God's image and is the sovereign of all creation, it is his prerogative to rule in all things. God had made these distinctions, and man's interference was a monstrosity.

For men like Corothers, the act of prophecy meant a human was a conduit of the Holy Spirit, speaking under direct inspiration. Such proclamation, he noted, did not involve the intellect. Because of the absence of any intellectual engagement in prophetic utterances, women were not exercising authority and, therefore, were not violating Scripture or God's ordained order of leadership. This position touches on a number of issues including how its followers, including the Assemblies of God leadership, viewed the inspiration of Scripture, as well as the role of women in the fellowship. Corothers' argument goes so far as to compare women's "ministry" in the prophetic with that of children who could also be filled with the Spirit, but who, obviously, were in no position to lead. When a woman seemed "anointed" to preach, like her male counterparts, Corothers and crew resorted to the Scriptures that forbid a woman to instruct men, concluding that women by their very nature had failed the test of the call.[2] Corothers' argument combined with the attitudes of leaders like Bell (who felt that relieving women of the heavy responsibility of ministry was actually a kind and thoughtful action) created an environment in which not only a woman's calling but also her value was in question. To equate a woman's intellectual capacity with that of a child denigrates a woman as a human being. Children, namely male children, could at least develop an intellect worthy of God's call to ministry, but women not only were to be subservient,

2. Blumhofer, *Restoring the Faith*, 172–73.

but also, according to Corothers, they were by divine order, physically and mentally deficient compared to men.

As the Assemblies of God entered into a season of sustained growth and development, women serving in positions of ministry did not easily give way to these arguments or to men who were called to rise up and take over the leadership of church ministries. However, their participation continued to be challenged and the discourse over their status to be muddled, which resulted in a discursive dissonance in which women were encouraged and affirmed on one hand and told to go away silently on the other. This chapter details the shifts that occurred specifically within the Assemblies of God from 1927 through the early 1990s, as the fellowship grew in both number and in institutional stature with more centralized power. It demonstrates the impact that this centralization had on the continued debate over a woman's place in ministry by examining the lives and positions of several key female leaders who significantly advanced the ministry of the Assemblies of God despite some very personal protests against their participation.

Several significant rhetorical events transpire during this time period. A significant shift occurs first in the perception of the prophetic versus the priestly function of ministry in the Pentecostal movement. The Assemblies of God was birthed out of a revival movement that focused on the mystical nature of a spiritual outpouring. The spiritual blessing resulted in prophetic revelation from both men and women. During this period, however, the leaders of the organization made strategic rhetorical choices that diminished its uniquely gender inclusive cultural and religious identity. As the Assemblies of God grew and became more established, the center of ministry moved from the laity to the professional clergy in what Barfoot and Sheppard refer to as a shift from the prophetic function of ministry to a priestly function of ministry. Simultaneously, the Assemblies of God placed more restrictions on the activities of women in ministry and created alliances with those who held more conservative and fundamentalist views on who could minister.[3] Second, the leadership of the Assemblies of God made a distinct shift in terminology used for the offices within the church, establishing hierarchical language that limited the offices available to women. Finally, in response to the number of women entering the Assemblies' Bible Institutes, the disproportionate number of women who served overseas as missionaries, and the number of women credential holders, the leadership of the Assemblies of God made specific calls for men to step up into these positions.

3. Barfoot and Sheppard, "Prophetic vs. Priestly Religion."

The challenge to the status of women within the Assemblies of God is only one aspect of the prophetic/priestly debate. A second key feature of this argument is the philosophical stance that birthed the Pentecostal movement in the first place. In discourse involving the nature of Pentecostalism, prophetic roles were not only a function of ministry but also a paradigm by which the movement called out a sinful society, challenged the activity of the church within that culture, and emerged from the dysfunction of the Civil War to proclaim a new paradigm for God's revelation to his people. The fledgling Assemblies of God was a voice crying in the wilderness against the status quo of religious understanding and practice. A change must be made if the mission of Jesus was to be accomplished on earth. The empowerment of women was pivotal to this prophetic stance as their very presence challenged established religious practice and their freedom to participate and lead reversed thousands of years of religious patriarchy.

Over time, the Assemblies of God severely undermined its prophetic role in religious culture. As it developed, the fellowship more closely resembled the religious denominations it once decried than it did a rogue prophet who spoke truth to power. The choices that led to this change were profoundly rhetorical and rooted in discourse used by the leadership. These rhetorical choices were the result of the subtle shifts that have been examined throughout the course of this study from the early position of John Wesley to the extraordinary work of women at the Azusa Street Revival. At each juncture, as the movement became more successful, the status of women was challenged. The discursive tension that dominated the formative years of the Assemblies of God (despite the desire of early leaders for the issue to fade into the background) follows a similar pattern. Women continued to create opportunities for service in ministry as a result of their spiritual empowerment through the experience of the baptism in the Holy Spirit. In response, the discourse on the level of engagement available to women continued to try the leadership of the Assemblies of God. During these years of growth and influence, the conflicts grew stronger as the secular world began to embrace a greater autonomy for women in the workplace and the marketplace.

Clearly, women presented a disproportionately prominent presence in the Pentecostal movement and, more specifically within the Assemblies of God. This dominance redefined how the work in the church was done and by whom, subverting centuries of religious ideology and practice. Women's participation in Pentecostal ministry reconceptualized who God is, how humans relate to him, and how his work on earth is carried out. As a result, the doctrinal stance that developed from the discourse surrounding the participation of women in the Assemblies of God was as distinctive as their position on the baptism in the Holy Spirit. The doctrine of empowerment for service not only defines Assemblies of God identity but also gives rise to the empowerment of women for service alongside their male counterparts.

Despite a doctrinal stance that seems to provide carte blanche to women's participation in the Assemblies of God, historical analysis reveals that practice was otherwise. Women in the fellowship have engaged in a constant negotiation and renegotiation of their role. In light of the historical, theological, and cultural contexts in which the Assemblies of God exists, the challenges women have faced and continue to face are profoundly rooted in a discourse that offers rhetorical encouragement on the one hand and dismissal on the other.

From the formative years of the Pentecostal movement to years of sustained growth and influence, specifically within the Assemblies of God, the movement lost sight of its unique cultural and religious identity. Despite a radical beginning and a unique theology and praxis, as the Assemblies of God developed into an individual institution, strategic choices precipitated rapid growth in the United States and around the world. In the process, however, these choices sacrificed elements of a distinctive history and ideology. These choices contributed to the tensions faced by women who sensed a calling to church ministry and leadership. This chapter examines how the function of ministry with the Assemblies of God shifted from prophetic to priestly, and as a result, a distinct call was made by the leadership for greater male participation. Next, continued centralization of power and institutionalization moved women away from the prominence they had held during the early years of the movement. Finally, shifts in the larger culture, including situations for women in the workplace and the marketplace, shaped the Assemblies of God's response to feminism. As previous sociological and theological scholars have argued, the Assemblies of God sacrificed its moment to be a catalyst for the changing role of women in the church and in American culture.

While the secular world began to shift social attitudes toward women following World War II and as the modern Women's Rights Movement gained momentum, the Assemblies of God was faced with a difficult series of choices over how to respond and speak to the growing concerns of women in the broader culture. By choosing to remain with their more conservative counterparts in the greater evangelical community, the Assemblies of God missed a crucial opportunity to be at the vanguard of women's liberation and sacrificed what sociologist Margaret Poloma has argued was their charismatic moment to lead cultural change and chose instead a reactionary stance that created further dissonance for women who desired to serve the church.

These observations are not new to the critique of the Pentecostal movement or the Assemblies of God. Some of the earliest scholarly analyses of Pentecostals began to identify these shifts as turning points in the history of organizations like the Assemblies of God and their impact on the unique identity of those who affiliated their lives and ministries with these organizations. Adherents expressed reservations even before the Hot Springs gathering in 1914 where the Assemblies of God was birthed. The choice to create a formal organizational structure had profound impact on the prophetic nature of the movement going forward. Thus far, the expressed reservations and following analysis have focused on the theological and sociological impact of these shifts on the organization specifically. I would argue, however, that early Pentecostals had engaged in profound symbol formation, establishing a unique rhetoric of who they were and what they stood for, and they had set the scene for a radical change not only in how their faith was practiced and expressed, but in who could share that faith and lead others into their own Pentecostal experiences. Pentecostals had also engaged in a period of rhetorical invention in which the cornerstone of their identity was how they expressed their faith and mission. The theological and sociological climate was certainly impacted, but in their rhetorical engagement a shift took place that moved them away from their more radical beginnings.

## THE PROPHETIC VS. PRIESTLY FUNCTION IN THE ASSEMBLIES OF GOD

According to Barfoot and Sheppard, when the symbolic function of Pentecostal leadership shifted in the 1920s from "prophet" to "priest," the number of women in leadership positions rapidly declined. Prophetic female figures were central to the genesis and subsequent growth of the movement.[4] The symbolic function of Pentecostal leadership as presented by Barfoot and Sheppard relies on the definition and use of the terms "prophetic" and "priestly." These terms, common among Pentecostals, were often used to defend Pentecostalism in general and then to distinguish elements of ministry specifically.

The ecstatic religious experience of Pentecostals, as manifested through speaking in other tongues and interpretation of those tongues as well as other mystical experiences, was clarified through the biblical depiction of prophecy and prophetic figures. This interpretation of the Pentecostal experience depended upon at least three factors that led to greater equality among men and women in Pentecostal ministry. The first factor was the

4. Ibid., 2.

establishment of a "calling." The call (prior to formal organization) was the only defining difference between ministers and laity. Second, the call was confirmed by the community's recognition of the charismatic gifts: specifically, the Baptism of the Holy Spirit, which would become known as "the initial physical evidence" of speaking in tongues as the identifying feature of the empowerment for service. The final factor included the eschatological belief that what was occurring was the outpouring of the "latter rain" according to the prophet Joel in which both "sons and daughters prophesy" according to Joel 2:28.

Early Pentecostals considered most pastoral and preaching duties as prophetic and identified priestly duties with only certain administrative functions, which may or may not have included the administration of the ordinances of the church: officiating at marriages and funerals, water baptism, and overseeing the giving and receiving of communion. Through this emphasis on prophecy, the Pentecostal experience opened the door to a dramatic change in the gender dynamic in Pentecostal churches. As the movement grew, however, these formerly prophetic functions began to be called "priestly," rhetorically limiting the participation of women in these activities. The only Pentecostal denomination not to place "priestly" restrictions on female ministers was the International Church of the Foursquare Gospel, which was founded by Aimee Semple McPherson, the female evangelist who affiliated with the Assemblies of God for three years before resigning to form her own organization.

A subtle, but distinguishing hierarchy had begun to emerge within the Assemblies of God. The term "elder" developed as category to curtail women's leadership. In the early years of the Assemblies of God, the practice of priestly functions limited to males peacefully coexisted with the idea of equal opportunity for women who could continue in their prophetic functions. Serious theological disputes, as addressed in the previous chapter, including the theology of Acts 2 as doctrine and the "Jesus Only" movement had led to the fracturing of the overall movement into smaller sects, but as the Assemblies of God moved on from these disputes and began to see several years of sustained growth, the challenges were less and less theological and more and more organizational.

## Establishing a Hierarchy of Ministry Roles

Barfoot and Sheppard claim that the easiest place to document the change in the function of Pentecostal ministry from the prophetic to the priestly occurs in these organizational shifts. Like the present study, Barfoot and

Sheppard specifically examined the Assemblies of God, but they note that many of the changes that occurred within the Assemblies were also typical of those in other Pentecostal organizations. Significantly, as Barfoot and Sheppard highlight, while organization clearly occurred in the Assemblies of God beginning in 1914, the leadership vehemently denied that this organization or the creation of a denomination or sect was occurring.

Beginning in 1917, however, a significant shift occurred that set up a gradation among the clergy in the Assemblies, which for the most part continues today. The socio-religious function of preaching was no longer solely rooted in the prophetic; it was shifting to priestly performance. Various levels of credentials began to be issued to distinguish a hierarchy of functions within the fellowship. Ordination was and is the highest level of credential offered. It provides its holder unlimited ability to serve as a leader in the local church, in district positions, and within the General Council. In the development of credentialing levels, women were severely limited in their ability to move from "credentialed or licensed" to "ordained." In addition, the Assemblies took a strong rhetorical stance that also severely limited the ministry of women: the education and training of ministers at an established Bible Institute (later College).

From 1927 to 1941, the Assemblies of God experienced significant growth, not only in membership, but also in the numbers serving as ministers and missionaries. Menzies cited a 285 percent growth in the number of ministers, a 321 percent growth in the number of churches, and a rise of 290 percent in church membership.[5] Then General Superintendent E. S. Williams attributed this growth to the number of graduates from Assemblies of God Bible schools, often called institutes, which by 1941 stood at 1,450 graduates who had entered full time ministry (stateside) or missionary service (abroad). This was approximately 50 percent of the total number of graduates at this time.[6]

Early Pentecostal ministers had little or no formal Bible school or seminary training, nor did the Assemblies of God require an education of any kind for ordination or licensure. While recognizing a need for a Bible training school from its inception, in practice the fledgling organization instead chose to espouse apprenticeships, fasting, and prayer as the marks of calling. The establishment of the first Assemblies of God school for ministerial training is another evidence of the increasing centralization of authority.[7]

5. General Council of the Assemblies of God, General Council Minutes (1927–1941) summarized and analyzed by Menzies, *Anointed to Serve*, 146–47.

6. General Council of the Assemblies of God, General Council Minutes, 1941, 73.

7. Central Bible Institute in 1922 was the first school established by the General

Six years after Central Bible Institute opened the coeducational school, the Dean reported a need for more male students. According to the General Council minutes, the report stated, "we take this opportunity to bring before our people, and especially the pastors, the need in their assemblies for encouraging and stimulating the interest of the young people in preparing themselves definitely, especially the young men, as there is a crying need everywhere for a more consecrated Spirit-filled young man."[8] The call for prophesying daughters, Spirit-filled young women, was not forthcoming. In addition, single women who were candidates for missionary appointment were asked to finish graduate degrees before reapplying for appointment, while this requirement was not made of their male counterparts. The shift to priesthood had begun.

## A Reversal of Policy

The strongest official reaction against women's ministry occurred at the 1931 General Council. A resolution questioned whether women should have the same rights as men in performing the ordinances of the church. This resolution reversed the flexibility the Council had shown since 1914 and denied the earlier rights of women to priestly acts in the church.

The resolution noted that while views continued to diverge on the roles of men and women in the Assemblies of God the previously established rights and offices of women were unacceptable to the General Council. The resolution explicitly forbade a woman from serving in any ministry capacity except evangelist, and the terminology, which had previously been added to allow for administering the ordinances of the church, was removed from certificates issued to women.

Then Missionary Secretary Noel Perkin, who himself was converted to Pentecostalism under the ministry of a woman, argued that "competent authorities" had advised him that "the work of the General Council of the Assemblies of God depends too much on women workers."[9] While he gave credit to those sisters who "stood in the gap," he implied that men were not fulfilling their call. Clearly, missionary women who responded so strongly

---

Council of the Assemblies of God. Regional or district training schools such as Southern California Bible Institute (now Vanguard University) were established as early as 1920, but these were owned and run by districts and were only loosely affiliated with the General Council.

8. General Council of the Assemblies of God, General Council Minutes, 1929, 75.

9. General Council of the Assemblies of God, General Council Minutes, 1931, 58.

to the call just a few years earlier when they petitioned the Council for credentialing rights did not feel they were simply "standing in the gap" until a suitable man could be found, but once again, in a public forum, women who were serving were deemed second class to men or married couples.

### The Ironic Relationship of Robert and Marie Burgess Brown

Ironically, women were invited to speak on the resolution, which they did, some for and some against the motion. The views of the women, however, were not the significant ones. Following the call for women to speak, the Reverend Robert Brown rose to give his position on the resolution. Brown was no ordinary Assemblies of God pastor; rather, he was the husband of Marie Burgess Brown, one of the most influential and highly respected female ministers within the Council. Brown observed that "he could not help but notice that in the scriptures there was no woman in the priesthood and none in the apostolic ministry. God chose men." He stated that his wife always refrained from "acts of priesthood." Brown hated to see women put on "a white garment and try to look like angels, and go into the baptismal pool to baptize converts."[10]

While Brown's position on women is not unique among men of his day, the woman to whom he was married and partnered with in ministry was certainly a force in ministry work. A graduate of Moody Bible Institute and a former stateside missionary, Marie Burgess founded a Pentecostal mission in New York City in 1907. Upon her marriage to Robert Brown in 1909, she asked her husband to join her in ministry, and together they pastored what by then was called Glad Tidings Hall, later Tabernacle. According to Brown's nephew, Dr. Robert Berg, Marie preached every Sunday morning service during her tenure at Glad Tidings, and her husband took on the preaching of Sunday evening services. However, Brown left the majority of the business functions of the church to her husband including the practice of baptism. She did, however, administer communion.[11]

Robert's death in 1948 brought Marie back to the pastorate alone. She served as Pastor for 23 years following her husband's death, asking her nephew, Stanley Berg to join her in ministry. As with the division of ministry she shared with her husband, Marie Burgess Brown also turned over the business functions of the church to her nephew.

A great irony exists in the ministry of Marie Burgess Brown. Clearly, Rev. Brown believed she had a calling to ministry, and she fulfilled this call

10. Frodsham, "Editor's General Council Notes," 4–5.

11. Berg, in discussion with the author, June 22, 2009.

as a single and a married woman. While she worked with her husband and later her nephew, she was clearly the spiritual leader of her church. This designation of leadership is a significant point regarding how women like Rev. Brown negotiated their roles. She delegated the "business" functions of the church to someone else so that she could focus on the spiritual needs of her congregation. We do not know what Brown's personal position was on her role versus that of her husband, but her actions speak volumes.

Gordon P. Gardiner writes in a booklet published for the 48th anniversary of Glad Tidings Tabernacle that while Brown had the assistance of her husband and later her nephew, the church will remember the "lady pastor" as "the minister whom God used to blaze the Pentecostal trail in this metropolis."[12] Gardiner goes on to state that forty-eight years is quite a tenure for any pastor to serve a single congregation, but his addition of "and a woman at that" distinguishes Brown as a force of nature in the Pentecostal ministry. One 1950s account surveying Christianity in New York City notes the success of Marie Burgess Brown's ministry, "Lady pastor Rev. Marie Brown . . . does an effective job according to the consensus of evangelical opinion. It is associated with the Assemblies of God, broadcasts Sunday morning, gets a large crowd most any time it opens its doors and gave $200,000 to missions in the last five years."[13] Marie Burgess Brown continued to serve Glad Tidings Tabernacle as its pastor until her death in 1971, concluding 64 years of pastoral ministry.

Like so many others in her position, Marie Burgess Brown was reluctant to accept the call to ministry; she was reluctant to pioneer a church; and she was reluctant to continue in ministry without her partner and husband. In the end, an act of obedience to a distinct call eventually enabled her to continue her work. This personal call, according to sociologist Max Weber was the decisive element that distinguished the prophet from the priest. Weber states, "The latter lays claim to authority by virtue of his service in a sacred tradition, while the prophet's claim is based on personal revelation and charisma."[14] Barfoot and Sheppard argue that for Pentecostals one must add the telling of one's call, which was modeled after the depiction of the biblical prophets. In nearly every instance, particularly with Old Testament prophets including Moses, Isaiah, Jeremiah, and Ezekiel as well as the Apostle Paul in the New Testament, the prophet experiences a divine confrontation, an introductory word, the commission, the objection, the

12. Gardiner, *Origin of Glad Tidings Tabernacle*, vi.

13. Flynn, "World's Greatest Mission Field" as cited in Gardiner, *Origin of Glad Tidings Tabernacle*, v.

14. Weber, *On Charisma and Institution Building*, 254.

reassurance, and the sign. The biblical descriptions of the prophets provided a powerful rhetorical tool by which women could make a claim to their rightful place in the Pentecostal pastorate. Like the prophets of old, prophetic stories were used to interpret aspects of a woman's call to preach or to fulfill other experiences in her life. For example, as with the case of Marie Burgess Brown, female Pentecostal ministers frequently reported that they had initially objected to God's call on the grounds that they were women. But commitment to the call, once accepted, continued to be the case with Brown following her husband's untimely death. Just hours after her husband's burial, Marie Burgess Brown returned to Glad Tidings Tabernacle and preached a Sunday morning church service despite her personal grief. Again obedience to the call was the priority over personal desires and in this case deep pain and loss.

The 1931 resolution that Robert Brown had spoken in favor of passed, denying rights of women that had been granted to them earlier. We do not know what Marie Burgess Brown's position on this issue was, nor do we have any record of her ever speaking on a woman's role in the church. She was never silenced in her own church, and in 1933, she preached the Memorial Service at that year's General Council.[15] The gauntlet, however, had been laid down. As Barfoot and Sheppard put it, "Male monopolization of the priestly functions was complete."[16]

The conflict between rhetoric and action of Robert and Marie Brown is a microcosm of that within the Assemblies of God as a whole. Robert Brown took a very strict and narrow position on the role of women verbally and in matters of policy, but continued to function as a co-minister with his wife. Marie Burgess Brown did not take a public stand on ministry policy or write articles espousing her views of women's roles. Rather, she took her calling seriously and let the men debate the matter while she did the work of spiritually guiding her congregation. Like many women before and after her, Brown was more focused on the call of God than on the official policy of an organization. Her silence on the issue is deafening. Her actions speak volumes about how she and women like her seized opportunities despite even the most personal of constraints placed before them. Brown is the personification of Weber's view of the prophetic role of ministry. Her husband, on the other hand, represents how Pentecostals, particularly those in the Assemblies of God worked out their view of the prophetic versus priestly.

---

15. Marie Brown would speak again at the 1951 General Council during a morning meeting, but she was the last woman to be invited to speak at a General Council until the late 1970s.

16. Barfoot and Sheppard, "Prophetic vs. Priestly Religion," 14.

His rhetoric stands in stark contrast to his actions, and yet it is the discourse, not the practice, which ultimately determined the policy.

## A Reversal of Policy . . . Again

In 1935, the General Council again reversed itself on women's status in the church by restoring to women the full rights to pastor and administer all the ordinances of the church. The 1935 resolution (which was then Article v, Section 4(b) of the bylaws and has only seen subtle changes over the years) began by noting that the Scriptures "plainly teach" that men and women had different ministry callings, but that "women may also serve the church in the ministry of the Word." Women were required to be 25 years of age and "matured" and were required to give evidence of both development in ministry and actual service. The right to administer the ordinances came with the qualifier "when such acts are necessary."[17]

While this reversal may seem like a victory that would settle the issue, Blumhofer argues that the "failure to address underlying reservations about women in leadership" and "deeply rooted prejudices both against women exercising authority over men and against married women assuming responsibilities outside the home" made the decision to offer ordination to women little more than a technical improvement.[18] And yet, while the General Council waffled on what the rights and offices of a woman should be, the number of ordained women in the Assemblies actually grew between 1925 and 1935 from 18.6 percent to 20 percent.[19]

Despite efforts to shift the discussion and redefine the context of Pentecostal ministry while maintaining the distinct nature of the prophetic, the Assemblies of God was failing to reconcile the counter-cultural nature of their movement with the cultural norms of traditional religious practice. The leaders of the Assemblies of God seemed to want it both ways. They wanted to be a prophetic movement, which could be a voice crying in the wilderness to usher in the latter days of human history with all its signs and wonders, but as time passed and the movement grew, they sacrificed their unique cultural identity to more closely relate to the very religious movements they had reviled, condemned, and ultimately abandoned. The challenge was that women in the Pentecostal movement and especially within the Assemblies of God took their callings seriously, and despite the

17. General Council of the Assemblies of God, General Council Minutes, 1935, 111–12.

18. Blumhofer, "Role of Women," 14–16.

19. Kenyon, "Analysis of Ethical Issues," 228–29.

formidable opposition, they continued to forge ahead in their work. When leaders of the movement could no longer limit women's involvement theologically or in many cases socially, they again resorted to rhetorical tactics to make their displeasure and discontentment known.

## MORE MEN NEEDED

In a 1935 article in the Assemblies of God's newly minted official publication the *Pentecostal Evangel*, Ralph Riggs decried the lack of men in the Assemblies of God. He maintained that Scriptures teach that "men are the God-ordained leaders in the home and in the work of God."[20] They are gifted with leadership qualities such as physical strength and analytical intellect. He postulated that the Assemblies of God needed "a strong dominant male element" in their churches. He backed up his view with what he notes are "alarming" statistics: 60 percent of Assemblies of God Bible school students, 67 percent of Assemblies of God church members and 75 percent of Assemblies of God missionaries were women.[21] What he fails to mention is that four out of five Assemblies of God ordained ministers were men.[22] While publicly, the Assemblies of God seemed to be moving in a more egalitarian direction in favor of women in ministry, the private feelings of individual leaders opposed to women in ministry surfaced several times in official publications of the Assemblies.[23] A perception persisted that men in the Assemblies of God were in short supply; yet, again, one of the most outspoken leaders who made the call for more men, J. Roswell Flower, was

20. Ralph Riggs served as Assistant General Superintendent from 1943 to 1953 and as General Superintendent from 1953 to 1959 and is best known within the Assemblies of God as the strongest and most vocal advocate for a denominational liberal arts college. In 1955, under his leadership, Evangel College, now Evangel University, opened its doors and continues to serve as the national liberal arts university within the Assemblies of God. At the time of this citation, he was serving as a pastor and his statistics were not corroborated from available data.

21. Riggs, "Place of Men in the Work," 16.

22. Barfoot and Sheppard cite 1936 statistics to show that women comprised 63 percent of Assemblies of God church members and 60.4 percent of Foursquare Church members. The former was an organization led by men and the latter by a woman. Cavaness cites 66 percent of missionaries in 1938 were women.

23. At least four *Pentecostal Evangel* articles were published appealing for a rise in men's involvement, including the Riggs article Flower, "Men Wanted," 12; Peters, "Help Wanted," 2; Keys, "Where Are the Young Men?" 6. Along a similar theme, see also Flower, "Liberia Needs Men," 12; and Guynes, "Kind of Men We Need," 1969, 18–19. Only one later article asked for women nurses in a particular foreign field: Perkin, "Appeal for Lady Missionaries," 8.

married to an influential and well respected woman who served most of her life in ministry.

### The Legacy of Alice Reynolds Flower

Alice Reynolds Flower, who was affectionately known as "Mother Flower," lived to be 100. Her life and ministry spanned most of the history of the Assemblies of God. Alice was licensed as a minister in 1910 and ordained in 1913. In 1911, she married J. Roswell Flower. By 1913, the Flowers began printing a small weekly newspaper called the *Christian Evangel*, which would later become the official publication of the Assemblies of God, the *Pentecostal Evangel*. When her husband was appointed General Secretary of the Assemblies of God in 1914 and was away from home for several weeks, Alice published the paper on her own. She wrote articles and children's stories in the newspaper and later served as an author of Sunday school literature for the Assemblies of God's Gospel Publishing House. Rev. Flower taught Christian Education classes until she was 90 years old, led a weekly prayer and study group for more than 45 years, and authored 17 books and more than 250 poems.[24] Like Marie Burgess Brown, she pastored churches with her husband, whom she outlived, and was a great influence in the Assemblies of God from its earliest years until the time of her death. The Flower's were leaders who exemplified the contradictions of rhetoric and practice. Clearly, Mother Flower, had great influence and was capable of engaging in ministry but her husband's rhetoric, specifically, seemed to undermine the roles she played and how she lead. Simplistically, one could argue that she operated as she did because of her marriage to another minister and leader, however, her work and ministry did not end upon his death. This disconnect between rhetoric and practice is amplified in the lives of early pioneers like the Flowers.

## MEMBERSHIP IN THE NATIONAL ASSOCIATION OF EVANGELICALS

While the rhetoric of ministry shifted from the prophetic to the priestly, and while the office of pastor became more and more a professional occupation, the Assemblies of God would also make a shift that would have surprised early leaders of the movement. The fellowship of like-minded believers, despite its best intentions, was beginning to look a lot more like a denomination.

---

24. Lee and Gohr, "Women in the Pentecostal Ministry," 3.

Leaders began to identify with the emerging fundamentalist movement, which had earlier rejected them, and authority within the movement was becoming more and more centralized.[25] This institutional shift occurred alongside the Assemblies of God's membership in a new organization, the National Association of Evangelicals for United Action more commonly known today as the National Association of Evangelicals (NAE).

The Assemblies of God and Pentecostals in general had previously been isolated from other collective bodies (often by their own choosing) including the Fundamentalists, who denounced the Assemblies at a 1928 gathering of the World's Christian Fundamental Association. The invitation from the NAE marked the first time any evangelical body had asked the Assemblies of God to participate. In 1943, the Assemblies of God officially voted on joining the new group.

Membership in the NAE was not without its controversies and ramifications. Several scholars like Kenyon, Dayton, and Blumhofer note that this affiliation signified a "search for respectability," "a drive for acceptance and recognition" and "a desire to shed their radical image." Howard Kenyon suggests that the Assemblies of God was attempting to "mainstream" itself or "accommodate itself in all non-essentials to prevailing fundamentalist/evangelical thought." These efforts resulted in the denomination's attempts at neutrality in most issues that were controversial and at times "produced a contradiction in the denomination's self-understanding."[26] Donald Dayton states that the traditions brought on by the alignment with the greater evangelical church had become "much like those whom their foremothers and forefathers had protested."[27]

Blumhofer contends that the leadership of the NAE influenced attitudes within the Assemblies "far more extensively" than the Assemblies of God influenced them.[28] Cecil Roebuck, Jr., concurs with Blumhofer and states that while the "evangelicalization" of Pentecostals brought them into dialogue with the greater evangelical community, it has not come without the loss of certain distinctives. In addition to moving away from social positions on pacifism and moving toward a more right-leaning political stance, doctrinal shifts on more traditional evangelical issues such as scriptural "inerrancy" and suspicion of other ecumenical organizations cut the Assemblies of God and other Pentecostal groups off from "meaningful interaction" with a greater cross section of the Protestant community, which may have

---

25. Wacker, "Assemblies of God," 10–11.

26. Kenyon, "Analysis of Ethical Issues."

27. Dayton, "Evangelical Roots of Feminism," 54.

28. Blumhofer, *Assemblies of God*, 101.

actually limited influence and diminished witness. But the issue of women's leadership is where the Assemblies of God sacrificed the most.

While not all Pentecostals took women's leadership even as far as the Assemblies of God had done, women historically have played a more distinct and influential role in Pentecostal ministry than in most evangelical traditions. As evangelical values were adopted by the Assemblies of God, the placement of women in ministry was sacrificed.[29]

## Trading Women for Influence

Harvey Cox makes a similar connection: "Ever since the beginning of the modern [Pentecostal] movement, both men and women have tried to undercut the Spirit's gender impartiality."[30] When the Assemblies of God aligned itself with fundamentalist ideology and evangelical theology, it undermined the blurring of gender lines practiced from the beginning of the Pentecostal movement. Cox continues, "But wherever the original Pentecostal fire breaks through the flame-extinguishing literalist theology, women shine."[31]

Poloma observed in her 1989 book that chronicled the institutional dilemmas faced by the Assemblies of God that the "marriage with non-Pentecostal conservative Protestantism is moving the Assemblies of God away from its historical ambivalence toward women in ministry and toward silencing its prophesying daughters." She continues, "These evangelical ties have been accompanied by an adoption of biblical interpretive principles from fundamentalism, rather than the development of a hermeneutic consistent with the experience of Pentecostals."[32]

By choosing to align themselves in an awkward marriage with both the greater evangelical community and the fundamentalist movement, the Assemblies of God was becoming more visible, and by many accounts, more successful about whom they might attract to their congregations, and in their ability to establish continued growth, but they were sacrificing the unique characteristics and distinctives that had created their initial success and attractiveness. Poloma argues that the "very success of the Assemblies" has made it more difficult for charisma to flow, "particularly if the Spirit should choose to rest on women."[33]

29. Robeck, "National Association of Evangelicals," 635.

30. Cox, *Fire from Heaven*, 125.

31. Ibid.

32. Poloma, *Assemblies of God at the Crossroads*, 119.

33. Ibid.

The Assemblies of God, as part of the larger Pentecostal movement, had a countercultural mentality that allowed women to find a place in ministry, but that mentality was replaced by its embracing one segment of culture and rejecting another. The benefits of this move were greater acceptance among the Christian community and the ability to attract and promote growth overall. The sacrifice was the movement's ability to be revolutionary for women and, by extension, continue to be revolutionary both inside and outside the church.

## From Counter-Cultural to Privileged Class

Poloma as well as Barfoot and Sheppard draw from sociological theorist Max Weber to address the shifting attitudes toward women ministers in the Assemblies of God. Weber contends that the "religion of the disprivileged classes" allows for the tendency to grant equality to women. However, when women began to use their prophetic gifts and gained a following, the equality of the sexes only existed in principle. Only men were considered for specialized training and were assumed to possess the natural qualifications; therefore, only men could carry out the priestly functions or the law of the gospel. The great receptivity of women as leaders was short-lived. Weber states: "Only in very rare cases does this practice continue beyond the first state of a religious community's formation, when the pneumatic manifestations of charisma are valued as hallmarks of specific religious exaltation. Thereafter, as routinization, and regimentation of community relationships set in, a reaction takes place against pneumatic manifestations amongst women."[34] It was no longer enough to look to the "initial physical evidence" of the baptism in the Holy Spirit as a confirmation of the call of God to ministry where women were concerned. As the Assemblies of God became more centralized in its organization and more middle- to upper-class in its appeal, women were no longer valued as a necessity to reach the masses. We see this shift in the specific call by the leadership of the Assemblies of God for more men to become educated and join the ministry ranks. It appears in the shifts in policy to limit women's involvement and allow men to come in and take their place. Once a movement in which color and gender lines were "washed away in the blood," the fellowship has become an institution in which authority structures are far more valued than the counter-cultural stance of the prophetic voice.

As was the case with early Pentecostals, the legitimacy of one's anointing and authority to speak came from personal charisma or what Weber

34. Weber, *Sociology of Religion*, 104.

calls that "certain quality of an individual personality by virtue of which he is set apart from ordinary men and treated as endowed with supernatural, superhuman, or at least specifically exceptional qualities."[35] As the movement took on a more structured stance, the argument for what set Pentecostals apart was replaced with what made them more acceptable to the culture they had previously rejected. Rather than stay a course of reformation, the Assemblies of God became reactionary and in turn robbed itself of the moment and the prophetic posture it once had to speak to the culture and instead became entrenched in the very cultural patterns that had been rejected by the pioneers of the movement.

Certainly, the culture had shifted. Following World War II, Assemblies of God adherents experienced the same rapid upward mobility as many of their secular counterparts. Members of the fellowship quickly became more middle class and established in their communities. They were no longer on the fringe of society socioeconomically, and this newfound affluence markedly changed the demographics of the Assemblies of God to a predominantly white, middle-class, conservative denomination.

While the war thrust women into changing social and cultural patterns, within the evangelical community, women were encouraged to reject this shift, and traditional female roles were reaffirmed. Within the Assemblies of God, specifically, as the men came home from the war to take over jobs and the pulpits, the opportunities for women in ministry declined.[36] Women could pioneer churches and remain on the foreign mission field, but less and less could they preach in their own home churches. While the founding fathers and mothers of the early movement had encouraged a relationship between social reform and religious revivalism, which had birthed the Women's Suffrage Movement and gave great power to the Abolitionist movement, the same would not be said of continuing the fight for gender and racial reconciliation in the twentieth century.[37]

Poloma goes so far as to argue that Pentecostalism could have led the charge for gender and racial equality by sparking an alternative to what would become the modern secular feminist and civil rights movements. However, both Cavaness and Kenyon note that Pentecostals had become complacent and seemed to lack awareness of what was going on in the world around them. As a result, they lacked a public discursive presence on the burning social issues that dominated the cultural dialogue. While publicly the Assemblies of God was silent on these burning issues, in meetings

35. Weber, *On Charisma and Institution Building*, xviii.
36. Wacker, "Assemblies of God," 11; and Blumhofer, *Assemblies of God*, 9–10.
37. Hestenes, "Women in Leadership," 4–10.

of the Executive Presbytery and in personal correspondence, General Superintendent Ralph Riggs was clear that the fellowship would not go on record favoring either integration or segregation, but rather would mark time until the matter had "developed further in the public consciousness and practice."[38] Blumhofer calls this decision a "willingness to wait for cultural accommodation."[39] I contend that the discourse shows more political posturing, a sort of finger-in-the-wind-mentality. The leadership were not willing to step out and be the voice of justice and righteousness for women or African-Americans as doing so might have once again alienated them from the greater evangelical community and appeared too liberal for what was and continues to be a more socially and politically conservative movement. The Assemblies of God would have once again been a fringe movement and respectability had become more important than standing up for what was right.

By 1965, the General Council was finally willing to take a public stand on the issue of segregation and passed a resolution affirming civil rights, but in an interesting use of exclusivist language, the author of the resolution reaffirmed "the intrinsic value of every man" and urged the Assemblies to discourage "unfair and discriminatory practices wherever they exist." The resolution further asserted, "Those in authority . . . particularly in evangelical groups, have a moral responsibility toward the creation of those situations which will provide equal rights and opportunities for every individual."[40]

The lack of moral clarity and prophetic imagination to speak into civil rights set the Assemblies of God outside of the culture in a way that diminished their influence and authority on the intrinsic value of every person. By the time a resolution was issued, the Assemblies of God was simply reacting to the shifting cultural landscape rather than shaping it as an act of spiritual leadership.


## FEMINISM AND CULTURAL ACCOMMODATION

While civil rights and women's rights have historically been linked, the Assemblies of God did not make the connection with larger social issues. The women's movement was altogether ignored, viewed with suspicion, or labeled sinful. Although the number of women serving was already in decline, fear of seeming alignment with the secular women's movement

38. Letter from Ralph Riggs to Kenneth Roper (January 24, 1956)

39. Blumhofer, *Assemblies of God*, 173–78.

40. General Council of the Assemblies of God, General Council Minutes, 1965, 60–61.

continued to reduce the numbers of women serving in Pentecostal ministry. Women's participation in church ministry at nearly every level saw rapid decline in the 1960s.

Mixed responses toward women in ministry continued among the Assemblies of God leadership and its constituency throughout the 1970s. In 1969, the term "elder"—which had created the earliest debate over the role of women in the Assemblies of God—was replaced with the more specific "ordained ministers," which forced some districts to rework their bylaws. This change brought up some latent conflict and "powerful sentiment against ordaining women" in some of these districts.[41] However, between 1975 and 1977 the General Council removed an assertion in the bylaws that the "Scriptures plainly teach that there is a difference between the ministry of men and of women in the church," removing the "difference" clause and changing the language to read, "The Scriptures plainly teach that divinely called and qualified women may also serve the church in the ministry of the Word."[42] At the 1977 General Council, a motion prevailed to once again "reaffirm its position on the ordination of women"[43]

## Ignore the Issue and It Will Go Away

As with the issue of civil rights, little was written in any official publication on the feminist movement or the campaign for passage of the Equal Rights Amendment (ERA). Previous scholarship shows that the Assemblies of God tended to follow the lead of the NEA on the issue whose attitudes were generally negative.[44] Lumping the issue together with the Vietnam War, student protest movements and other activist causes, the Executive Presbytery issued what they termed a "social statement" in 1968. They concluded that the fundamental problem was sin and the most significant course of action the church could take would be to mobilize for evangelism. Given the prophetic history of the Assemblies of God and the Pentecostal movement, this refusal to engage the culture on significant issues is both interesting and

41. Kenyon, "Analysis of Ethical Issues," 249.

42. It is unclear exactly when these changes were made, but they were in place by the time of the 1977 resolution. In her analysis of official documents, Cavaness notes that other editing had also taken place since the 1935 version of the bylaws, but this change was clearly the most significant. Cavaness also notes that the change perhaps could be credited to Joseph R. Flower, the eldest son of J. Roswell and Alice Reynolds Flower.

43. General Council of the Assemblies of God, General Council Minutes, 1977, 100.

44. Kenyon, "Analysis of Ethical Issues," 272–77.

distressing. The perceived indifference toward speaking to these issues is further evidence that a paradigm shift had taken hold in the Assemblies of God and its prophetic role had diminished.

## The Feminist Threat

These "activist movements," especially the women's movement, were increasingly viewed as a threat. The ultraconservative response, including the subjugation of women in the home and the workplace by the evangelical community including the Assemblies of God, was justified as the biblical response. General Superintendent Thomas F. Zimmerman and other leaders viewed feminism and other social issues that seemed to dominate the movement as a "serious threat to traditional social institutions."[45] They linked the women's movement to rising divorce rates, the breakdown of the family, and problems of immorality in the church. Yet, a number of college-aged women within the Assemblies of God voiced frustration over the fellowship's "failure to address or even acknowledge both the ambivalence in its own stance on women and the issues raised by evangelical feminists."[46]

In a 1978 letter to Zimmerman, Virginia Hogan, an instructor at Evangel College and the wife of J. Phillip Hogan who served as Executive Director of Foreign Missions, reported her concerns over trends she was observing among her female students who were opting for "independent careers" rather than having a "complete dedication to God and to their husband's calling."[47] Liberation movements, especially those that claimed to be biblical in nature, she lamented, were a growing challenge.

The fears that an "evangelical" feminism was becoming a negative influence seemed justified when several wives of Assemblies of God executives reported to Zimmerman after a 1978 conference at Fuller Theological Seminary in California. In an address (obtained for Zimmerman by Virginia Hogan) on "Women and Evangelical Movements," Faith Sand, a missionary to Brazil, called on her audience to acknowledge that cultural bias influenced how they communicated God's message. Sand noted several inconsistencies in how evangelicals used Scripture. She issued an indictment of "our worship of capitalism," called the audience to boycott religious institutions that gave only lip service to women's rights, and insisted that "women's liberation portend the end of evangelical chauvinism."[48]

45. Thomas Zimmeran to Mr. and Mrs. R. T. Highfill, February 10, 1977.

46. Ibid.

47. Virginia Hogan to Thomas F. Zimmerman, July 31, 1978.

48. These quotations are taken from a draft of Sand's address, which the women

The reactions of these women and Zimmerman's response made it abundantly clear that feminism of any kind, including that which may be presented from a biblical worldview, would not be accepted in the Assemblies of God and was led to a slippery slope of other moral challenges facing the culture.[49] Pastors at the local level and some of the laity also picked up this line of argumentation, linking the women's movement to higher divorce rates, the breakdown of the family, and a widening array of marital problems that plagued the church and culture. Curiously, they appeared to absolve men of any responsibility for these trends. Considering the backlash against the changing roles of women within the culture, the intensified decline in the number of women within church leadership is not at all surprising. A 1988 report on ministerial statistics cited that in 1936, one female was ordained a minister for every four males. By 1986, the number was one female for every eight of her male counterparts.[50]

## The Church as the Vanguard of Women's Liberation

Despite the Assemblies of God's fierce opposition to the women's movement and the potentially harmful trends that in their view resulted from it, in 1978, Joseph R. Flower, General Secretary of the Assemblies of God and son of J. Roswell and Alice Reynolds Flower, published a 22-page paper titled, "Does God Deny Spiritual Manifestations and Ministry Gifts to Women?"[51] The most extensive treatment of the subject to come from an Assemblies of God official to that point, the document not only cited statistics of the day, but also presented a systematic discourse on both sides of the women-in-ministry argument.

Flower's conclusions affirm the ministry of women on several points. Flower defends women's rights by stating that "in no way could any of them be accused of an arrogation of powers or usurpation of authority over the

in attendance were able to obtain. The copy of the draft can be found in the Women's Movement File at the Flower Pentecostal Heritage Center, Springfield, MO, 4–5.

49. Thomas Zimmerman to Mr. and Mrs. R. T. Highfill, February 10, 1977.

50. These statistics are also misleading and are a bit like comparing apples and oranges. The earliest statistics only included ordained women. After 1917, most stats included both licensed and ordained women. As the years progressed, the statistics would also include retirees (active or inactive) and after 1988, the lowest category, which was at the time Christian worker (now Certified Minister), was also included. These changes in who was counted prevent a true picture of the situation and often the categories of inclusion were different for men and women. Whether intentional or not, there is no way to get an accurate picture of the overall decline.

51. The paper itself was not widely distributed. The copy held in the Assemblies of God Archives is stamped "not an official General Council Document."

man." He draws this conclusion based on the ministerial recognition women in the past had received by properly constituted credentialing committees who granted them the right to minister. Flower continues, "Even those serving as pastors are doing so by the free choice of those whom they serve."

Flower articulates Old and New Testament Scriptures and provides positive examples of women in public roles and addresses the so-called "problem" passages in the New Testament that are often used to discredit women in church leadership. Flower calls readers back to the "priesthood of all believers, as over against a special ruling priestly class" while making a striking admission. "Unfortunately, although we have doctrine, we do not always have it in the experience and life of the church." He concludes by stating that he can find "no good reason to exclude spiritual gifts and ministries"[52] from Christian women, going so far as to advocate for women to serve as deacons, elders, and presbyters. The "church should be in the vanguard of any movement promoting true spiritual liberty for womanhood."[53]

While the document that Flower wrote was never published in full as an official position paper of the fellowship, a condensed version was published in a later issue of *Advance*, a periodical sent to all Assemblies of God ministers. Over the course of several years, Joseph Flower updated the statistics in the paper and sent it to anyone who requested it. In a 1988 interview, Flower admitted that while "no gender distinction is made from 'headquarters' regarding eldership . . . prejudice exists."[54]

In the mid-1980s, the General Council elected G. Raymond Carlson to serve as general Superintendent. Carlson desired to be a different kind of leader than his predecessor and sought to give the constituency of the Assemblies of God more freedom to exercise initiative, but he stopped short of advocating changes in specific policy. Despite the well-argued position paper from Joseph Flower, Carlson did not use the pulpit to speak about political issues or to draw more women into the ministry. This absence of activism is striking considering Carlson's personal history with the Assemblies of God and his willingness to affirm women in ministry, including women as preachers, missionaries, and evangelists. My personal history with Carlson is consistent with this affirmation. I was raised in the same Assemblies of God Church as Carlson and his wife, Mae Steffler Carlson, and my parents were mentored by them while students at Central Bible College. I recall often hearing "Grandpa" Carlson recount the story of his salvation and spiritual upbringing in North Dakota, and I never left an encounter

---

52. Flower, "Does God Deny Spiritual Manifestations?" 1–22.

53. Ibid.

54. Kenyon, "Analysis of Ethical Issues," 269.

with him or his wife where he did not speak directly to me about being obedient to the call of God on my life whatever that might be. The story of his salvation and Pentecostal experience is like many of the others I have profiled in which a woman played a significant role.

## The Influence of Blanche Brittain

Blanche Elizabeth Brittain, an Assemblies of God pastor and evangelist, was widely acclaimed as the denomination's most prolific church planter in North Dakota where she founded and pastored at least 25 churches around the entire state. According to Carlson, "The name of Blanche Brittain is synonymous with the Assemblies of God in North Dakota." [55] Licensed as a missionary evangelist by the Assemblies in August of 1915, she held meetings across the northern plains. She came to North Dakota in 1918 where she would spend the bulk of her ministry years. One of the first places where Brittain established her ministry was in Divide County where she assisted Etta Reckley in pioneering a church in the mining town of Noonan. Known as the "sod buster," Blanche Brittain had foresight and pioneered numerous churches in areas previously untouched by Pentecost, including some that were less than hospitable to the message. For several years, evangelists from nearby Noonan and Ambrose had tried to establish a mission in Crosby, but they were either discouraged or overtly resisted when the tent they had erected on Main Street was burned to the ground. Finally, in 1925, Brittain, against the advice of her congregation in Ambrose, was able to start a church in Crosby. The small congregation met in several locations before building a tabernacle on the site where the original meeting tent had burned to the ground. At the meetings in Crosby, a five-year-old Raymond Carlson would hear the Gospel message and be called into ministry. Brittain's vision was also amazingly foresighted with regard to the mission in Crosby. While the people from Ambrose could not see the church ever being successful, within a few years, the railroad established a base in Crosby, and the town became the county seat and center of commerce. The church in Ambrose closed its doors in the late 1930s or early 1940s, and today that community barely exists while Crosby Assembly of God remains a fixture in the small farming town and the only Assemblies of God church within a sixty-mile radius.[56] Had Brittain not insisted on trying again to start a mission in Cros-

55. Carlson, "When Pentecost Came," 5.

56. I am deeply indebted to Darrin Rodgers, the Director of the Flower Pentecostal Heritage Center and fellow North Dakotan, for his historical analysis of the Assemblies of God in North Dakota. Much of the information recounted here I had heard as stories

by, the Pentecostal message would be non-existent, the leadership of the Assemblies of God would not have included Carlson, and my own personal spiritual history changed forever.

A powerful speaker, Brittain did not stay long in any of the communities in which she pioneered churches, but she left in her wake powerful testimonies of spiritual outpouring that accompanied her ministry. Carlson, in an interview with Assemblies of God historian Darrin Rodgers, notes that Brittain preached with a "rich anointing and with a compassion. . . . When she preached, tears would flow and sinners would get under conviction. Quite a passion for the lost [sic]. She would just grab a hold of you and you would get under conviction."[57] Another story recalled a group of miners who came to be entertained by a lady preacher; they heckled and taunted Brittain throughout the service. Despite the negativity, she seemed to thrive on the attention. She offered clever responses with biblical admonitions and earned the respect of these miners, some of whom ended up on their knees at the makeshift altar that evening. In 1945, Brittain married her second husband, Osmund Urdahl, who, unlike her first husband who had rejected her call to ministry until his deathbed, joined her in her evangelistic efforts until her death in 1952.[58]

Like so many early leaders of Pentecostalism, Carlson's life and ministry was deeply influenced by a woman who, despite rhetorical and often physical constraints, found opportunities to continue their ministry. While many chose to view the feminist movement as a threat to traditional families and to the church, the female leaders of Pentecostalism found the backlash to their work a threat to the Kingdom of God and defied the constraints placed in their way.

After leaving office, Carlson wrote in *Advance* magazine, "With Christ's coming to earth came a liberation of womanhood and the restoration of her dignity. . . . Women have had an important place in the growth of the Assemblies of God. My wife and I were brought into the Pentecostal experience through the ministry of Blanche Brittain, a godly woman preacher. . . . Women were first at the cradle and last at the cross."[59] It is unfortunate that Carlson, like so many of the Assemblies of God leaders who had gone before him, were unwilling to take a stronger official stand and use the power of their position to bring women into the ministry as a result of their own

passed down at church reunions and family gatherings; however, Rodgers was able to do the accurate and scholarly research that produced *Northern Harvest*, 43.

57. Rodgers, *Northern Harvest*, 43.

58. Brittain Ministerial File; and Rodgers, *Northern Harvest*, 43.

59. Carlson, "From the Cradle to the Cross," 24–25.

experience under the leadership of women. While the personal sentiments of these former leaders is striking, one can only imagine what a powerful expression could have done for women who desired to serve as Brittain did, but were met with a less than welcoming fellowship.

## The Debate Continues

Several authors and ministers published articles in Assemblies of God publications during the 1980s affirming women in ministry and provoking letters and opposition to the notion. The debate raged among men and women, old and young, those opposed to and those in favor of women's leadership in the church. One such article was written by Richard Champion, editor of the *Pentecostal Evangel*, who wrote, "If we are going to continue to accept women into our Bible colleges and theological school for ministerial training then we have an obligation to make available all areas of ministry to them. . . . [S]ome of our people have been guilty of limiting the possibilities open to women."[60]

Richard Dresselhaus, an Executive Presbyter, took on the issue of resistance to women deacons and elders, calling it prejudice that questions God's wisdom and seeks after self-justification. He went so far as to claim that repentance was the only way to deal with such prejudice. "It is sin," Dresselhaus stated.[61] Whether Joseph Flower's "position paper" increased the discourse on the subject or not, at the very least the discussion was once again open, centering less upon the secular world and more on the appropriate response within the Assemblies of God itself. The double-speak on women in ministry had created a dissonance between where the Assemblies of God stood and what that meant to the women among its ranks. Whether by what was happening in the broader American culture and the evangelical response to it or by indictments such as those issued by Flower, the Assemblies of God once again needed to examine the attitudes toward women and attempt to speak prophetically on women's roles in ministry.

## An Official Position Paper

Beginning in the late 1980s and early 1990s, a series of white papers was published by the General Council of the Assemblies of God to clarify the official position of the fellowship on issues such as abortion, alcohol

60. Champion, "Editor's Note," 3.
61. Dresselhaus, "Place of Women in the Church," 4–5.

consumption, and gambling. Others addressed the Assemblies of God's teaching on divine healing, the rapture of the church, eternal security, and the initial physical evidence of the baptism in the Holy Spirit. The intention of what would become known as the Assemblies of God Position Papers was to steer the faithful away from false teaching on issues as well as to articulate opposition to or support of cultural and social issues.

Around the same time as the position papers were first published, a "letter" (exact authorship is unknown and not given on the document itself) titled, "A Request for a Clear Delineation of the Role of Women in the Assemblies of God" was circulated. The letter cited women's church planting and missionary work throughout the history of the Assemblies and noted the declining number of women entering ministry work. The writer expressed grave concern over pastors, professors, district, and national leaders who were attempting to silence women and keep them from teaching and ministering. The letter contended that the negative or perceived negative attitude toward women leaders was driving women to other denominations that had become more welcoming. It called for an official reiteration of the biblical rights of women who were faced with criticism from those who objected to their ministry. Readers who were in favor of the request were asked to contact the office of General Secretary Joseph R. Flower.

A committee was appointed by the Executive Presbytery almost immediately in order to respond and formulate a position paper similar to the others. The position paper titled, "The Role of Women in Ministry as Described in Holy Scripture," was released in 1990. Like the unofficial position paper written by Flower, this official paper, outlined the historical activities of women in ministry in the Assemblies of God and expressed appreciation for their service. The paper discussed Old and New Testament role models. A more detailed exegesis of the Scriptural texts that seem to restrict women is presented and those arguments refuted. Unlike Flower's original document, this paper finally carried the weight of an official Assemblies of God position. Like the Statement of Fundamental Truths, these position papers had come to represent the official doctrines and positions of the fellowship: a final word on the values and beliefs of the Assemblies of God. This particular position paper is quite possibly the only one that ministers can publicly preach against without being sanctioned, it has helped to clarify the issue for many who have honest questions. It also contains some of the strongest language on the subject over the entire history of the movement. The paper concludes:

The Pentecostal ministry is not a profession to which men or women merely aspire. It must always be a divine calling, confirmed by the Spirit with a special gifting. . . . To the degree that we are convinced of our Pentecostal distinctives—that it is God who divinely calls and supernaturally anoints for ministry—we must continue to be open to the full use of women's gifts in ministry and spiritual leadership. As we look on the fields ripe for the harvest, may we not be guilty of sending away any of the reapers God calls.[62]

By the mid-1990s only 8.6 percent of the Assemblies of God ordained ministers were women. Dr. Opal Reddin, who spent 24 years as a Professor of Biblical Studies at Central Bible College, noted that "there is a definite lapse between what we have on paper and what we practice." She continued, "The more institutionalized a movement becomes, the more difficult it is for women's calling to be recognized."[63] Dr. Reddin and Dr. Billie Davis, who was one of the first women with a doctoral degree to teach at Evangel College and the Assemblies of God Theological Seminary, spoke optimistically about more women being accepted into positions of decision-making and greater authority. Both women acknowledged, however, that they had "willingly accepted restrictions so they could do God's work."[64]

Nearly the entire first century of Pentecostalism had passed, and the desire of Assemblies of God leaders like E. N. Bell to move on to subjects other than women in leadership was not met. Women were a distinct and unique part of what made Pentecostalism the gr eat movement of the twentieth century. As the movement grew and birthed organizations like the Assemblies of God, women were present and ready to fulfill their calling as prophesying daughters. Women who were called and anointed in their ministry found the justification and the means to forge a head in ministry in spite of confusing and what must have been insulting arguments about the proper role for them in the work of the Gospel.

Argument after argument and justification after justification have been made to both accept and deny women as a part of the mission of the Assemblies of God, and through it all, women have continued to work. Some accepted the restrictions placed on them in order to do what they had been called to do; some sat silently while their husbands debated the issue publicly; some simply forged ahead as "cloud-bursters [sic]"[65] who saw great spiritual outpourings on the Northern Plains. Women have been and continue to be a vital part of the work of Pentecost in the United States and around the world. One writer notes,

The kinds of discrimination that bar women from the opportunity to serve to their fullest capacity are, moreover, no easier for the well-trained

62. General Council of the Assemblies of God, *Role of Women in Ministry*, 16.

63. Edwards, "Woman Up for A/G Post," 6A.

64. Ibid.

65. Carlson, "When Pentecost Came," 5.

and devoted woman to accept in the denomination where women have, theoretically, all rights and privileges, but where they have been completely and effectively ignored, than they are in those churches which in age-old rites and rituals find irrevocable barriers to women entering into significant ministries.[66]

The discrimination faced by women throughout the history of the Assemblies of God has been intensified by the inconsistent discourse of those in leadership. Privately, women were often personally praised and affirmed only to see the very same people degrade and challenge their right to speak in the public square. The Assemblies of God as a movement lost their opportunity to shape and inform the public discourse on the role of women, which not only put them at a disadvantage once the culture caught up to their revolutionary history, but also put them in awkward opposition to the very arguments they had used to justify their existence in the first place. Therefore, they sacrificed their ability to speak truth to power when it might have mattered most.

66. Culver, *Women in the World of Religion*, 201.

# 5

# The Enemy at the Gate

## Women and Evangelical Rhetoric

*Without blushing, Paul is simply stating that when it comes to leading in the church, women are unfit because they are more gullible and easier to deceive than men. While many irate women have disagreed with his assessment through the years, it does appear from this that such women who fail to trust his instruction and follow his teaching are much like their mother Eve and are well-intended but ill-informed.*[1]

—Mark Driscoll, Pastor, Mars Hill Church, on the role of
   women in leadership at Mars Hill Church according to
   1 Tim 2:12–14

*The commands of God in Scripture clearly delineate the structures of the Church. . . . We cannot have it both ways. The Church must choose between the ordination and the subordination of women.*[2]

—Elisabeth Elliot, author and spouse of martyred missionary
   Jim Elliot

1. Driscoll, *Church Leadership.*
2. Elliot, "Why I Oppose Women's Ordination," 16.

BLUMHOFER WARNED THAT SCHOLARS who choose to examine the subject of women in the Pentecostal movement would be met with multiple narratives, competing voices and an array of discrepancies as to the actual role women played in the founding and shaping of the movement. Like the story of women's involvement throughout church history, no single narrative explicitly defines where a woman's voice fits into the grand narrative of Christianity. Could this absence of clarity be a result of the cultural oppression of women that denied them a formal education, proper teaching on the Scriptures, and a lack of opportunity to discover their place on their own? As a result of these conditions, men penned the histories, examined the texts, and wrote the doctrines upon which thousands of years of church history and hierarchy has been formed. Do we simply lack the female perspective and, therefore, cannot truly know what roles women played or the influence they brought to bear on the development on the church? Or is it something far worse? Could God himself have chosen to exclude women and raise up only a select remnant of chosen men to spread his message of redemption and the Gospel of eternal life through Christ?

These questions are not new. Throughout the history of Christ's church, these questions have been pondered, questioned, challenged. John Wesley wrestled with them after being discipled and deeply influenced by the teachings of his mother, Susanna. Phoebe Palmer argued for the public speaking and ministry of women based on careful biblical study and presented one of the more sustained critiques on the role of women ever presented in her day. Yet, Palmer remained steadfastly committed to the cultural and social norms prescribed for women in the home and within the marriage relationship. The issue continues to be taken up by the Southern Baptist Convention. In their denominational meetings they chose to remain steadfastly committed to the position that ministry work is reserved for men. The Roman Catholic Church, faced with a shortage of priests entering the ministry, revisits this issue often, and it is well debated in the public square, yet the Vatican continues to excommunicate women who seek ordination in rogue parishes. Growing non-denominational movements whose charismatic leaders seek to appeal to the popular culture in their dress, their proclamation of the gospel, and their mega-church growth plans dismiss the notion of women as ministers and argue fervently for a male-dominated priesthood within the evangelical church.

For every tale of frustration and repression, stories arise of women and men who reject the historical precedent and look to God himself both in His written Word and in the pouring out of His Spirit to reconceptualize who God is and through whom He is willing to work. While women have been celebrated in the mythology of Pentecostalism: the movement birthed in the outpouring of the Holy Spirit to the oppressed, the societally rejected, and the underclasses; they were privately doubted and their qualifications questioned. Men expressed reservations over the impact on the church, society, and the family of women's involvement in ministry. For every rhetorical opportunity, often more powerful rhetorical constraints arose.

The tension seems not to be firmly grounded in theology or the Scriptures, but rather in the historical context and in relationship to the prevailing culture. The friction manifests itself in the way the church uses words. Language and symbols are used to construct, shape, and naturalize very particular ways of seeing that may or may not exist in the broad counsel of the Scripture. The relationship between the church and women is distinct, and as a result of their unique ideology and practice, how Pentecostals have talked about women in ministry is even more distinct. Yet, the challenges faced by Pentecostals, specifically, mirror the challenges faced by the larger evangelical community. The idea of women in church leadership opposes religious convention, but it also defies American conservative evangelical culture, which places strict limitations on the role of women outside of the domestic sphere. Evangelical rhetoric creates and shapes both policy and perception of the place of women in the public, private, and religious spheres. Several voices compete on the roles women may play in their homes, in society, and most importantly in the church.

This chapter argues that the role of women in the church speaks directly to the nature of who God is and how he relates to his people. When women are excluded from formally sharing the Gospel of Jesus and in serving his people, then they are excluded from the very center of Christianity.

I contend that the role of women in the Assemblies of God is symptomatic of greater issues at play in evangelical rhetoric. These concerns include a lack of reconciliation of past affiliations and historical patriarchy, a desire for greater cultural acceptance in the evangelical community, and a reaction to the secular women's movement, which was perceived as an assault on the family and traditional values.

These issues are significant because they speak directly to how the Assemblies of God moved from the fringe of American evangelical culture to the largest denominational member of the National Association of Evangelicals. Given this shift in influence, these remaining challenges to women in both the Assemblies of God, specifically, and in the evangelical community more broadly are significant. Presumably, the Assemblies of God would have had a greater influence in freeing women to serve in the ministry of the church, given the historical precedent set by women in the Pentecostal movement. Instead, the Assemblies of God appears to have been molded and shaped by the standards of evangelical propriety regarding women's leadership.

As the Assemblies of God grew into the middle-class and waded into the mainstream of American religion by aligning themselves with organizations such as the National Association of Evangelicals, they began to sacrifice distinct, identifying traits that had set the movement apart at its birth, including racial diversity, pacifism, and some might argue a strong emphasis on the physical manifestations of the Holy Spirit. These losses dramatically affected how the Assemblies of God addressed the issue of women and their approach to a woman's ministry. The number of women serving in ministry positions including those of evangelist and missionary (which had historically remained strong despite challenges to their call and questions surrounding their proper roles) declined significantly. What might appear to be the most devastating era for the number of women serving in ministry positions in the Assemblies of God also saw the official position on women becoming more refined and accommodating and the discourse more prevalent as the secular culture also wrestled with the issue of women's roles in other major professions. The discursive tension surrounding the opportunities for women in the Assemblies of God would again emerge means of restraining them dominated the discourse.

While Blumhofer's warning of the lack of a single narrative is true, within the conflicting narratives, we are able to trace the threads that created the tapestry of the Assemblies of God and place them in the context of the rhetorical situation. Out of this unraveling, I believe a more complete picture of attitudes toward the role of women emerges. Within the conflicting narratives, one unified message remains constant: women who experienced a distinct call to ministry and an empowerment for service via the theology of the Pentecostal movement and the doctrine of the Assemblies of God could have served as a prototype for women in the greater evangelical community to also take responsibility for their calling and be poured out in their service to God. I contend that while the challenges facing the Assemblies of God continue to mirror those in the greater evangelical community, the Assemblies of God can address these challenges, regain their charismatic moment, and lead on this issue rather than follow.

## WOMEN AND THE SOCIOECONOMICS OF SERVICE

The story of Pentecostalism and the Assemblies of God, as we have seen throughout previous chapters, is the story of the discontented. It is the story of people who were not satisfied with the way religion and the world in general was functioning. According to James Davison Hunter, much of the evangelical culture was initially created in reaction to a perceived secularization of mainline protestant institutions.[3] The Assemblies of God shares a similar reactionary history. At least initially, Pentecostals were rejected both by the mainline of American religion and by their evangelical counterparts. This rejection positioned the Pentecostal movement to establish itself as counter to the greater religious culture within the United States. Their message was one that challenged all religious convention and created an opportunity for their rhetoric to take on a prophetic tone to both the secular "lost" world as well as to "dead" churches. Like the movement itself, women in the Assemblies of God operated in a capacity that blew apart the culture of their day and challenged the notions of conventional wisdom and church hierarchy.

Yet, the arguments used against them sound surprisingly similar to the discourse on the role of women today. Some opponents argued that the very fabric of the family, the foundation of society itself would crumble if women dared to proclaim their message and live their calling. Others championed the empowerment of women through Holy Spirit infilling as a means of building the church on earth in anticipation of Christ's return; the harvest is ready, but the workers are few, and women are needed if the world is to be persuaded to the cause of Christ. Over a century since the founding of Assemblies of God and nearly a century after women's suffrage, the church is still debating the place of women while the secular world is hiring them as CEOs of major corporations, appointing them as university presidents, and nominating them to national political tickets. Women have become a pawn in the "culture war" where their motivations are continually questioned and their pursuits are suspect.

A movement that ran counter to the culture, including the religious establishment, has been absorbed by the culture and the politics of the day. The Assemblies of God emerged from the cultural, ecclesiastical, and theological margins of American society and over time moved to the center, middle class of society.[4] In their progression to middle-class acceptance, the Assemblies of God either toned down or all together changed their perspectives on the nature of Scripture, millennialism, and the roles of women. To some degree, these changes were the result of the rapid growth of the movement. As more people were brought into the Assemblies of God, many of whom were reaping the benefits of the rise of the American middle class, the "outsider" values that had played a dominant role in the success of the

3. Hunter, *To Change the World*, 86.
4. Tackett, "Embourgeoisement of the Assemblies of God," 1.

movement succumbed to the American consumer culture. Not only were these new adherents more representative of mainstream American culture (e.g., Caucasian, white-collar, suburban, etc.), they were also more likely to have come into the Assemblies of God by way of prior evangelical affiliation. And with these past affiliations came theological differences that, over time, blended with the Pentecostal ethos.

In the early years, Pentecostalism was committed to all people as equal participants, especially the marginalized. Women, the poor, those with little formal education, and people of color worked and worshiped with people of financial means and cultural status. Each had a place, an obligation, in spreading the Pentecostal message.

According to theologian Cheryl Bridges Johns, "This subversive and revolutionary movement . . . had a dual prophetic role: denouncing the dominant patterns of the status quo and announcing the patterns of God's order."[5] As a result, Pentecostalism and Pentecostals were rejected and opposed by society at large and by established religious organizations. For Pentecostals to be accepted in the larger culture, they would have to be willing to make some compromises and accommodations to that culture. These choices continue to have a dramatic impact especially on the role of women and amplified the tensions that already existed within the movement.

Theologian and historian Mark A. Noll argues that the evangelical revivals of the eighteenth century disrupted traditional gender roles, but as the heat of revivals cooled, the blurring of gender lines receded.[6] While female missionary activity was and continues to be vibrant among evangelicals such as the Southern Baptists (similar to what we saw amongst Pentecostals in the Assemblies of God), these same groups present one of the more conservative positions on broader issues of gender roles both in the church and in the outside world. Women were often empowered, used, and then silenced.

### Engaging the Culture War and Drawing the Battle Lines

As the "culture wars" ramped up and the secular feminist movement grew, more mobilization occurred within the evangelical ranks with a dramatic move to a more right-wing stance. Evangelical leaders became prominent in these wars and enlisted many followers into organizations such as Concerned Women for America, the Christian Coalition, and Focus on the

---

5. Johns, "Adolescence of Pentecostalism," 4–5.

6. Noll, *American Evangelical Christianity*.

Family. Noll states that such mobilization "obscures historical evangelical attitudes toward gender, which were sometimes quite radical."[7]

This mobilization has also resulted in the emergence and solidification of boundary drawing within the evangelical subculture and can be seen as an attempt to establish or reestablish the community's self-definition. Several recent scholarly examinations of evangelical culture and rhetoric have highlighted what is called boundary work or what Charles Alan Taylor has termed "demarcation rhetoric."[8] According to Pauley, a culture that engages in boundary work or the rhetoric of demarcation is one that is feeling disrupted and is forced to look internally at its communal assumptions. When those within the culture challenge the beliefs and norms, then these rogue members of the group must be addressed and limits and boundaries articulated.[9]

We can see this demarcation occur, however subtly, over time with regard to the role of women. As the Assemblies of God was initially attempting to establish their community's self-definition of shared common beliefs, values, and social patterns, they first had to contend with those who had come from "the outside" and brought with them differing definitions of cultural acceptability. This challenge continued with the joining of the Assemblies of God with the greater evangelical community. The Assemblies of God absorbed evangelicalism more fully than the culture of Pentecostalism influenced evangelicalism.

As a result, the challenges to evangelical culture represented in the role of women became an internal threat to the community and like Pauley describes, once this aberrant practice is discovered, the community undertakes a process of clarifying and marking out its boundaries. The result for women in the Assemblies of God was the sustained effort to diminish their presence in the ministry and to avoid engaging the evangelical community in any form of reevaluation of the defining characteristics of who is called and what it means to serve in ministry. Essentially, the Assemblies of God abandoned the promotion and empowerment of women ministers rather than be excluded from the evangelical community.

Sociologist Christian Smith takes the analysis of boundary work further to include not only internal threats from within the community, but also the establishment of these rhetorical boundaries by those outside the community who pose a threat to the stability of the culture. According to Smith, evangelicals have and continue to operate with a very strong sense

7. Ibid., 83.

8. Taylor, *Defining Science*; see also Pauley, "Jesus in a Chevy?" 73.

9. Pauley, "Jesus in a Chevy?" 76.

of boundaries that distinguish themselves not only from the non-Christian, but from the non-evangelical. A distinct "us versus them" mentality is "omnipresent in evangelical thought and speech," which shapes evangelical consciousness and discourse.[10]

The secular feminist movement, in particular, represents a hostile outside threat to the community if for no other reason than they represent the "them" of "the world" that operates outside of the boundaries of evangelical Christianity. The perceived threat by the feminist movement to the stability and structure of the family and an undermining of traditional gender roles places them at odds with evangelicalism and therefore makes not only the movement itself but also anything that resembles a feminist approach an enemy. Smith argues that while evangelicals do not spend a great deal of time talking about what is so "worldly" about social movements like the feminist movement, they are keenly aware of the threats that are represented by feminists, and they must stand in opposition to these threats and interact only in a redemptive manner. The appropriate response to opposition is not often contemplated, but it is, in Smith's view, a lived experience. As a result of the lack of contemplation over these perceived outside threats, very little thought or discourse is then given to what attitudes toward issues like gender may have existed historically within the evangelical community.[11]

Noll continues that the mobilization and boundary drawing also obscures the surprising similarities and the interest shared by some leading feminist voices and many rhetorically anti-feminist evangelicals. Evangelical women's organizations took up issues that were not that far removed from their feminist counterparts such as experiences of severe wounding by men, growth in a shared female consciousness, and the ability to control their own lives. While evangelical women tend to criticize the humanism of the secular movement and uphold tenets such as inerrancy of Scripture, they share a belief in the ability of women to accomplish great things and make an impact on the world including a desire to work outside of the home and a desire for equality amongst the sexes in society at large. It would seem then that feminism is more compatible with conservative religious belief and practice than is often argued.

As we have seen, following World War II American society underwent significant changes, including middle class women entering the work place and feminist voices pushing attitudes about gender to the forefront of public discussion. What occurred in the Assemblies of God was reminiscent of what occurred amongst Baptists and Methodists following the

10. Smith, *American Evangelicalism*, 124.

11. Ibid., 125.

early revivals of the eighteenth and nineteenth centuries. Distinctions between male and female roles grew as the intensity of the movement was replaced by institution building. According to Noll and as evidenced by what has been presented in earlier chapters of this study, the result was not an out and out repudiation of women in ministry, but a steady elimination of women from public places of visibility. Over time, the Assemblies of God grew closer to the fundamentalist and neo-evangelical strands as the twentieth century progressed.

## THE APOSTLE PAUL, FEMINIST OR FOE

While nineteenth and twentieth century evangelicals and early twentieth century Pentecostals advocated women's full participation in ministry and viewed Acts 2 and Joel 2:28 as the "magna carta" for proof of the biblical evidence for women's ministry, other Scripture that seemed to limit the liberty of women was destined to be interpreted through the lens of Pentecostal proclamation and experience.

However, a tract written by Frank M. Boyd, who at the time was one of the fellowship's most respected Bible institute instructors, and published by the Assemblies of God's Gospel Publishing House, broke from the earlier traditions of the fellowship and focused the argument concerning women's ministry on the Pauline "limitations" of 1 Cor 14:34 and 1 Tim 2:11–12. Boyd emphasized his position that these limitations were not cultural or temporary conditions, but were for all believers in all time periods. These limitations, in Boyd's view, were not to exclude women from ministry, but to provide safe parameters for the Lord's handmaidens. Boyd's argument focused on the differences in roles for men and women in the divine economy and the headship of women by men, especially their husbands. Therefore, women were to serve under the headship or leadership of male pastors and denominational leaders and ministry work was to vary according to her marital status. Unmarried women were "unencumbered by the duties of wifehood and the responsibilities of motherhood"[12] and were then able to devote their time and energy to ministry. Married women, however, are to submit to their husbands and place their focus on their homes.

---

12. Boyd, *Women's Ministry*, 4.

## Authority versus Submission

As has been noted in Chapter Three, the official policy of the Assemblies of God on the role of women was revised in 1935 and has changed very little in the years that have followed. If anything, the refining of the language actually strengthened the position of women, unlike previous revisions such as the 1931 limitations. Yet, from the late 1930s through the 1960s, official publications, including the *Pentecostal Evangel* and Christian education curriculum, took on a perspective that was closer to Frank Boyd's position. From illustrated messages to articles and lessons, the message coming from the Assemblies of God was clear: women are to be allowed to participate in ministry, but men are to be the authority of the church.

This posture is significant because the argument about authority shifted away from the empowerment of the Holy Spirit to the empowerment of institutions. For Pentecostals in the Assemblies of God, authority had always been derived from the Holy Spirit. It initially prevented organization among the membership because the formation of organized denominations symbolized a removal of the Holy Spirit as Empowerer and moved adherents closer to the "dead" religious organizations they had left. Again, Poloma argues that the adoption of biblical interpretive principles from fundamentalism and evangelicalism, rather than the development of a hermeneutic consistent with the experience of Pentecostals has silenced the Assemblies of God's prophesying daughters.[13]

I would take Poloma's assertions further by arguing that the rhetorical shift away from the empowerment found in the Books of Acts and Joel to the perceived limitations presented by the Apostle Paul created a situation in which women were not only excluded from church leadership but also relegated to other spheres. I would argue that what Poloma sees and what I assert are both reactions to the perceived threat to the evangelical culture. Further boundaries were created with increasing emphasis placed on limiting a woman's authority in every sphere. The primary role of a woman was to be married and her sphere was in the home. Within her marriage and as a means of maintaining her proper sphere, a woman's obligation was to submit to her husband. According to one author in the *Pentecostal Evangel*, "Too much 'spunk' here is a sure cause of trouble; it is well nigh impossible for a man to respond amiably to a bossy wife." Rather, she should "maintain the equilibrium with a meek and quiet spirit."[14] Adult Sunday school curriculum presented lessons that noted the "most far-reaching advancements

13. Poloma, *Assemblies of God*, 119.
14. Hinman, "Happiness in Marriage," 21.

achieved in this century of progress is the prominence to which woman-hood has steadily climbed."[15] Yet, the curriculum claims, this progress resulted in "an overbalanced emphasis upon women's rights which, while claiming equality with men, demands an absolute independence contrary to the scriptural standing regarding the relationship of the sexes."[16] The Christian model, the lesson argues, is of a husband and wife working together as long as the man is in charge.

Here again, we see the rhetorical boundary lines being tightened with regard to women's roles in the Assemblies of God. Not only had emphasis shifted in the scriptural hermeneutic to stress greater limitations for women in leadership, the rhetorical boundaries were further tightened to emphasize a woman's place outside of the church. Women were not explicitly prevented from serving in the church, but the words, language, and symbols expressed by the Assemblies of God established a clear message that women were to be subject to men and as a result, anything that challenged this subordination amounted to rebellion. For a woman called into pastoral ministry, especially those whose husbands were not also serving in the church (so she could remain subject to his leadership), this position presents a real problem and rather than finding empowerment in her call, the message was reinforced that her call was suspect.

While a subtle shift occurred from the 1960s through the 1990s toward encouraging women in a variety of social roles, the primary emphasis remained on women as wives and mothers. In the early 1980s, the *Pentecostal Evangel* published an issue that "honored" mothers who were employed outside the home. In this issue, a writer admonished members of the church to reconsider its attitudes toward women: "Nowhere does the Bible extol a mother because she refuses employment. On the contrary, the capable wife described in Proverbs 31 seems to be engaged in business as well as efficient homemaking."[17] While response to the issue was mixed, even those who expressed some support were troubled that the article "seems to encourage mothers to work" or emphasizes those who were "forced" to work. The church would not then "force" a woman into full time ministry when it might create a situation in which her primary function as wife and mother might be called into question. "The world" outside of Christianity might seek to undermine this core value of family and motherhood, but the church would not be participate in this societal breakdown by promoting women within their ministry ranks.

15. Pearlman, "Christian Ideal of Marriage," 44–50.

16. Ibid.

17. Caldwell, "Let Us Honor Our Job-Holding Mothers," 12–13.

These messages are consistent with those marketed by leaders in the greater evangelical community, including Dr. James Dobson founder of the Focus on the Family organization and author Elisabeth Elliot who championed the notion of women's submission. Unlike Frank Boyd, who argued that women's submission was rooted in the fall of mankind, Elliot argues for submission at the moment of creation and as an established hierarchy created by God from moment one as a means of protection for women. Rather, she argues that the secular women's movement was responsible for placing guilt and shame upon women in the church.

In an article published in *Christianity Today*, Elliot argues against the ordination of women and states the question was raised because of the women's liberation movement and the concepts of authority, submission, and obedience have fallen "into disrepute in the secular world."[18] She continues to argue that women's ordination is a means for the secular world to imbue guilt to the church for denying women equal status to men. The church is, according to Elliot, in "painful self-doubt" and deciding to jettison certain principles and practices that have become distasteful to the society at large. "The exclusion of women from ordination is based on the order established in creation. . . . Quite simply, woman was made for man. Man was not made for woman."[19] The natural order of creation did not change at the fall or through Christ's redemption and the church negates the truth of what it teaches when it ordains women to the office of "minister of Word proclaimer."

Elliot states that if a woman "'feels called' to do a work that on scriptural grounds is outside the 'idea of God in the making' of her, it is the duty of the church theologically . . . to judge her vocation. No one merely because he or she has the Spirit, may disregard the judgment of the congregation."[20] She concludes her argument by stating, "The commands of God in Scripture clearly delineate the structures of the Church. . . . We cannot have it both ways. The Church must choose between the ordination and the subordination of women."[21]

Again, we see the dominant language used by Elliot is one that focuses on a battle, an "us versus them" encounter with the world. She includes no discussion of historical attitudes towards women or the roles women have played in Scripture and within the modern-day church to spread the gospel message. The idea of women as ordained ministers of the church, she

18. Elliot, "Why I Oppose," 12.
19. Ibid., 14.
20. Ibid.
21. Ibid., 16.

suggests, could not have come from within the church or by the virtue of scriptural authority, but rather, it is the result of the deception of women and those who would seek to promote them by the evil secular forces that seek the church's destruction. As a result, she implies, the church and its members should discourage this deception and prevent women from engaging in heretical behavior.

Whereas Elisabeth Elliot places the blame for the desire of women to participate in ministry work at the feet of the feminist movement, Poloma argues that the Pentecostal movement could have built on the work of nineteenth century evangelical women who advocated women's suffrage and sparked an alternative to the secular feminist movement. Poloma argues that the Pentecostal movement had an opportunity to be revolutionary and create a place for women in ministry, but Pentecostals chose instead to remain with their brothers and sisters in more conservative Christianity, and as a result, they also chose a reactionary course.

It would seem that the rhetoric of early Pentecostals was revolutionary in its openness to women's participation while attempting to maintain a balanced perspective of traditional family roles, but over time, the argument for a woman's role in the family structure began to dominate the discussion. The leadership of the Assemblies of God may have been looking for a way to deal with those women who were already amongst their ranks as ministers and simultaneously subvert any growth in the ranks, thus promoting a more conservative view of womanhood in their popular publications. They managed to do so while maintaining a quasi-supportive stance of women already engaged in ministry work, thus exacerbating the tension women felt and continue to feel with regard to their place in ministry. This type of double-talk creates dissonance for those who support women's ordination and ministry and sends the message that Pentecostalism was not, in fact, the revolutionary movement it claimed to be, but that it is more like the culture Pentecostalism emerged from and sought to revolutionize.

The Assemblies of God appears to have engaged in nothing more than a school-yard game of wanting to be part of the "popular" crowd. Originally rejected, they were now part of the evangelical "in" group, and with that acceptance came pressure to conform to the ideas and action of the rest of the group. Assemblies of God General Superintendent George O. Wood acknowledged this peer pressure when he was asked what factor contributed most to the challenges that women have faced in the Assemblies of God. Wood replied, "Culture. We tended to succumb to the prevailing culture."[22]

22. Wood in discussion with the author, November 2007.

## MODERNISTIC INFLUENCE
## AND RHETORICAL PRACTICE

While the Assemblies of God undoubtedly engaged in cultural accommodation that was detrimental to its distinctive doctrines and practices, its stance was more than a simple position in a popularity contest. The root of this accommodation comes from the shared epistemological roots of the Assemblies of God and their evangelical brothers and sisters. As historians George Marsden and Mark Noll have argued, these groups were profoundly influenced by a particular set of Enlightenment-based assumptions on American religious thought that began in the eighteenth and nineteenth centuries and that continue in large part today. This "Scottish Common Sense Realism" or as Noll calls it "didactic Enlightenment" assumes the plain and transparent nature of truth and wisdom, the workings of the universe, and the meaning of the Bible. To continue to the school-yard metaphor, the Bible is reduced to a divinely inspired "third grade answer book." Evangelicals, then, know *how* they know by looking at truth and wisdom as uncomplicated and by placing emphasis on literal, "common-sense" understandings of biblical truth. These epistemological assumptions about how to interpret Scripture first led to a dangerous impasse on how to arrive at a biblical position on the question of slavery during the Civil War and caused great damage to the church. These same assumptions are at play in how the evangelical community, including the Assemblies of God, have created and reinforced a scriptural impasse to arrive at a position on the role of women in church leadership.

As Mark Steiner notes, one of the challenges that stands out in evangelical rhetoric (and the theology from which it is formed) is that it has blindly accepted the epistemological assumptions of modern thought. He stresses Marsden's point that American Protestantism featured notions that "the common sense of mankind, whether of the man behind the plow or the man behind the desk, was the surest guide to truth."[23] Noll builds on Marsden's point by acknowledging the initial effectiveness of this intellectual framework as it made evangelical Protestantism "so dynamically powerful in the early history of the United States," but in the end fostered a "weak intellectual legacy" that resulted in a dysfunctional and anti-intellectual response to social, intellectual, and theological challenges.[24]

These assumptions, according to Steiner, are still very much entrenched in the evangelical tradition and rhetorical practice. The result of

23. Steiner, "Reconceptualizing Christian Public Engagement," 299.
24. Noll, *Scandal*, 105–7.

these assumptions in evangelical discourse is a strident, boundary-drawing, cultural warfare that reduces the complexities and ambiguity of faith to a simplistic formula. Those who question, challenge, or seek to engage these complexities are labeled enemies of biblical truth. Warfare engages an "either for us or against us" type of rhetoric.

This "us versus them" rhetoric accelerated as women found more acceptance in the larger culture. Whereas the discussion in the early days of the Assemblies of God publications gave at least lip-service to questions of the theology of women's leadership, as the evangelical community chose to engage evolving roles for women as a battle against the church of Christ, the rhetoric changed dramatically. The rhetoric focused instead on the assault against "tradition" and against the family. Feminism, not the call of God on their lives, was driving women to seek out opportunities where they might lead and direct. The rhetorical shift within the Assemblies of God was no different. The emphasis moves from the empowerment of women for service to the protection of their role in the domestic sphere and the battle against being "forced" into something that might take them outside of the home.

By naming the enemy "feminism," a battle could then be waged with a defeat-at-all-cost rhetorical stance so as to save the family and restore order and "right" to the world. Rhetorical positions such as Elisabeth Elliot's draw a clear line in the sand over which the church is forced to make a choice. The correct choice is clear, and the congregation must take a stand against any woman who might proclaim a calling from God. No middle ground exists. For women, subordination was ordered at the moment of creation. Clearly, a fallen world (an enemy) works to subvert the natural order of God's design and put an idea into the mind of a woman that she might have a role to play in spreading the Christian message rather than gazing lovingly upon her husband while he ministers At best she may teach her children's Sunday school class or participate in a women's Bible study group. Anything outside of this "acceptable" realm is an attack on the church, rather than a contribution.

At one time, Pentecostals rejected culture (both religious and secular). Evangelicalism determined to wage war with culture. When the Assemblies of God chose to embrace the activist stance and demarcation lines established by their evangelical counterparts, they also took on the consequences of their war, and women became collateral damage. Rather than examining historical attitudes on gender and finding common ground, the evangelical community chose to be combative. What is more, the evangelical community including the Assemblies of God sacrificed something even greater than women's rights when they engaged the culture war over the role of women. They sacrificed their ability to stand in prophetic resistance and lost an opportunity to become revolutionary.

## The Loss of Prophetic Resistance

While the political choices of evangelicals, specifically their alignment with one political ideology is outside the purview of this study, it is important to note that when evangelicals sought to battle issues like feminism, they often did so by engaging the enemy on political grounds. Yale scholar Stephen L. Carter argues that the prophetic religious voice, calling us to account, pointing the culture in the right direction of God's will is very different from the one telling us who should be in charge. The Old Testament prophets simply presented the message of righteousness; they never had a hand in the building of kingdoms or the downfall of those who did not heed their message.[25]

Religion is inherently subversive to culture and politics. Carter argues that the church must avoid the temptation to join its authority to the authority of the state.[26] The American political system is not averse to those who are radical in their message. Rather, the American political system invites radicalism, in order to tame it and refocus its energy on minor triumphs within the political system. This co-opting is only possible, however, when the radicals are willing to be co-opted. Once the decision is made to become a part of the system, the power of the prophetic is lost.

I contend that the Assemblies of God is facing the choice Carter presents. By aligning the fellowship with the greater evangelical community and embracing a more conservative political position, the Assemblies of God has sacrificed the prophetic nature of their message and diminished the impact of their role in the culture. An opportunity to challenge the mainstream church culture on how God views women in the family, society, and the church became a reaction to the culture's empowering of women as a means of subverting God's plan.

The Assemblies of God was once an antagonist of the status quo (both within the church and those outside of the church), but among her people today are impassioned patriots who have chosen to battle the culture via politics and who have adopted nationalism as a religious creed. What was once a radically inclusive spiritual fellowship in which race and gender virtually disappeared, today's predominantly white, middle- to upper-class adherents are skeptical of what they view as radical feminism and multiculturalism fraught with the challenges of immigration and cultural change.

25. Carter, *God's Name in Vain*, 32–39.
26. Ibid.

These issues faced by the Assemblies of God mirror broader rhetorical problems in the evangelical community. As in the early days of the Assemblies of God, the world is an uncertain place. This uncertainty drives questions about the role of religion in the public square. The presence of women in church leadership challenges religious convention and American culture. Voices compete to describe the role women have to play within the home, the society, and the church.

While some within the evangelical community supported female candidates for political office, leaders of their denominations were removing magazines from their bookstores that featured female pastors on the cover. According to Richard Land, then President of the Southern Baptist Ethics and Religious Liberty Commission, no disconnect or inconsistency exists in their position on the role of women. Land states that leadership in public office is different than leadership in the home or the church.[27]

Land's failure to see a disconnect between the position of women in the church and in the public square does not mean a discrepancy does not exist. The discourse on women's roles in the church remains contentious, the boundary lines are strictly drawn, and the evangelical community maintains a position of insular cultural production that feeds this discourse. Women who believe they are called to serve in the world of the church continue to be left behind.

Pentecostals stand again at a cultural crossroads. If, as George Wood stated, the problems faced by women have been the result of the movement's succumbing to the attitudes, actions, and beliefs of evangelical culture, then the direction of future discourse on the role of women depends upon how willingly Pentecostals stand in prophetic resistance to that prevailing culture on this issue.

27. Baker, "Southern Baptists Back Palin."

# 6

## Benevolent Neglect

### Overcoming Rhetorical Circumstance

*The decline [of women serving in ministry] may be the cumulative result of the ambiguity of leaders' attitudes toward women in ministry as seen in the previous historical events. The attitude could be labeled "benevolent neglect" of the problem, or perhaps a failing to perceive even that there was a problem. Some might have even seen the decline as a good thing.*[1]

—Dr. Barbara Cavaness

*My identity isn't wrapped up in any one of those [ministry] roles; it doesn't depend on a specific title or position or what people call me. My identity is in Christ, as a follower of Jesus and a woman called to minister to people.*[2]

—Dr. A. Elizabeth Grant

AS THE TWENTIETH CENTURY ended, Pentecostalism appeared to be a very different movement than when the century dawned. In a relatively short amount of time, the movement had grown beyond the fringe of the

1. Cavaness, "Biographical Study."
2. McClure, "Many Roles, One Call," 11.

American religious class and spawned several organized fellowships and denominations. One of these was the Assemblies of God, arguably the largest and most widely recognized Pentecostal organization in the United States and around the world. Once excluded from the evangelical community, the Assemblies of God is now the largest member of the National Association of Evangelicals and has, since its inclusion in the organization, been recognized by its members holding positions of national prominence within the organization.

Growth and influence have not come without a price. During the 1980s the Assemblies of God was forced to endure scandals created by two of its most well-known ministers when both the Rev. Jim Bakker and the Rev. Jimmy Swaggart, television evangelists affiliated with the Assemblies of God, were found to be engaging in sexual and financial misconduct. In addition to Bakker and Swaggart, several others credentialed with the Assemblies of God were caught up in the scandals, which resulted in both disciplinary action by the Assemblies as well as legal action.

Facing deeper challenges than just those associated with the Bakker and Swaggart scandals, the Assemblies of God was described as "beset by bureaucratization and bewildered by cultural change."[3] The Assemblies of God responded in a very dysfunctional manner to these challenges, especially where women and more specifically women leaders were concerned. The fellowship's evolving rhetorical stance toward women throughout the twentieth century, in significant part, explains the nature and consequences of this dysfunction. Historically unwilling to subject themselves to critical scrutiny, particularly self-critical analysis, the Assemblies of God suffered from stagnation more typically associated with the "dead" religious culture they had once decried. While most Americans had at one time been suspicious of Pentecostals and had ignored the movement, white, middle-class growth and favorable media coverage revealed that those in the Assemblies of God behaved more like evangelicals and less like radicals. This discovery dispelled the myths that being Pentecostal meant participating in bizarre conduct, living like a pauper, or believing in strange theology. It also dismissed any notion that the Assemblies of God was in the vanguard on social issues that had plagued the United States during the same period. When women and minorities began to gain a place within society, the Assemblies of God was at best rhetorically absent or at worst, battling the movements that sought to promote more inclusive participation. Most Assemblies of God constituents were, in fact, white, middle-class evangelicals whose churches, districts, and national offices were led nearly exclusively by white

---

3. Tinlin and Blumhofer, "Decade of Decline or Harvest?" 684.

men. While this situation might have brought about a greater comfort level in the evangelical community, it did not reveal an adequate picture of what was truly happening within the fellowship. The Assemblies of God was at a place where self-evaluation was necessary, and the timing seemed right to deflect attention away from the scandals and re-evaluate the perception of who and what the Assemblies represented.

## The Decade of Harvest

In the 1990s, the Assemblies of God launched "The Decade of Harvest" as a means of both self-evaluation as well as a program of mobilized growth to take the fellowship into the next century as a stronger and more influential force. The program called for the addition of 20,000 new ministers, 5,000 new churches, 5 million new converts, and 1 million prayer partners to the ranks of the Assemblies of God membership rolls within 10 years.[4]

The program was meant to demonstrate just how far the Assemblies of God had come from its humble roots. The message that had once seemed so pure because it had been at odds with the culture now seemed credible because so many people believed it. At one time, adherents were called to live in prophetic tension with society, but by the Decade of Harvest they were typically representative of other Americans of similar socioeconomic standing. Success, which at one time had been defined as being uneasy in this world, was assigned a numerical designation as defined by the goals of the program.

Unfortunately, the energy poured into the Decade of Harvest merely maintained or slightly improved the status quo. In an article published in *The Christian Century*, Assemblies of God Pastor Paul Tinlin and historian Edith Blumhofer associated the dismal results of the Decade of Harvest campaign to a lack of serious self-critique, an abandonment of spiritual disciplines that allowed for spiritual formation (but required time and effort) for an overemphasis on mega-church development, media stars, and faltering programs. The problems lay with an uncertain denominational identity, the struggle to expand while conserving their Pentecostal essence, a detachment of the grassroots from the national leadership and difficult theological and social issues that the Assemblies of God refused to adequately address. One of those theological issues cited by Tinlin and Blumhofer included where the Assemblies of God really stood on the role of women in ministry.[5]

4. Ibid., 685.
5. Ibid., 684–85.

While it appeared on the surface that the Assemblies of God had made the most progress among evangelical denominations in affirming the ministry of women, the experiences of women within the fellowship did not confirm this progress. Toward the end of the twentieth century, the supposed increase of women within the fellowship was based largely on the methods of reporting data and not on any socio-cultural change.[6] In trying to navigate the difficult waters between a distinctive Pentecostal identity and greater acceptance among its evangelical peers, the Assemblies of God failed to create an environment in which women could find a true place to fulfill their call to minister and serve side-by-side with their male counterparts in leadership. Rather than address the challenges facing women in the fellowship, the Assemblies of God adjusted how they reported the number of women serving and once again created a rhetorical situation that veiled the true state of affairs. Tinlin and Blumhofer confirm what has been evident throughout this book: progress on questions relating to women in ministry has been slow, painful, and less than transparent.

## Rhetorical History as a Process of Social Construction, Maintenance, and Change

A look at the rhetorical history of women in the Pentecostal movement does more than simply expose a mixed historical record. Historian Grant Wacker, addressing the disproportionate role of women and the conflicting constraints they faced from the movement's inception, contends that the real question was not that this conflict of opportunity and constraint existed, but rather "why?" Answers to why are found in the rhetorical invention of the movement itself, the women who participated in it, and in those who challenged their involvement. The conflict is inherent in the language of the movement and the role this language played, and to an extent, continues to play in the formation and shaping of a distinctive position on

6. A 1990 report by the National Council of Churches seemed to reveal that the Assemblies of God had seen dramatic change in the number of women serving in ministry. However, this progress was due in large part to methods of reporting. In earlier studies, the Assemblies of God only submitted the names of women who were ordained, but in the 1990 study, the numbers submitted included those who held a license to preach in addition to those who were ordained. These are two of the four forms of credentials issued in the Assemblies at the time. While the comparisons seemed to show dramatic change, the numbers are questionable as the majority of credentialed women held licenses rather than ordination certificates and more than half of these women were retired and not actively serving as pastors, evangelists, or missionaries. See also Tinlin and Blumhofer, "Decade of Decline or Harvest?" 685.

women's leadership and the context in which people think about the role of women in the church.

In the conflict of the narrative, women who have experienced both a distinct call to ministry and an empowerment for service via the theology of the Assemblies of God speak uniformly. The feminine voice does not call for a chance to rule for the sake of personal power; rather, in the words of Beth Grant, an Executive Presbyter who represents credentialed women, women seek an opportunity to take responsibility for their calling and to be poured out in their service to God.[7]

What began as a movement counter to the culture, however, has been absorbed by the rhetoric of the evangelical culture and its politics. The Pentecostal people of the Assemblies of God were once rhetorically radical. Today, they fight for relevance among competing voices in the evangelical community. They seek a place in the larger culture and among their own people who often question the necessity for a distinctive identity or movement at all. Therefore, women have faced dissonance in the messages concerning their place within the Assemblies of God.

The Pentecostal movement created an exigency or a sense of urgency: to spread the messages of Jesus as Savior, Baptizer, Healer and soon-coming King. This sense of urgency created a space for women and provided them empowerment for service. However, among their fellow laborers, in their gatherings, and within the evangelical community were an audience bound up with varying constraints of what ministry looked like and who could legitimately present the discourse. These constraints play a significant role in the social construction of Pentecostal culture and discourse.

A more fundamental theological tension inheres in the Pentecostal movement. The tension between radicalism and conservatism is a continuing exigency that needs to be negotiated and renegotiated. A constant and very fundamental "imperfection" exists among core denominational distinctives, such as the role of women, and in the larger movement that requires a continual rhetorical effort to engage—whether to ameliorate the imperfections or to strategically amplify the imperfections so as to increase pressure for some sort of social or theological change. This tension touches the core of Pentecostalism's relationship to the larger evangelical community and American religious culture. At every major juncture of Assemblies of God history, the role of women continues to surface as a significant issue that has both made the Assemblies of God what it is while at the same time creating the greatest amount of dissonance both within the movement and in its relationship with evangelicalism.

7. Grant, "Celebration and Commitment to Community."

When the Pentecostal movement broke forth and birthed the Assemblies of God, Americans were asking themselves who they were and who they wanted to be.[8] The turn of the century was fraught with changes, and the United States was on the verge of emerging as a major worldwide power. A shift in power, wealth, and military might was about to take place, and Americans were making the choices that would lead to this change. The rise of the Assemblies of God was not the accomplishment of the elite or the powerful, but rather emerged from a gathering up of the poor and outcast, taking the despised things and seeing God glorified in them. Pentecostals have not prospered in the twentieth century by blending into its cosmopolitan ethos. They succeeded by criticizing that ethos and suggesting alternatives.[9] At each juncture, the greatest challenges faced by the Assemblies of God came when they tried to be both subversive and "just one of the boys" in an old boys club.

The context for women of the Assemblies of God in the twenty-first century does not seem much different than it did during most of the twentieth century despite cultural accommodation. While several opportunities were taken to temper issues like race, address faulty perceptions of Pentecostal identity, and assert a position of influence within the evangelical community, the challenges to women desiring a place in ministry and leadership of the Assemblies of God still exist, and the rhetoric surrounding these issues is circular and eerily similar to that of their foremothers. Ironically, women in Pentecostal ministry are central to the Assemblies of God theological practice.

Several changes within the leadership of the Assemblies of God, specifically the election of Dr. George O. Wood to the office of General Superintendent of the Assemblies of God in 2007, signaled a significant change in rhetorical practice with regard to the role of women in ministry. His election resulted in the adoption of a resolution at the 2007 General Council in Indianapolis, Indiana, to appoint one woman and one minister under the age of forty to the Executive Presbytery, the highest governing body within the fellowship. His inclusion of auditors (a rotating group of women and ministers under the age of forty) in meetings prior to the resolution taking effect in 2009 created a cultural shift within the leadership of the Assemblies of God. Prior to the inclusion of these auditors, no one other than the members of the Executive Presbytery had participated in these meetings. Just having the auditors present changed the dynamic of the group and brought an awareness of to the insight these participants

8. Cox, *Fire from Heaven*, 32.
9. Ibid., 106.

provided. In addition, Dr. Wood's administration oversaw the creation and implementation of the Network of Women Ministers (originally named the Network of Women in Ministry), the first officially endorsed and funded department within the Assemblies of God organization to focus specifically on the support and promotion of women in all ministry areas of the Assemblies of God. The discourse surrounding this "network" could develop an entirely new generation of Assemblies of God churches and women serving in vocational ministry.

The rhetoric of women's involvement has been reframed by male and female ministers who have chosen to bring the issue of women's leadership once again to the forefront of denominational discourse. The shift in this discussion occurs through the language of authority versus service. When a rhetoric of service is employed, greater opportunity for women abounds and the opposite is true when a rhetoric of authority is employed.

Finally, denominational leadership have created new opportunities for women's leadership, and the implications of these opportunities are unfolding. Specifically, the discourse of denominational officers such as General Superintendents Thomas Trask and George O. Wood as well as some key women "activists" expose key changes in the rhetorical landscape of the Assemblies' discursive culture. The reality for women, however, remains significantly constrained by important continuities in that landscape.

## REFRAMING THE MESSAGE

Although the programmatic Decade of Harvest proved to be a less-than-stellar system for evaluation and change for the Assemblies of God, the 1990s did bring about several changes in national leadership and a renewed focus on advocacy for women as leaders and ministers. One example of this renewed focus was a series of white papers published by the General Council referred to as "position papers."

### *The Role of Women as Described in Holy Scripture*

In 1990, the General Presbytery issued one such position paper that affirmed the ministry roles of women, including language that confirmed women's authority to serve in any and all leadership roles at the local, district, and national levels. The title of the paper is rhetorically significant as it does not simply say, "What we believe on the role of women in ministry." Rather, the title, "The Role of Women as Described in Holy Scripture," explicitly states that the position taken by the Assemblies of

God is not their own construction, but rather the position demanded of them by Scriptural mandate.

Building on this title, the position taken by the leaders of the Assemblies of God reaffirmed the official policy and appealed to the eschatological commitment of Pentecostal's proclamation of Holy Spirit empowerment. The paper begins with the creation narrative and argues that men and women were created equal. The paper extends the argument that Paul's theology, particularly Gal 3:28, has universal application, and calls for the equality of all people. The paper concludes with an eschatological argument for women's roles in ministry. It says, "As we look on the fields ripe for the harvest, may we not be guilty of sending away any of the reapers God calls. Let us entrust to these women of God the sacred sickle, and with our sincerest blessings thrust them out into the whitened fields."[10]

One distinction in this paper is the incorporation of the creation narrative as evidence of the equality of men and women. This inclusion significantly contradicts the interpretation of the creation narrative found among most mainstream evangelicals as argued by men and women like Elisabeth Elliot. Evangelicals such as Elliot argue that equality does not exist because women were created second to men and were "given" to men who were intended to lead female followers. The Assemblies of God's narrative places the fissure of inequality at the fall of mankind into sinfulness away from the original intention of God at the moment of creation as espoused by many mainstream evangelicals.

Second, this position paper places a priority on the Apostle Paul's commitment to the equality of people beyond the availability of salvation. Rather than prohibiting women's equality, the position paper takes the viewpoint that the Pauline limitations are to be viewed in light of Paul's statement that there is neither Jew nor Greek, male nor female, but all are one in Christ Jesus. In naming examples of ministers, both Old and New Testament women are mentioned, including women to whom Paul refers as fellow laborers. The emphasis on Paul's affirming of women counters the argument that the limitations he advocates are universal. This position is also a shift from evangelical arguments that limit the roles of woman by focusing solely on restrictive verses and then interpret through that lens the work of women Paul mentions by name.

Unfortunately, the position paper does not give attention to the gospel narratives and does not fully incorporate the role that women played in Jesus' life and ministry. This omission is ironic because other position papers, specifically those on the "theology of ministry," present Jesus as the model

---

10. General Council of the Assemblies of God, *Role of Women.*

for ministry by beginning with Jesus and the gospel narrative.[11] While this absence is a weakness in the position paper on women, it does not negate the strength of the arguments presented and the shift in the rhetoric from what has been argued historically by the leadership in the Assemblies of God as well as their evangelical counterparts.

Not only does this position paper, which was updated and reaffirmed in 2010, lay out a rhetoric that argues from an inherently Scriptural position for the role of women, its tone reaches back to the earliest arguments for Pentecostalism's own existence.[12] The Assemblies of God uses the language of Holy Spirit baptism and speaking in tongues as an empowerment for service (its doctrine that distinguishes it from its counterparts in evangelicalism) and employs the eschatological language of saving souls and the desperate need for workers willing to take up the task of reaching the lost. The language used is not unique to women empowered for the "harvest work" God has given them, but its terms have historically been used both to justify Pentecostal distinction and to create space for women within the ranks of those harvesters. By aligning the language in the policy with the Constitution and Bylaws of the Assemblies of God, the position paper creates an argument accessible to the constituents within the fellowship and renews a commitment to its Pentecostal distinctives and to the women who were present from the very beginning.

## A Reclamation of Pentecostal Rhetorical Invention

David Zarefsky argues that perspective distinguishes the rhetorical historian from others who examine historical events. This position paper reframes the message regarding women's roles in the Assemblies of God, yet it is directly in line with Pentecostal rhetorical invention as laid out by rhetorician Martin Medhurst. Therefore, it is important to identify principles of rhetorical invention that are inherent to Pentecostal thinking and, in turn, Pentecostal talk.

Medhurst, himself the product of a Pentecostal upbringing, has identified a set of rhetorical principles grounded in doctrinal positions of the Assemblies of God. As with Pentecostal theology, Medhurst argues that Pentecostal rhetoric is informed by experience, and these experiences affect the way Pentecostals communicate. While Pentecostals share a common adherence to doctrines such as creation, fall, and redemption, they have also created a self-identity and public personae through a system of interrelated

11. .Tackett, "Embourgeoisement of the Assemblies of God."

12. General Council of the Assemblies of God, *Role of Women*.

enthymemes and examples. In enthymematic form, Medhurst presents five premises: First, *God is in control* because in Rom 8:28, "all things work together for good to them that love God, to them who are called according to the will of God." Second, *pray without ceasing* as 1 Thess 5:17 says, for "this is the will of God in Christ Jesus concerning you." Third, *expect a miracle* for in Isa 53:5 we are told that "by his stripes we are healed." Fourth, *trust and obey* as is stated in Heb 11:6, "without faith it is impossible to please Him." Finally, *work*, for in John 9:4 the Scripture tells us that "the night cometh, when no man can work."[13]

As is evidenced in the position paper and in this enthymematic structure, the Bible is the authorizing agent of the Pentecostal worldview and is guaranteed by God. Medhurst argues that these premises are inexorably linked because Pentecostals live in the constant expectation that God will act in history, even if it is outside the norm of everyday experiences. A constant awareness of God' presence and power shapes the way a Pentecostal thinks and approaches everything. No matter what the situation, God can change it.

According to Medhurst, the "primary task for the Pentecostal is to *trust and obey*."[14] This faith includes an unfettered trust in the Bible as the verbally inspired word of God. It is both the grand narrative of salvation, but it also offers specific promises to mankind from God. Pentecostals are also taught to trust and obey those in authority including the local pastor. Because this authority is ordained by God, one risks relationship with the Divine by questioning or disobeying the pastor's instruction.[15]

I would expand on Medhurst's explanation of this point to note that to trust and obey also means that those called into the ministry of the gospel must trust that their calling is valid; they are empowered through their Pentecostal experience, and they must be obedient to the call as well as the God who called them. This principle consistently creates dissonance for women in the Assemblies of God. It is inherent in their Pentecostal DNA to trust God and to obey his calling on their lives according to the Scriptures and the empowerment of the Holy Spirit, yet they are also to look to the authority of those God has already placed into service. When those in authority, at the local or national level, discourage a call or place roadblocks in the path to ministry service, they create insecurity and dissonance.

The action of obedience is found in the fifth premise: *work*. More than anything, the Pentecostal is "admonished to work." Pentecostals from the

13. Medhurst, "Filled with the Spirit," 565.

14. Ibid., 567.

15. Ibid., 568.

time of the early church were to be about the Father's business and use all the available means of persuasion to spread God's word before it is too late. Medhurst argues that a sense of urgency pervades all Pentecostals' works. Time is running out and the work must be done before it is too late.[16]

This premise also speaks directly to the calling of women. It does not designate only men to do this work. If you were baptized in the Holy Spirit, then you were to be about the work of God regardless of your gender, race, or socioeconomic status. The work is great and the workers are few, so those who are called and empowered must use everything at their disposal to see the work completed. I would argue that as time passed and the Assemblies of God grew both in number and status, the sense of urgency diminished. This premise was used to whip up Pentecostal fervor more so than it was used to embolden those who were called into active service. Time might have been running out, but there was more than enough time to limit those who could serve and in what capacity.

The first act of rhetorical invention is to invent the Self. Medhurst affirms Kenneth Burke's contention that we invent language and the negative, and they in turn invent us. This interaction takes place over many years, and in this formation, a worldview develops with a set of assumptions, beliefs, and presuppositions. This worldview functions like ideology to guide not only the content of thought, but its processes, and our approach to a topic or a problem. How we think about things and the motives that lead us to embrace them are critical to the invention of Self and the way we will engage in rhetorical practice.

Ultimately, the Assemblies of God returned to an earlier worldview and its original assumptions, beliefs, and presuppositions to create this position paper and argue for an equal place for women. The ideology of Pentecostal belief and rhetorical invention affected not only how the Assemblies of God thinks about women in ministry but also how they approach the problem of moving this ideology into reality. By reframing the message and arguing from a distinctive scriptural position outside the evangelical mainstream, the Assemblies of God once again set itself apart with a paradigm on the role of women. The question that remains today is this: Has the publication of this position paper done anything more than provide lip-service to the issue and to those women who question if they really are welcome in the ranks of clergy within the Assemblies of God?

I would argue that it has not. Rather, this document is more often than not another paper on a shelf that creates a false sense of well-being while not making a lot of difference in the practice of women being hired

16. Ibid.

or allowed to fulfill their calling. While the rhetoric employed in this position paper is one more means of strengthening the policy positions of the Assemblies of God, it has not translated into more women finding a sense of belonging in their call.

Although the position paper on the role of women communicated a position on women to the general population in the Assemblies of God, other publications reframed the message regarding women specifically to the ministerial class. In addition to a renewed emphasis on women in ministry, research included in these publications confirms my argument that despite the publication of an "official" position on women, the reality of women's leadership was not in line with the rhetoric of this paper.

In 1997, the *Enrichment* journal, which served as a professional publication for the Assemblies of God until 2015, dedicated an entire issue to the subject of women who were creating ministry opportunities for themselves, many of whom were outside of the traditional roles of pastoring churches or serving on the foreign mission field. The issue highlighted the variety of ministry areas where women were thriving, including a feature story about four Assemblies of God women ministers creating their own opportunities for ministry: Janie Boulware-Wead, whom I will discuss in more detail later in this chapter, is a single mother who planted six Hispanic churches in Northwest Arkansas in five years and who, as a result of her success, would be tapped to direct a missionary program targeting the Hispanic peoples both in the United States and around the world. Patricia Cote served as a U.S. Army Chaplain and was the first female ever assigned to an infantry unit. Cynthia Smith pioneered a church with a strong commitment to social action in an African-American community, including a home for AIDS victims, a program to feed the poor, a transitional home for men, a short-term shelter, and a clothing outreach. Angie Thomson left a lucrative corporate position to establish an orphanage in Romania. Each of these women found ministry niches consistent with the example set by women early on in the Pentecostal movement. They found opportunities to take responsibility for their calling and carry it out. To herald their work in a "professional" media tool designed for pastors demonstrates a distinct change from much of the dissonance-laden rhetoric perpetuated by the Assemblies of God to that point in its history.[17]

17. Booze, "God Who Calls is Faithful," 17–21.

## A Rhetoric of Women's Service Requires Obedience and Men

The 1997 edition of *Enrichment* also includes a critical analysis of the situation facing women in the Assemblies of God written by Deborah Menken Gill. At the time, Gill was one of the few women in the Assemblies of God serving as a senior pastor of a church. In addition to her pastoral role, she also served as a professor of pastoral ministries at North Central Bible College (now North Central University), an Assemblies of God affiliated college in Minneapolis, Minnesota.[18] Gill notes statistics consistent with those highlighted in other reports that seem to indicate that there is a strong presence of women serving in the Assemblies of God. For example, from 1977 to 1993, it would appear that the number of women pastors showed gradual increase, but this increase is suspect when one looks beyond the raw numbers. Gill notes that in the official reporting by the General Council these gains include a disproportionate number of women who were 65 years or older (approximately 40 percent of the total number of women reported) and who were most likely retired or nearing retirement. The number of women who sought ordination had steadily decreased during this same period. Gill rightly points out that despite a perceived openness to women in a variety of ministry areas, "this generation has the lowest percentage of female ministers of any in the history of our Fellowship."[19]

Gill makes it a point several times throughout her writing that it is the responsibility of women to pursue their calling fervently and repeats the question, "What's a woman to do?" Her response to this question is to emphasize the Pentecostal rhetoric of work, trust, and obedience. Still, Gill notes that few opportunities have been presented to women to obey their call, which can create a sense of disillusionment, cause them to question the call itself, and give rise to a strong sense of discouragement, leading women to leave the fellowship in order to pursue their call elsewhere. As a result, Gill challenges male pastors to become "armor-bearers" for women by encouraging women to follow their calling into all areas of ministry and to provide those opportunities to succeed.

18. Dr. Gill now serves as a professor of biblical studies and exposition at the Assemblies of God Theological Seminary at Evangel University. In 2009, Gill became the first female to be appointed to the position of full professor at the Assemblies of God's only denominationally owned seminary. In addition to her academic work, Dr. Gill is a founding member of Christians for Biblical Equality, an interdenominational organization that promotes gender equality. She is also a published author on the subject of women in ministry, having several articles in academic and popular periodicals, co-authoring a book with Dr. Barbara Cavaness and speaking publicly on the biblical and theological position for women in ministry.

19. Gill, "Called by God," 35.

Gill also takes her advocacy one step further when giving the charge to her fellow pastors. She asserts that ministers need to do better work in understanding the biblical basis of women in ministry and to study the Assemblies of God's policy statement that provides for the full participation of women. Finally, Gill admonishes her colleagues to articulate their personal endorsements of preaching women. This plea is significant because Gill reiterates arguments that have been made several times throughout the history of the Assemblies of God. Women are supposed to "just do it," regardless of how they are treated or what opportunities are available to them. For the most part, as noted above, that is exactly what women have done by carving out their own opportunities or being creative in how they have acted out their calling. However, Gill also calls out the men who need to be more encouraging and empowering in both actions and words. The challenge she levels last is the key to her argument—Gill's fellow pastors must articulate their endorsement of women. What Gill does not differentiate, but I would argue is also vital to this challenge is that this articulation cannot simply be in private, polite conversation in the presence of a woman who is struggling with her call. This articulation must be made publicly in teachings, sermons, and in their endorsement of women candidates for ministry positions at all levels of the Assemblies of God ministry structure.

This public advocacy is lacking throughout the history of the Assemblies of God and has created a significant amount of dissonance in the messages surrounding women in ministry. From the earliest days of the movement, to the organization of the Assemblies of God in 1914, and continually as the fellowship grew and became more accepted, a "two-faced" approach to the question of women persists. On one hand, women have been affirmed in private conversations or through official policy positions, but when pressed to be advocates for women, the leadership of the Assemblies of God has fallen significantly short.

However, it is difficult to articulate a position and engage in advocacy if the arguments in favor of a position are not clear. Over time, the arguments in favor of a Pentecostal position for women's leadership became muddled. At every juncture where formal organizations were established, the freedom of women to participate in ministry was limited. William Seymour began to establish boundaries against women's leadership that eventually led to fissures with several women including Florence Crawford and Clara Lum and leaving his wife, Jennie, as the only woman in any form of leadership position. At the formation of the Assemblies of God, E. N. Bell, the first General Superintendent privately argued that women did not have the ability to serve effectively in ministry because they were too weak to handle the difficulties ministry service required. Even after the establishment of an official position on women within the constitution and bylaws of the Assemblies of God after years of revisions, men like Robert Brown spoke openly about their disdain for women who might officiate over the ordinances of the church. Brown's position was filled with irony given the fact that his wife, Marie Burgess Brown was the founding pastor of the church they served in together and would continue to serve long past his death.

Cultural accommodation also played a significant role in muddling the message on a woman's place in Pentecostal ministry. This accommodation came from within the religious culture and as a result of changes in the secular culture. As more converts to Pentecostalism came into leadership positions, they brought with them previous theological baggage, which would seep into the rhetoric and be used to argue against women's participation regardless of the number of women already serving under the banner of the fellowship. When the secular women's movement from suffrage to feminism gained momentum, the roles of women were challenged to combat what some saw as an evil attempt to destroy the family structure and to undermine the moral fabric of the church and the nation. These social movements were seen as an affront to the church, rather than an opportunity to demonstrate that the Pentecostal church had actually been at the forefront of advancing a woman's rise to full citizenship as well as her role within the church. While women's positions in the Pentecostal movement were questioned and challenged even in the earliest days, the discourse that had initially focused on empowerment for service had become less about serving and more about power. Arguments focused on theological positions of power and authority as well as a revolt against changing societal roles that seemed to undermine centuries of religious patriarchy and family structures. The official position of the Assemblies of God had become lost amongst the clamor of these constraints and created rhetorical dissonance for the women caught in these cross-currents.

## THE QUESTION OF AUTHORITY

The opportunities that Pentecostal belief had provided for women began with a foundational understanding that the purpose of a Pentecostal experience was not simply personal edification, but sharing the gospel of Jesus Christ. Because God chose women to participate in the New Testament Holy Spirit baptism experience, then it was only logical that they should also carry the gospel message.

During the earliest years of the Pentecostal movement, validation of women's roles in ministry were based on the eschatological Pentecostal proclamation found in Acts 2 and the prophecy found in Joel 2. A herme-neutical shift developed in which the Pauline limitations in the Corinthian and Timothy letters were emphasized more with less regard for how women were perceived in other New Testament writings.[20] This shift parallels the position found in many other evangelical traditions including the Southern Baptist Convention, which continues to deny women a place in official min-istry positions. Several founding members of the Assemblies of God who rose to prominence, including Bell discussed above, came into Pentecos-talism from these traditions. As the Assemblies became more accepted in the evangelical community, these arguments against women's involvement grew in prominence. According to Assemblies of God theologian Sherilyn Benvenuti, the reaction against Pentecostalism's prophesying daughters was based entirely upon the question of authority.

The use of authority rather than Spirit-empowerment to determine calling directly reverses the position taken by the earliest pioneers of the movement. Initially, servant hood, not authority, was the paradigm by which Pentecostals measured calling. The Holy Spirit held the authority, and the Spirit anointed whomever he chose to serve the body. Authority is not derived by position alone, but rather it is found in the individual who serves though the power of the Holy Spirit. As a result, gender becomes irrelevant because there is little debate over gender when it comes to who can and who cannot serve.[21]

These challenges to women within the Assemblies of God are out-weighed only by the reality that they live in a world desperately in need of every anointed person who can preach the gospel to do so. This reality is manifested in Pentecostal rhetorical invention with the premise to *work*. The sense of urgency that is coupled with the great work of "winning" souls to Jesus demands an immediate and swift response when one is called to engage in the work of the church. A commonly used colloquial phrase amongst Pentecostals has been that "the fields are white for the harvest but the workers are few." If this statement is more than a figure of speech, then women not only *can* be chosen to serve, but *must* be. Women who reject this command and those who encourage them to ignore it do so at their own peril. Unfortunately, the church has chosen to remain preoccupied with never-ending doctrinal debates over who is qualified to present this gospel message and in what position. Benvenuti states, "We are, in a sense, watch-ing the house burn down while arguing which fire truck to use. The time has

20. Booze, "Jesus and Women," 4.
21. Benvenuti, "Anointed, Gifted and Called," 231.

come for Pentecostal women to leave the arena of debate and simply be who they are and do what God has called them to do."[22]

## Reclaiming the Prophesying Daughters

During the last decade of the twentieth century, Pentecostals began to again revisit their commitment to women and the Assemblies of God furthered their emphasis on the multiplicity of women's ministry roles. This renewal appears in multiple publications specifically aimed at ministers and scholars as well as local church members dedicating issues to the subject. Some of these publications include the position paper on women's roles, entire issues of *Enrichment* journal, and *PNEUMA: The Journal of the Society for Pentecostal Studies*. As an extension of the arguments made by Gill in *Enrichment* and Benvenuti in *PNEUMA*, the Assemblies of God established a task force to examine once again the roles of women in the fellowship and to reconcile what is written in policy papers with what is practiced at the local church. According to Beth Grant, who was appointed National Chairperson of the taskforce in 1998, "We find ourselves at a point in which the role of women in the church and ministry is being debated within the evangelical community and within our ranks."[23]

The taskforce was not established to address gender issues, but rather it was an attempt by the General Council to raise the visibility of women in ministry and to keep faith with the roots of the Pentecostal movement. Grant argued that the future of the Assemblies of God depends on the faithfulness of both men and women to do what God has called them to do and to be empowered by the fellowship to do so. She stated, "This initiative brings together the best of what our Assemblies of God executive leadership, our national task force . . . have to offer women ministers of all ages. Each partner is contributing creativity, resources and ministries in the areas of their greatest strengths because of their shared commitment to empowering women of God."[24] Wood, then General Secretary of the Assemblies of God, articulated that "We [the General Council] want to do everything we can to encourage the development of women in ministry, and encourage young women who are in training for ministry in our schools."[25]

22. Ibid., 230.

23. Attanasi, "Fellowship Convenes Conference for Women."

24. Assemblies of God Women in Ministry Task Force, "National Conferences for Women in Ministry Slate."

25. Attanasi, "Fellowship Convenes Conference for Women."

Byron Klaus, former President of the Assemblies of God Theological Seminary, speaking at a biennial conference sponsored by the taskforce stated, "This is not about feminism; it's about the call. How dare we not be good stewards of what God has ordained? Redemption knows no limits!" Klaus added, "I am not hearing from the young women in our Movement that 'I deserve this' [position of ministry]. I am hearing 'God called me!' I am not championing equality but asking for righteousness!"[26] This statement is a distinct shift in the rhetoric by leaders in the Assemblies of God from previous generations. Through these efforts, the Assemblies of God, as a body, was making a deliberate choice to articulate support for women and to create an environment that encouraged their participation.

This move is significant for several reasons, but for one in particular, the way the Assemblies of God is organized. As a cooperative fellowship, the leadership of the Assemblies of God, namely the General Superintendent and the Executive Presbytery, do not have the power to issue a decree about a position or policy so that the member clergy and their district leadership must see that it is carried out. Rather, power within the Assemblies of God is based in the autonomy of the local church. Yet, unlike the leadership of the Assemblies of God historically, Wood believed that he could serve as an advocate for a "full employment act" for women's service including in roles of senior pastor, elder, or any number of ministry positions.[27] Unlike during previous attempts to reconcile the issue of women's roles, Wood took a stand rhetorically and then backed up that rhetoric with action. He encouraged women to become educated, credentialed, and ordained. This combination empowered them to serve and opened doors that had previously been closed by the double-speak of leaders who said one thing and did another.

The establishment of the taskforce provided an opportunity for the Assemblies of God to engage in self-critical analysis while at the same time establishing a forward momentum. The language used by the leadership within the fellowship and in the taskforce returned to a rhetoric in which the language of calling was rooted in empowerment of the Holy Spirit and not in authority, and a rhetoric of service was once again given prominence. The task force continues to serve as a means for the Assemblies of God to put their rhetoric into action. Unlike the Decade of Harvest initiative, the taskforce was not a top-down program of change and growth; instead, it is a way for the local church to partner with the fellowship to examine how the roles of women play out both in terms of policy and practice.

26. Knoth, "Women in Ministry a Reality at Conference."

27. Wood, Question and Answer Forum, *Conversations '08 Conference*, presented on November 1, 2008, Phoenix, Arizona.

The Women in Ministry Taskforce would never have come to be had it not been for a shift in leadership within the fellowship. These leaders were committed to seeing the Assemblies of God reclaim its prophesying daughters and give them a renewed voice. This reclamation and renewal did not occur quickly, but it has been a sustained effort over the course of nearly a quarter of a century. I contend that just as the leaders of the past have created dissonance on the issue of women's roles, these shifts in leadership have created an opportunity to clear away the dissonant voices and replace them with a unified rhetoric.

## CHANGING LEADERSHIP, CHANGING RHETORIC

Leadership changes in the fellowship also renewed the focus on the roles of women when, in 1993, Thomas Trask was elected General Superintendent of the Assemblies of God. During his tenure, Trask seemed to encourage the Assemblies of God constituency toward a greater acceptance of women in a larger multiplicity of ministry roles than had previously been espoused by national leaders. In an interview for the ministerial journal, *Enrichment*, Trask stated, "I would encourage them [male pastors] to open their hearts and pulpits to women whom God has gifted in preaching, teaching, exhortation, and other abilities." He contended that such action would have lasting benefits for everyone involved. Women would find fulfillment in their calling, and the church would benefit from their participation.[28] This position anticipated the call made by Gill a handful of years later that male pastors are a key component of the rhetoric of women's roles if the Assemblies of God is going to be in line with the policy positions outlined by the fellowship. Those pastors are the last line of defense between the policy positions and the acceptance of women by congregants who had most likely never seen a woman active in a ministry role or knew of the history of women's roles in the Assemblies of God outside of the position paper—that is assuming these congregations had access to or had ever read the position paper.

### *Thomas Trask and the Priority of Women*

At the same General Council meeting where Trask was elected, the first woman in Assemblies of God history was nominated to the Executive Presbytery. Carmen H. Perez, a minister from Puerto Rico, ran as one of fourteen for a position held by a Presbyter who was also up for re-election.

28. Trask, "Ask the Superintendent," 8.

While Perez was not elected, her nomination was a precedent- setting event that drew the attention of the media. One reporter noted that while women were able to serve in any capacity within the fellowship's hierarchy, there appeared to be some hostility toward women. The article assumed this hostility was the result of the rise of feminism, but I would contend that it ran deeper than just a feminist backlash. The perceived hostility felt by the author of this article is rooted in a dissonance-filled rhetoric that began long before the Assemblies of God became a player in American evangelicalism. As a result of this dissonance, women struggle to be accepted and hired as pastors, which in turn limits their ability to reach the point of being elected to regional or national leadership positions. It was noted in the article that, at the time, only 8.6 percent of the Assemblies' ordained ministers were women.[29]

While this perceived backlash was fiction than reality, within a couple of years, the message coming out of the General Council was very different. In 1997, the General Council speakers docket included only the third woman ever to serve as a keynote speaker in the main session of the meetings and the first woman to do so in eighteen years. Her message: women preachers in the Assemblies of God can succeed, and they can receive respect and recognition for their work. Janie Boulware-Wead, who had been featured in the *Enrichment Journal* as one of five women changing the perception of women in ministry, had just been appointed the director of Hispanic Project 2000, a new part of the Division of Home Missions (now called US Missions), was that speaker. In addition to her service as a foreign and home missionary for the Assemblies of God, Boulware-Wead was a single mother who had gained the attention of the fellowship's leaders by pioneering six Hispanic churches in Northwest Arkansas in five years.[30]

In her address, Boulware-Wead stated emphatically, "Women, there has never been a greater day of opportunity than today. The Lord of the harvest is an equal opportunity employer!"[31] She went on to point out that women in the Assemblies of God have had the best success when they have pioneered ministry works such as planting churches, establishing missionary posts, and embarking on evangelistic tours. Clearly by her actions, Boulware-Wead had taken her own advice and rather than wait to be hired, she had gone out on her own and found opportunities to take ownership of her calling. This decision is very like that of her sisters throughout the history of the Assemblies of God; however, her sermon defined a distinct

29. Edwards, "Woman Up for A/G Post," 6A.
30. Floyd, "Janie Wead," 8–9.
31. Boulware-Wead, "Lord Send a Revival."

shift in the rhetoric of the General Council that had spent years haggling over policy and ways to "fit women in" to the ministry model of the Assemblies of God. While women had often pioneered works, they were limited in what functions they were allowed to perform in a flourishing work or, often at the behest of leadership, women were replaced by male counterparts once the work was established. What makes Boulware-Wead stand out in this particular period was that her pioneering spirit had caught the attention of Trask. Unlike his predecessors, Trask did not simply pay lip service to the work of Boulware-Wead; instead, he gave her a platform to share her message and a position with which she could carry out more than just rhetoric. Rather than immediately place a rhetorical constraint in the way of this self-created opportunity, Trask opened the opportunity further and made an example of her for others. Trask did not merely advocate that local pastors create opportunities for women, he gave a woman a national platform to speak for herself on the value and necessity of the female voice within the Assemblies of God. No General Superintendent before him had given a female speaker at a General Council meeting such a platform with the explicit purpose of encouraging women to take responsibility for their calling and empowerment.

## The Election of George O. Wood, the Son of a Preacher Woman

In 2007, another shift within the Assemblies of God's highest positions of leadership would continue to renew the rhetoric on the role of women. Just prior to the General Council gathering in the summer of 2007, General Superintendent Trask announced that he would retire and leave his term early. Wood, who previously had served as General Secretary, was elected to serve out the remaining two years of Trask's term. While Wood had served for several years as an executive in the national leadership as well as at the local and district levels of the Assemblies of God, his selection ushered in several unique changes to the fellowship. Unlike his predecessors, Wood held both a doctoral degree in pastoral theology and a juris doctorate in law, and he was arguably the most educated chief executive in the history of the Assemblies of God. This distinction is significant because historically Pentecostals have not placed an emphasis on formal education, particularly graduate education, and have been criticized for being almost hostile toward intellectualism. However, that approach began to shift as the Assemblies of God embraced a liberal arts model within their own colleges and universities and a new appreciation for education rose in tandem with a growing educated class of Pentecostals. Younger and more educated Pente-costals, both men and women took notice that within the early days of the movement their forefathers and mothers were heavily involved in many ar-eas of social reform. Historically, Pentecostals were pacifists, conscientious objectors, advocates for civil rights in the African-American community, and early leaders in the women's suffrage movement. This rediscovered appreciation of the role that early Pentecostals played in significant social reform movements created a population within the Assemblies of God that was less reactionary to these movements. They were more likely to connect Pentecostalism with social reform movements than to view social reform as antithetical to their own religious belief and practice.

As Wood's educational status lent credibility to a more educated con-stituency so did his personal experience with women ministers. In speeches, articles, and interviews on the subject of women's service, he was quick to point out that the greatest influence on his views on women came from his mother who served as a single missionary in Tibet for several years before marrying and continuing her ministry with her husband in China. As a re-sult, he has an extensive record of promoting women within his own sphere of ministerial influence, including working to formulate the constitution and bylaws at churches in which he served to allow for women to serve as elders and deacons and hiring women to serve on his pastoral staff.

## The Ethos of Credentialed Women

As General Secretary, Wood wrote extensively on the need for women to become credentialed. The reason, he argued, is not gender specific, but it is the same for men and women: credentials complete a process of prepara-tion, the culture desires that professionals demonstrate their qualifications, and the credential provides a means for ministers to participate in the deci-sions that affect the direction of the Assemblies of God through their vote at district and general councils. The bottom line is this: credentials provide credibility and the wellbeing of the fellowship is dependent on the involve-ment and wise counsel of all (men and women) who serve.[32]

Wood's arguments on credentials reach back to a more educated and thoughtful approach to ministry. While Wood's Pentecostal theology accepted that the Holy Spirit empowers one for ministry, he recognized a need for preparation and acceptance within the culture as endorsements for ministry. This broad view was a significant rhetorical shift from previ-ous leaders in the Assemblies of God because it did not distinguish women

32. Wood, "Why Credentials Are Important."

as a separate entity in ministry. A woman's opportunity for full participation in Pentecostal ministry became equal to that of a man's, required all of the same preparation, and that preparation required full consecration as a minister of the gospel. Rhetorically, Wood created space for women's full participation and rather than immediately placing constraints on this space, he expanded the rhetorical space by not distinguishing the requirements for ministry as being gender specific.

## A Distinctive Doctrine of Women in Ministry

Finally, Wood's position on women's roles that returned to the earliest ideology of Pentecostal practice. According to Wood, the Assemblies of God tilts differently than other denominations in the evangelical tradition on two specific areas: pneumatology and women. He claimed a specific theology is at play where the text informs experience and experience informs the text. Wood believed that this theology must be emphasized and re-emphasized. He argued that some in the Assemblies of God have been too influenced by the voices of conservative evangelicalism and fundamentalism. In his assessment, the hierarchical model of leadership does not work. The unique theology of the Assemblies of God, which depends upon the anointing of the Holy Spirit as empowerment for service, assumes that women can receive this empowerment and, therefore, demands their service. Women do not need to prove their call to ministry, they need to do ministry.[33]

Wood's admonition for women to become credentialed and his elevation of women to the doctrinal level of pneumatology also signals a significant shift in the rhetoric of the Assemblies of God. For decades, leaders in the Assemblies continually placed rhetorical constraints in the way of women who served or sought to serve within the fellowship by specifically limiting their ability to become credentialed in the same manner as their male counterparts and dismissing their beliefs on pneumatology by restricting female voices within the fellowship. George Wood's sustained vocal support for women and his involvement in establishing positions for women in the local churches, at the district level, and within the General Council at each point in his service distinctly boosted the opportunities for women to once again find empowerment to serve in their callings.

33. Ibid.

*A Woman Shall Lead With Them*

Further evidence of this shift came the very same year Wood was elected to serve out the remainder of Trask's tenure as General Superintendent. A change in policy adopted at the 2005 General Council meeting added representatives to the Executive Presbytery from non-Hispanic foreign language districts and ethnic fellowships. This new group of Presbytery members provided wide-ranging contributions and diversity to the body of leadership. What the Presbytery still lacked was gender diversity and youth. As a result, the Executive Presbytery sponsored a resolution that recommended that the Executive branch expand again to include one ordained minister under the age of 40 and one ordained woman.[34]

The sponsorship of this resolution should not be overlooked. The need to continue to diversify the highest levels of leadership within the Assemblies of God was not something that was brought to the General Council by a women's group or by any one specific district that might be more open to the voice of women and younger leaders. This resolution was written and sponsored by the Executive Presbytery as a recognition of where they were lacking in perspective and in demonstrating action and not simply language that allows for women to serve at any level of ministry office.

The resolution was not without controversy. Debate over the resolution included a sustained theological discussion by one delegate who objected to the resolution on the grounds of the Pauline limitations in 2 Timothy as well as discussion as to the need for "affirmative-action" to promote women to positions that they should have naturally ascended to like their male counterparts. However, following the conclusion of this debate and a corrective issued to the delegate who insisted that biblically women were ineligible to serve in such a capacity, the resolution was adopted. In 2009, for the first time in the history of the Assemblies of God, a woman would be elected to the highest leadership board in the fellowship.

While women like Carmen Perez and Beth Grant had seen their names put forward as nominees to serve in various national capacities, no woman had ever been elected to these offices. This action by the leadership of the Assemblies of God was the most far-reaching opportunity for women throughout the history of the fellowship. However, it would be another two years before the election would take place. While this historic vote to change policy was significant, policy alone had never been enough for the women in the Assemblies of God.

34. General Council of the Assemblies of God, 52nd General Council, August 8–11, 2007.

Once again, Wood's leadership made a significant impact in creating opportunities for women beyond what mere policy had been able to accomplish. Wood, along with the Executive Presbytery, determined to invite one woman and one minister under the age of 40 to serve as auditors at each of the executive meetings held between the conclusion of the 2007 General Council meeting and the permanent election of these representatives in 2009. These auditors would not have the vote of full membership on the Executive Presbytery, but would be able to provide counsel and perspective to the meetings and decisions before the governing board. Once again, where opportunity had too often been met with immediate constraint, a shift in policy as well as practice had taken place. Opportunity now seemed to mean just that: an opportunity for women to have a literal seat at the table of leadership and service within the movement that has been one of the first to open the door to the female voice.

While the election of a woman to the Executive Presbytery would create a position of full leadership at the national level, the inclusion of auditors to Presbytery meetings in the interim is also significant. At each of the nine meetings between 2007 and 2009, a different woman was chosen to represent the female point of view. While one might argue that it was constraining to these women to be token representatives with no vote, I would contend that the variety of women from different areas of ministry and their ability to be more than mere observers was a unique opportunity for women's service and exerted influence within the executive leadership. The two-year time span between the passing of the resolution authorizing a woman's service and the election of a woman to the Executive Presbytery could have been a time when the voice of women was essentially put aside. The leadership of the Assemblies of God, however, made a distinct choice to create further opportunity for women where none had previously existed.

### The Female Voice of Leadership 100 Years in the Making

On August 5, 2009, at the 53rd gathering of the General Council of the Assemblies of God, following nearly 100 years of mixed history and rhetoric surrounding the role of women, the council voted to elect Dr. A. Elizabeth (Beth) Grant to the Executive Presbytery. Grant was one of four women including Dr. Deborah Gill, Linda Stamps-Dismore, and Jane Boulware-Wead who were nominated after each district submitted potential candidates and the Executive Presbytery nominated and narrowed the group for the vote. It took three ballots to achieve the required majority ending 95 years of male-only leadership in the national ranks of the Assemblies of God.

While the shift in direction is distinct, old habits also seemed to die hard. The districts also submitted potential nominees for the Executive position for a minister under the age of 40. This position could also have been held by a female minister, but all of the names submitted by the districts were male. This remnant of male dominance is striking because of the organizational nature of the Assemblies of God. While argument persists on the need for "affirmative action" with regard to promoting women within the fellowship, the autonomy of the local church represented in the power of the district offices demonstrates that when given the freedom to promote a female without compulsion, local structures show little support for women's leadership. Much work remains to create a more affirming culture for women at the district level. These opportunities will only materialize if more women are allowed the freedom to minister in the local church. A more detailed analysis of the cultures that exist at the local and district levels of the Assemblies of God is necessary. The greatest constraints to women's ministry work resides in these cultures, and the constraints at that level are deeper than those exposed through this study.

Recognition of the challenges faced by women at the local and district level did not go unnoticed by the first woman elected to a national position in the Assemblies of God. In her acceptance speech upon the electing ballot, Grant appealed to her male counterparts on the local church level by encouraging them to recognize the call of God on women in their churches, particularly little girls and young women. Grant exhorted these pastors to verbally say, "We see God's hand on you. He has called you. He is with you." This appeal is consistent with the one made to fellow pastors by Gill in her seminal article published in the *Enrichment* journal. Pastors in the local church and the district officials who oversee these ministers play a crucial role in changing the opportunities for women to serve and in eliminating the constraints that have plagued their work since the earliest days of the Pentecostal movement.

To her female counterparts, Grant also appealed to inspire the fellowship by their obedience to the call to ministry by stating, "We live in strategic days. It is time to say yes to God. Men and women together [sic]." Grant continued, "God is who calls and who orders our steps. We have a history of one hundred years of women who heard the call and obeyed," she included, with a hint of sarcasm at the election process. She concluded her thoughts using some humor in saying, "Thank you for hanging in there [through a long election process], after 95 years, what's a few hours? Spouses will never look the same in the Assemblies of God."[35]

35. Grant, "Executive Presbytery Election Speech."

The rhetorical approach in this appeal is also significant. Grant does not appeal to her female colleagues with the language of power overcoming oppression. She does not single women out as a driving force in ministry apart from men. Rather, in her appeal to women, she turns her language back to that of classical Pentecostal calling: empowered by the Holy Spirit and trusting that the God who has called them will not allow the rhetorical constraints of mankind to inhibit their call. But, she adds, women must be obedient to this call. By employing strong, yet historically driven rhetorical invention, Grant enables women to engage in the work of Pentecostal ministry, but she does not negate the men whom they will need to come alongside them. The most effective form of ministry includes both men and women if it is going to be successful at reclaiming a sense of urgency to see a lost world come to a saving knowledge of Jesus Christ.

By engaging in a hint of sarcasm and humor, Grant reminds the constituency that this partnership in ministry is not limited to men as the pastoral leader and the woman as the dutiful spouse. Rather, this partnership in ministry can also be achieved when the dutiful spouse is, in fact, the husband of the Pastor.

In an article highlighting her multiple ministry roles, including her work as co-founder of Project Rescue (a ministry focused on women and children caught up in sex trafficking), serving on the Executive Presbytery, and chairing the Network for Women Ministers (then known as the Network for Women in Ministry), Grant highlights why the female voice is so necessary in the Assemblies of God. She states, "When more than 6,000 women are credentialed—and many more are not, but week after week are doing what God has called them to do—that is quite a group of women." She continues, "To me, this is a very treasured responsibility and a privilege to represent that body of women, many of whom inspire me."[36]

The significance of Grant's election and her influence over the policy and practice of the Assemblies of God with regard to women's roles will take several years of history to assess fully. However, her election alone is a significant shift in the application of policy and practice within the Assemblies of God and ends nearly a century of constraints for women seeking to take responsibility for their call and the empowerment for service they believed they had been given by their Pentecostal experience.

36. McClure, "Many Roles, One Call," 11.

## The Network for Women in Ministry

In addition to Grant's election to the Executive Presbytery, she also continued to serve as the national Chairperson for what was then called "The Network for Women in Ministry" or simply, "The Network." Originally named the Taskforce for Women in Ministry, "The Network" was moved in 2008 from the status of taskforce to that of an official department within the national headquarters of the Assemblies of God. With this new designation, specific funds and national sponsorship of biennial conferences were supplied by the General Council and provided a level of credibility to the gatherings as official ministry endeavors on par with other national departments, including the Alliance for Higher Education, U.S. Missions, and Assemblies of God World Missions.

In 2016, the Network was renamed The Network of Women Ministers in order to further distinguish this department from the national Women's Ministries Department. While their efforts may overlap in some areas, their purposes and focus are entirely different. According to the website, the Network of Women Ministers exists to

> Connect and inspire credentialed women ministers, and those seeking credentials. We are dedicated to building community among our women ministers and providing leadership development opportunities. Our aim is to model biblical leadership through the various ministries in which we serve. We want to equip districts and the local church body to empower women to leadership within their churches and allow younger generations to see God's spirit poured out on all flesh."[37]

This statement is distinct from the Women's Ministries Department whose purpose is ministry *to* women as opposed to the ministry *of* women. These distinct purposes are separate and yet, their histories are intertwined. In 1925, Etta Calhoun formed the Women's Missionary Council, the organization that would become the Women's Ministries Department, when her own opportunities for ministry were constrained. In what would become a pattern for women like Calhoun, when constraints were placed on women's roles and opportunities, women who were convinced of their call moved past those constraints and created opportunities, as Grant states, to take responsibility for their calling. According to Grant, the call to ministry is not a call to women to rule or to seek positions of power, but rather a call to pour oneself

---

37. The Network for Women Ministers, General Council of the Assemblies of God, July 15, 2017. http://www.womenministers.ag.org.

out in ministry. In other words, the call to ministry is about giving of oneself in service rather than focusing on a hierarchy of leadership.

The rhetorical approach taken by Grant is also of interest. In 2008, the General Council sponsored a national conference that took on the moniker of "conversations." Playing on the social needs of women and the concept of networking, the conference was planned around conversations among women who serve in specific areas of ministry as well as mixes of these groups to discourse and respond to the various speakers and workshops presented during the course of the three-day event. Specific groups of ministry were identified including those who serve as senior or lead pastors, youth pastors, children's pastors, missionaries (both foreign and domestic), and educators to name a select few. These "conversations" took place around circular tables with a discussion facilitator and were in response to sessions termed "narrative sessions" where the stories of women actively engaged in various stages and types of ministry were shared. On the final morning of the conference a "dialogue" session was held with then General Superintendent George Wood participating in what was sub-titled, "Everything we ever wanted to know about women in ministry, but were afraid to ask." This question-and-answer session with Wood allowed him to share his vision regarding the role of women in the Assemblies both in terms of theology and practice as well as to answer specific questions about how this practice could be carried out more fully in the future compared with past experiences.

The conference rhetoric was replete with language that focused on community, mentoring, narrative, and discourse in a manner both female-centered as well as utilizing feminine strengths in communication such as relationship and service. Billed as a "unique experience for women in ministry" the conference both affirmed the multiplicity of ministry areas where women serve, but created an environment where women's voices were heard in a context that women understand best.

In a letter of greeting included in the *Conversations '08* program book, Wood stated, "Women have been at the heart of the diverse ministries of the Assemblies of God since it's founding. It is the desire of the executive leadership to see a growing army of women mobilized . . . to fulfill God's call with excellence and a greater anointing."[38] This desire as expressed by Wood on behalf of the executive leadership of the Assemblies of God again signaled a significant shift of purpose specifically directed to women. This purposeful change in the rhetorical stance of the leadership of the Assemblies of God allowed for a greater opportunity to see the rhetorical topography changed and in turn a greater opportunity for the female voice

---

38. Wood, "Welcome Letter," *Conversations '08*, November 1, 2008.

to be heard. The Network held another Conversations conference in 2010 opposite the General Council meetings to bring a specific focus to women in ministry, but later the Network added events to the Council week rather than hosting a separate conference.

## Breaking Down the Rhetorical
## Barriers to Successful Service

While these changes and shifts are dramatic and certainly seem to indicate a culture change at the highest levels with the Assemblies of God, challenges remain. Kate Cory, a presenter at the *Conversations '08* conference and a nationally appointed U.S. missionary, rose to question Wood during the question and answer session with an issue that continues to haunt women in the Assemblies of God: acceptance at the local level. Cory expressed the challenges faced by women such as herself who are required to raise funds to support their missionary work. She described in detail the obstacles she faces in meeting with male pastors upon whom she and others like her depend for opportunities to share their vision for ministry and appeal for funds. Cory expressed frustration at being told by her male counterparts that they would not be able to meet with her because it would be inappropriate for them to be seen in public or to meet privately with a female. Having come from a background in corporate America, this assumption was a foreign concept to Cory who found it remarkable that excuses such these were tolerated within the fellowship. Cory went so far as to assert that she found this stance taken by male pastors to objectify men more than women, which is the claim that seems so commonplace in media and the workplace.

Wood's response to the narrative Cory laid out was sympathetic, but while he affirmed her work and her right to serve as a woman within the Assemblies of God, he could offer little by way of change. As has been discussed over and over in this chapter, the greatest constraint women continue to face with regard to their ministry opportunities falls at the feet of the local church. The autonomy of the local church and, therefore, the autonomy of the pastor of that church prevents the General Council from specifically dictating how women will be treated. This situation goes beyond the issues presented by Cory with regard to the raising of funds for her work, and presents a challenge to those who desire employment as staff members at these churches. However, rather than dismissing Cory's frustration, Wood asked her to write a piece for the *Enrichment* journal on the challenges she faces and why the local church is so important in bringing about a full embrace of women within the church.[39]

While these constraints are significant and can be as discouraging as any other placed in the path of women throughout the history of the Assemblies of God, the rhetorical position taken by Wood seems to maintain a willingness to find even the smallest of open doors. In order to create opportunities in places where constraint remains dominant, Wood sought to be proactive in utilizing the tools and resources to continually send the message that women are welcome in the ministry of the Assemblies of God.

In the twenty-four years of Wood's executive leadership in the Assemblies of God first as General Secretary and then later as General Superintendent, he set out to encourage a shift in the make up of the leadership face of the Assemblies of God. The Network of Women Ministers, while it has struggled to gain a significant place of influence in the overall fellowship, is just one of those areas. The establishment of the Network creates a presence in the national office, but until the appointment of Crystal Martin in 2017, the chairperson for the Network was a non-resident appointee (meaning she did not work at the National Leadership and Resource Center located in Springfield, Missouri), and in addition to being led by a non-resident, the Network has not been led by a woman who has served as a lead pastor or in a significant ministry position apart from the position held by her husband. This scenario also has created significant challenges to the functional purpose and the influence of the Network beyond being a place for women to seek resources. For the Network to have significant impact, more work will need to be done to develop it as a department not just for women to seek information and support but also as a means of education and resourcing for male pastors, local church boards, and district offices.

## FROM BENEVOLENT NEGLECT TO FULL EMPOWERMENT FOR SERVICE

If the culture of the Assemblies of God is to become a place where women can thrive in ministry positions, issues such as those addressed by Cory as well as theological and scriptural challenges to women's roles in the church must continue to be confronted with a strong rhetorical stance. Anything less will only serve to set the Assemblies of God back rather than setting it apart as a vanguard of example to other evangelical traditions.

The implications of the rhetorical shift occurring within the Assemblies of God are numerous and profound. Not since the earliest days of

39. Wood, "Everything We Ever Wanted to Know."

the Pentecostal movement has such a sustained effort been engaged on the part of women for women along with the affirmation of those who lead the fellowship. It would seem that the argument presented by Benvenuti, Gill and others has not fallen on deaf ears, but rather the mantle of ministry has been placed firmly on the shoulders of women who not only are strong enough to bear its weight, but also who are no longer interested in arguing for their right to participate in ministry. They join a new generation of male leaders who are willing to engage the past, submit to examination, and use their rhetoric to affirm their sisters in the empowerment of the Holy Spirit for the work they have been called to do. The rhetorical opportunity is not limited to simply acknowledging the female voice within Pentecostalism. It extends to create the possibility for the Assemblies of God to stand out within the evangelical community and set the example rather than being swallowed up by the culture. This opportunity came during the General Council in 2017 where Dr. Melissa J. Alfaro was the first woman elected to the national governing body, to serve as the executive presbyter for ministers under the age of 40, a position not specifically intended to represent women. Alfaro is a product of the Assemblies of God from her childhood through her education at Southwestern Assemblies of God University. Alfaro, a Latina woman who is a pastor ordained in a language and ethnic district, is the first in her family to graduate both high school and college along with graduate and postgraduate degrees. Her presence on the executive presbytery marks a distinct shift not only in who can but also who does serve in this national role. In addition, Alfaro is now one of two women to serve as executive presbyter as well as one of two people of Hispanic descent in that body. She serves alongside an African-American executive presbyter, one ethnic/language executive presbyter, and she is one of 6 out of 21 executive presbyters who are not Caucasian and male.

As a result of the intentional promotion of women and other underrepresented people by leaders such as Dr. George O. Wood, the role of women can no longer be left to benevolent neglect. Rather, what the Assemblies of God now seeks to do is lead by example so that the Pentecostal tradition provides options for women who seek to reconcile their calling with an empowerment for service. Progress and influence come slowly, but change is afoot in the Assemblies of God, and now is the time to set the standard for others in the tradition as well as those in other areas of the evangelical community to see this change come to fruition. Speaking in a business session during the General Council in 2017, George Wood addressed this change specifically as he noted the representation in the executive as well as the general presbytery and that intentional legislative action helped make the change possible. Wood proclaimed that at one time the Assemblies of God did have a quota system. To be a national leader in the Assemblies of God, you had to be white and male. "No more!" he proclaimed! "That era is over in the governing structures in the Assemblies of God!"[40]

40. Wood, Business Session.

# 7

# What am I Supposed to Do?
# Let People Go to Hell?

## A Rhetoric of Empowered Women

*So in spite of opposition, examples and visible models of women ministers who were a part of the initial fabric of our Fellowship encouraged younger women. Sure, there was opposition, but the sheer fact is so many were called.*

—Dr. Byron Klaus, President, Assemblies of God Theological
    Seminary

*When people would say, "Women shouldn't be doing this," my response was "God called me. What am I supposed to do? Let people go to hell?"*

—Rev. Martha Klaus, recounting to her son, Byron,
    on opposition to her ministry

THE LIFE AND MINISTRY of Martha Klaus is reminiscent of others of her generation of Assemblies of God women called to the ministry work of the church. Her call to a life of ministry was not dramatic. Rather, in a private moment warming her hands over the family stove in the dead of Nebraska winter, sixteen-year-old Martha heard the voice of the Lord prompt her to dedicate her life to serve the church. Credentialed in 1937 at age eighteen, Martha traveled and held revivals and vacation Bible schools throughout the Midwest and up and down the coast of California. She held services in mining camps, at cattle sale barns, and in places even the burliest of cowboys would have found a little rough.

When she first applied for ordination, she was denied because her husband (whom she married in 1945) was not yet credentialed, and it would be unseemly for a wife to be ordained before her husband. Yet, despite this obstacle, Martha and her husband Arthur set out together to pastor on the plains of North Dakota, ministering primarily to German-Russian immigrants. They would be ordained together in 1949 and continue to serve as co-pastors. Wherever they served together in their 40-plus-year ministry career, their names both appeared on the marquee with Arthur preaching in the morning and Martha in the evening. According to their son, Byron, who recently retired as the president of the Assemblies of God Theological Seminary, "Mom's ministry really occurred before my dad's. The parishioners in the churches they pastored never questioned whether she was fully a minister. At times my father's role was more prominent because she took on a mother's role. But even though that was the case, there was never anyone who would have said when my mom preached, 'Oh we're getting the B team.' My mom was called; dad never doubted that."[1]

Narrative after narrative has provided a similar account. Women, called into the unlikeliest of vocations during the unlikeliest of times, faced challenges and constraints dictated not by those outside their faith communities but from within their own ranks, their fellow ministers. In spite of the unlikely circumstances that provided opportunity where none was culturally granted and despite the constraints that seemed to come more from those who also claimed to be among the called, these women persevered and forged a legacy that serves to inspire and challenge a new generation of women who believe that they too have heard the voice of God calling them to a life of service to his Kingdom within the Pentecostal tradition. How these young women will be received remains to be seen. While the times have certainly changed vocationally for women who seek opportunity in medicine, politics, or law, the discourse on women in ministry remains complex. For every story of acceptance and success another tells of rejection and discontent.

1. Byron Klaus interview by Crabtree, "'Mr. and Mrs.' On the Church Marquee," July 2005. See also, Martha Klaus interview by Crabtree, "He Preached Morning and She Preached Nights," July 2005.

## A REVIEW OF PURPOSE

I have set out to explore the impact of tensions generated in the rhetoric of opportunity and constraint faced by women seeking positions of ministry in the Pentecostal movement and more specifically in the Assemblies of God. This tension manifests itself in the historical context and in relationship to the prevailing culture. These discrepancies and the resulting tensions are profoundly rhetorical. They are primarily rooted in the way people talk—or how they use words, language, and symbols and are, in turn, used by them. The historical, cultural, and theological context in which the Pentecostal movement emerges contributes to this discourse and permeates the formation of ideology and practice that creates dissonance and tension both within the fellowship and to the outside observer. The challenge for me as a rhetorical scholar is how and how well people invented and deployed these messages in response to each situation. The relationship between the church and women is distinct and how Pentecostals have talked about this relationship has several implications.

I demonstrate that women have played and continue to play a disproportionately prominent role in the Pentecostal movement as compared to their counterparts in Evangelicalism. I have explored how the role of women in leadership within the Pentecostal church is about more than feminism and more than garnering women a seat at the table. Rather, women empowered to lead in the church is a total reconceptualization of who God is and how we approach the work of the church in our culture as well as a quiet subversion of centuries of religious identity and ideology.

I have argued that the inclusion of women in leadership positions within the Assemblies of God is doctrinally as distinctive as their pneumatology. I contend that the shift the Assemblies of God made in their distinctive theology and pneumatology creates a greater rhetorical space for women in the church. If the Baptism in the Holy Spirit is an empowerment for service and the Spirit pours out on daughters, what are they empowered to do in their service? I demonstrate that theologically and rhetorically, the fathers of the Assemblies of God saw it both ways. Theologically, the Spirit was available to these prophesying daughters, but when it came to creating both physical and rhetorical space for women to serve, their previous theological leanings and cultural norms weighed heavily against granting women a new place in the emerging hierarchy of the fellowship.

I have argued that the Assemblies of God lost sight of its unique cultural and religious identity. Despite a radical beginning and a unique approach to theology, as the Assemblies of God grew and developed into an individual institution, strategic choices were made that may have precipitated rapid growth and development in the United States and around the world. Yet, in the process these choices sacrificed distinct elements of their unique history and ideology. These choices contributed to the tensions faced by women who sensed a calling to church ministry and leadership. I built upon previous scholarship, which argues that the Pentecostal tradition, as exemplified in the Assemblies of God sacrificed its moment in time to be a catalyst for the changing role of women in the church and in American culture.

Finally, I have argued that these issues faced by the Assemblies of God mirror broader rhetorical problems in the evangelical community. The idea of women in church leadership challenges religious convention and American culture. Several competing voices emerge on the role women have to play within the home, the society and the church. I examined the way evangelical rhetoric creates and shapes both policy and perception on the place of women in public, private, and religious spheres.

My purpose in writing this book is to heed the warning of Blumhofer regarding dissonance and mixed messages in multiple narratives. At the same time, I have also exposed and addressed the rhetorical underpinnings of the discrepancies that I believe have existed and continue to permeate the role of women in American religion and church leadership. The vast narrative of history could not be ignored, but I have focused my research on the history of the Pentecostal movement in the United States, with sustained examination of the Assemblies of God. The history and exigence of the Pentecostal movement and the birth of the Assemblies of God is an extraordinary event and noteworthy from a rhetorical perspective.

While I believe that my work contributes substantially to the body of gender theory and rhetorical criticism, rather than use a feminist rhetorical approach that engages in critical analysis of patriarchy and power, I have focused my examination on the ways women negotiate and renegotiate rhetorical space throughout the history of the Assemblies of God. I have examined how they used and were used by symbols as they conceptualized their theology and practiced their faith. I have examined what their theology means and how they practice it authentically and try to do proper justice to it as they engage in public life.

It was important to first provide a foundation for understanding the Pentecostal movement, the Assemblies of God, and the cultural landscape in which this movement was birthed. In so doing, I have provided a detailed historical account of the theological foundations of Pentecostal belief as well as an account of the development and growth of the Assemblies of God with particular focus on their approach to women's leadership. Finally, I have created a more complete picture of the role women have played in the Assemblies of God by providing a narrative account of specific women who have created, shaped, and left a legacy in their contributions to the work of the church that extends beyond their gender or the time period in which they served.

The Assemblies of God stands today at a critical moment in which the role of women in ministry is again at the forefront of denominational policy and discourse. How the Assemblies handles the situation rhetorically and practically will determine whether the dissonance felt by women who are currently serving or considering service in ministry will continue or the counter-cultural revolution of the past will be redeemed. Therefore, the significance of this book goes beyond the historic place of the Assemblies of God and the greater Pentecostal movement and seeks a better understanding of the influence of rhetoric on shaping the role of women in Pentecostal ministry for the present and into the future.

The Pentecostal movement and the Assemblies of God specifically have made a significant impact in the United States and abroad and their practices are uniquely centered in tensions that are critical to understanding this movement as well as greater evangelical Christian culture. They are caught up in the tensions of theological conservatism driven by certain assumptions about the nature of mankind and their ability to experience God versus a history of restorationism, revivalism, anti-elitism, and the countercultural nature of their own movement. Historians have noted that the strength of evangelical movements has been in their identification with people and their passion about communicating their message.[2] Pentecostalism is democratic in structure and spirit and therefore belongs to the people rather than to the elites. The result is a measure of the importance of an issue by its popular reception or the adequacy of a method by the number of people it attracts. Therefore, messages receive a greater value based on the quantity rather than the quality of the message being sent.

The focus of my work has revolved around this tension and how women have worked through it to create and maintain rhetorical space in spite of the dissonance. The role of women in the Assemblies of God is centered in the pull between what is popular and what is possible. The tension exists in the rhetoric of the Assemblies of God and their prophesying daughters both past and present.

These challenges are created, shaped, reinforced and naturalized by how people in the early days of the Pentecostal movement and how members of the Assemblies of God in the present day use words, language, and symbols and are in turn used by them. My work analyzes how the rhetoric of Pentecostals as a whole and within the Assemblies of God specifically,

---

2. Hatch, *Democratization of American Christianity*, 214–19.

has created a gap of dissonance with regard to the role of women in leadership positions and has damaged the ability of the movement to continue in the vanguard of restorationism. This position has created a mistrust within the organization as well as in the greater culture they are trying to reach with their message.

The construction of this rhetorical history has provided a unique lens for describing and assessing actors, events, and cultures within the Pentecostal movement and the Assemblies of God as they wrestled to shape their theology and witness in the American religious landscape. Rhetorical history concerns itself with the role of persuasion and allows a closer look at those engaged as actors of persuasion. Rhetorical history is a lens for assessing the theological and cultural legacies of those who have led in Pentecostalism as well as those who have found a way to navigate through the tensions to create rhetorical space for women who participate in the work of spreading the Pentecostal message.

Women like Martha Klaus and her sisters in ministry were and continue to be agents who are called to spread the gospel in the context of ordained ministry wherever and whenever possible through preaching and leading. Listening to their male counterparts argue over the matter creates a rhetorical tension that challenges women's identification with men as ministers and vice versa.

The holiness and later Pentecostal revivals created an exigency or a sense of urgency to spread the message of Jesus as Savior, Baptizer, Healer and Soon-coming King. This sense of urgency created a space for women and provided an empowerment for service. However, among fellow laborers and in religious gatherings was an audience bound up with varying perceptions of what ministry looked like and who could legitimately present the discourse. These constraints have played a significant role in the social construction of Pentecostal culture and discourse.

In addition, a more fundamental theological tension exists inherently in the Pentecostal movement. The tension between radicalism and conservatism is a continuing exigence that also needed to be negotiated and renegotiated. The result is a constant and very fundamental "imperfection" that exists among core denominational distinctives and in the larger movement that requires a continual rhetorical effort to engage—whether to ameliorate the imperfections or to strategically amplify the imperfections so as to increase pressure for some sort of social or theological change. This tension touches the core of Pentecostalism's relationship to the larger evangelical community as well as American religious culture.

I have attempted to fully examine the constraints and social construction of Pentecostal discourse, unpack the history of the movement, and to take on the responsibility as a rhetorical critic to reconstruct the goals, strategies, and vision of the movement through a careful study of the surviving artifacts of the participants. It has not been my intention to simply examine the history of the Assemblies of God from the standpoint of the evolution of ideas, but from the perspective of how messages are created and used by people to influence and relate to one another.[3]

By engaging in this perspective, as a critic, I have been able to gain an insight into how the adherents to the Pentecostal movement and the founding fathers and mothers of the Assemblies of God used rhetoric to both create a space for women as active participants in ministry while at the same time creating a dissonance through that same rhetorical practice by the dichotomy of their policy and practice. It has been my contention that key rhetors including ministers at the local level as well as denominational officials used rhetoric to ameliorate the theological tensions in the Assemblies of God by closing and/or preempting those same spaces. While this dissonance falls outside the confines of the present work, it does speak to an important aspect of the context in which this rhetorical space was negotiated and renegotiated. The rhetoric employed by ministers within the local church who have acted as agents of this amelioration and preemption of theological tension and rhetorical space remains an area where further study must be conducted.

As Turner has argued, rhetorical history provides an understanding of rhetoric as a process; it creates an appreciation of both the commonalities and the distinctiveness of rhetorical situations and responses. Rhetorical history tests theory and compliments criticism while at the same time standing alone as a unique approach to scholarship.[4] This position runs counter to the notion that history is simply a mirror of the past. Rather than looking at isolated instances that are static in time, rhetorical history allows the scholar and the reader to view rhetoric as a dynamic process of social construction, maintenance, and change. Rhetorical scholars replace the mirror to reveal people who are "working within their societal context to create stories about the past."[5]

The value of my study is not in the mirror of Pentecostalism's past, but rather in the description and analysis of a dynamic process that has created and shaped the construction of Pentecostal culture and rhetorical practice. The delicate dance between those who favor a greater role for women and those who favor a more traditional approach to women's involvement is

---

3. Zarefsky, "Four Senses of Rhetorical History," 30.

4. Turner, Doing Rhetorical History, 15.

5. Ibid., 8.

inherently rhetorical. The time has come to put down the mirror of reflection and engage the rhetorical situation so as to see what has been, what is,
and what can be. As a rhetorical scholar, my intention is to work within the
context of the present to create stories about the past in an effort to move
toward a better understanding of how rhetoric creates both opportunities
and constraints that have resulted and continue to result in discursive tension and dissonance for women leaders in the Assemblies of God.

I have used as my guide to analyzing the rhetorical history of the Assemblies of God, Zarefsky's seminal work on the four senses of rhetorical
history. It is Zarefsky's final sense—the study of historical events from a
rhetorical perspective—that I have used to reveal the challenges and in-
sights into the rhetoric of the Assemblies of God with regard to the role of
women. As Zarefsky instructs, I have engaged this sense by starting with the
assumption that the rhetorical historian has the same subject matter as any
other historian, but the perspective focused not on facts and figures, but on
the messages created by early Pentecostals and used by them to both influence and relate to one another.

As a rhetorical historian approaching my texts from this perspective,
I have endeavored to view history as a series of rhetorical problems that
call for public persuasion to advance a cause or overcome some impasse.
How and how well did people in these rhetorical situations invent and
deploy messages in response to the situation? I have attempted to fulfill
Zarefsky's charge that studies of this type may offer a powerful answer to
the elusive "so what?" question. Through this analysis I believe that I have
been able to see significant aspects about the history of the Assemblies of
God and the role of women that other perspectives may have missed or
did not know existed.[6]

This analysis of historical events from a rhetorical perspective has
revealed the forces of history; the visions, goals, and strategies employed
by the Assemblies of God to both create a space for women, while at the
same time creating a rhetorical tension that continues to permeate the
culture. These challenges to women's empowerment have been present in
the rhetoric regarding the role of women in the Assemblies of God and
in the fabric of American culture. What does this work on women in the
Assemblies of God contribute to the larger issues of a woman's role in the
home and the community? And in turn, how does that impact the place
of the Assemblies of God and the Pentecostal movement in American culture? What does this work tell us about rhetorical history and about the
role of gender in contributing to the public moral argument? It has been

6. Zarefsky, "Four Senses of Rhetorical History," 30.

my desire to do more than hold up a mirror of reflection, but to offer up a critique by which we can move toward a better understanding of the power of rhetoric and its impact on the role of women in leadership within the Assemblies of God. As a result of asking these questions and offering up this critique, I believe that I have demonstrated a more consistent case for their distinct and necessary contribution.

Multiple challenges exist with regard to women in the Assemblies of God including those examined here. First, a perception persists that a "Golden Age" for women in ministry positions in the Assemblies of God once existed.[7] While the numbers of women, per capita, serving in the fellowship may have been greater in the early, formative years of the movement, contradictions in message still existed regarding their role, abilities, and freedom to function within the organization.

Second, the tradition of the Pentecostal movement and the Assemblies of God is full of multiple narratives and competing messages. The nature of the organization itself contributes to this challenge. The lack of a strong central organization makes the Assemblies of God unique and, at the same time, allows for dissonance in both the theological and cultural practices of the organization.

Third, the culture in which the Assemblies of God exists also provides challenges to the role(s) of women. Within this challenge resides the role of religion in American culture and how women are perceived and accepted in American religious life. The Assemblies of God is relatively young in the story of American religion and its exigence requires our attention. As a result, I have examined the role the Assemblies of God plays within the Evangelical community and how this relationship contributes to the rhetoric of women's leadership. Even more so than within the Pentecostal tradition, the Evangelical movement has a long history of rejecting women in roles of leadership, specifically leadership outside the domestic sphere and especially within the church. How the Assemblies of God has functioned and continues to function within the greater Evangelical community demands our attention.

Finally, I have spent considerable time looking at the problem noted by Sociologist Margaret Poloma: the Assemblies of God and Pentecostal movement as a whole was at one time a counter-cultural social movement that challenged the notions of the secular culture as much as that of the religious culture. I have also focused on the reaction to the rise of secular social movements such as the modern feminist and the growth of the "religious

---

7. Barfoot and Sheppard, "Prophetic vs. Priestly Religion," 2–17.

right." These movements have had a powerful impact on the rhetoric surrounding women's leadership.

## CONTRIBUTING TO RHETORICAL THEORY

As a result of this analysis, I believe that my examination of the history of the
role of women in the Assemblies of God from a rhetorical perspective provides a significant contribution to rhetorical theory. Specifically, I believe that
my study contributes to the rhetorical study of gender, evangelical rhetoric,
and expands the role of rhetorical history as a means of inquiry.

While this is not specifically a study in feminist theory, I believe that it
does contribute significantly to the study of gender and rhetoric. The Assemblies of God demonstrates the formation of a rhetoric of gender identity that
despite significant constraints reveals and affirms the voices and experiences
of women. The rhetorical history presented in this study reveals women as
rhetors who bear the mark of empowered servants of their God and are not
victims of a power struggle, but rather presents them as creators of their
own rhetorical space despite the social, cultural, and rhetorical constraints
placed in their way. This rhetorical history is about more than feminism and
the examination of power and oppression, but rather this study is about how
women used their belief in a Pentecostal paradigm to rhetorically negotiate
and renegotiate their role in the church, and as a result, many were successful in maintaining a rhetorical space for their daughters, granddaughters,
and generations to come. As I have stated several times, the empowerment
of women for service and the rhetorical negotiation these women engaged
in as a result is a reconceptualization of who God is and how he relates to
his people, what it means to be a woman, and how we relate to one another
as being co-created in the image of God.

This study provides an alternative to a traditional understanding of
gender study. The purpose is not simply to garner women a seat at the table
and increase the number of women on the ministry rolls within the Assemblies of God. Rather, the purpose is to look at how women used the unique
perspective of Pentecostal theology and practice to create rhetorical space
that had previously not existed and how this unique perspective challenged
the religious dynamic, the cultural landscape, and the relationship between
men and women.

Inherent in Pentecostal theology is an affirming and empowering
paradigm that provides an identity beyond what the modern church had
ever encountered. It is relevant to men and women as well as those within
and outside of the Pentecostal tradition. Pentecostal theology reveals more

about the nature of who God is and what is possible when we as human beings set aside our preconceived notions and allow God to reveal himself through us in sacred symbolic action. The power of the call of God on men and women, Pentecostal, Reformed, Catholic, or Non-Denominational is one that is both intensely personal and authoritative—it demands that we both contemplate and act. For anyone who has felt the call of God on their life but questioned how they might be chosen to represent the God of Abraham, Isaac, and Jacob to the world, I want to provide an opportunity to engage in a narrative that is affirming of that call, restores a sense of sacred pursuit, and demonstrates that in spite of the challenges of mankind, it is the Spirit of God who provides empowerment and the language for negotiating the rhetorical space necessary. When one operates in that empowerment, opportunities can be created where they did not previously exist and constraints can be negotiated to create a space for those who have previously been prevented from full participation in the Great Commission.

Throughout this history the rhetorical position of the women called to serve has remained consistent. They were empowered by the Spirit of God and not the preconceived ideas of mankind. Reluctance to this call is a strong theme throughout the history of women in the Assemblies of God; however, when women answered the call and engaged in ministry service, they were more reluctant to be quiet and to leave their work. These women and many men who embraced the Pentecostal empowerment of women were more determined to engage in their ministry when their roles were questioned. In the constraints, women found their voice and the ability to create new and unique means of ministry service. The history of the Assemblies of God and the narrative of women who have identified themselves with this fellowship is a dramatic example of how gender can on the surface appear to be a disqualifier for full participation. Instead, it emerged as a means to engage in discourse regarding an understanding of how God relates to his people and to ask who would not have received the gospel message without the presence of the female voice.

In addition to gender studies, a growing body of scholarship examines evangelical religious rhetoric. The evangelical community is a force to be reckoned with in the study of culture, politics, and religious understanding. Rhetoric has played a role in moving the Assemblies of God from the fringes of religious society to one of the largest and most influential organizations within the evangelical community. As a result of this move toward the mainstream, the Assemblies of God has adopted the rhetoric of evangelicalism, which has meant a diminishing of distinctive doctrines like the open-ended position of women's authority. Within the history of the Pentecostal movement and the Assemblies of God is a shared inheritance with much of the evangelical world including an acceptance of modernist epistemology and a shared engagement in what has been termed the "culture wars." Whereas the Assemblies of God may have been in a position of prophetic resistance in relationship to the rest of American religious culture, they have sacrificed much of what has made them unique and become a power player within the culture.

I have set out to provide a more sustained examination of the Pentecostal movement and the Assemblies of God from a rhetorical perspective. How women have engaged in rhetoric to negotiate and renegotiate their role in the Assemblies of God and the Pentecostal tradition serves as a foundational case study to examine the opportunities and constraints that women have been presented with in the whole of evangelicalism.

While certainly the challenges faced by the Assemblies of God mirror those present in the greater evangelical community, as I have argued, this mirror does not tell the complete story. By focusing on the Assemblies of God as a unique player in the evangelical community, I have been able to demonstrate that evangelical influence does not tell the entire story. Simply to lump all of the perspectives present in evangelicalism into one category does a disservice to the depth of diversity of belief and practice that resides within those denominations and fellowships. I have attempted to reveal the unique doctrine and practices present in the Assemblies of God that serve as a catalyst for addressing the challenges faced by evangelical women. Unfortunately, the analysis of this history reveals a cultural accommodation that has stifled and, in some cases, sacrificed completely these unique doctrines and practices. By bringing the history of women in the Assemblies of God back to the forefront of scholarly inquiry, I hope my analysis presents an opportunity to see how a shift in rhetorical practice could provide an opportunity for the Assemblies of God to engage their evangelical brothers and sisters on the subject of women and nourish a shift in perspective throughout the entire community. If the greatest challenge to women desiring to serve in ministry is, as George Wood says, a succumbing to cultural pressure, the Assemblies of God stands at a unique place of power and influence to reverse this accommodation and again be at the forefront of cultural change.

Finally, the rhetorical historian engages the known historical record from the perspective of how messages are created and used by people to influence and relate to one another.[8] A study of rhetorical history runs counter to the notion that history is simply a mirror of the past. Rather than looking at isolated instances that are static in time, this inquiry views rhetoric as a

---

8. Zarefsky, "Four Senses of Rhetorical History," 30.

dynamic process of social construction, maintenance, and change. Rhetorical scholars reveal people who are "working within their societal context to create stories about the past"[9] and in these narratives, the more complete picture emerges of how women in the Assemblies of God were able to embrace the paradigm of Pentecostalism and work within their context to engage a dynamic process of social construction, maintenance and change. Their efforts did not always yield the numerical success we would expect to see from a successful social change, but in spite of constant constraint and a lack of institutional empowerment, women remained a part of and an influence in the formation and success of the Assemblies of God.

My work is not simply centered on Pentecostalism's past, but rather this work explores the dynamic process that has created and shaped the rhetorical construction of Pentecostal culture. The delicate dance between those who favor a greater role for women and those who favor a more traditional approach to women's involvement is inherently rhetorical. Through a historical lens, I have taken my inquiry one step further to engage the rhetorical situation so as to see what has been, what is, and what can be. I have worked within the context of the present to tell the stories about the past in an effort to move toward a new rhetoric for women leaders in the Assemblies of God. While the purpose of this book is not one of advocacy, inherent in the context of this examination is the desire to see the Assemblies of God move from a rhetorical perspective that speaks richly of the history of women ministers as though their contribution is something of the past to a rhetoric that encourages and inspires future generations of women whose participation is present and active going forward. I believe that by presenting this perspective I have begun to offer a powerful answer to the elusive "so what?" question. It is my belief that through analysis of important historical events viewed from a rhetorical perspective, one can see significant aspects about those events that other perspectives might have missed.[10] This approach enhances the richness of rhetorical scholarship and provides an opportunity to highlight the truly interdisciplinary nature of rhetorical scholarship.

## IMPLICATIONS OF THE PRESENT STUDY
## FOR FUTURE RESEARCH

It has been my intention from the beginning to engage in a scholarly endeavor that was not only contemplative but also rich with practical application

9. Turner, *Doing Rhetorical History*, 8.
10. Zarefsky, "Four Senses of Rhetorical History," 30.

and implications. I desire that this study not only further rhetorical schol-arship, but also foster discourse and understanding of how we engage in rhetoric and what that means for how we practice our faith and try to live it authentically in the public square.

What I see as the final objective is to reveal the past in order to increase our understanding that rhetoric has consequences. In this case, the rhetoric of the women's roles within the Assemblies of God has provided opportu-nity that defied religious convention, challenged the culture, and created space for the message of Pentecostalism to be presented with a female voice. At the very same time, some actors who engaged in a rhetoric of empow-erment used their discourse to create serious constraints for the women of their generation and generations to come. This dissonance created a rhetorical tension that robbed the Assemblies of God and the Pentecostal movement from truly changing the religious landscape, providing a catalyst for women's involvement in other aspects of the culture, and expanding the influence of that feminine voice.

This book does not solve the challenges faced by women, nor does it answer all of the questions raised in this inquiry. What it does is begin the journey toward further discourse on the importance of the female voice to the Pentecostal identity. It has been my intention to better answer the "so what" question, but not shut the door on the questions that remain. The ex-ploration of the intersection of women, Pentecostalism, and evangelicalism is just beginning, and the interplay of these constituencies demands future scholarly inquiry. I have offered up what I see as the topography of the rhe-torical landscape over the course of a given history, and I offer this rhetorical landscape to others as opportunities for future research and study.

I believe this study has implications for theological reflection, specifi-cally in the area of gender reconciliation and the definition of leadership. It also has significant implications for the Assemblies of God. By focusing on the Assemblies of God as a representation of the Pentecostal tradition, this book provides a look at how the issue of women's roles has impacted the fel-lowship and those who choose the Assemblies of God as their ecclesiastical home. As is often the case, this book does not provide prescriptive answers, and in some ways, it creates additional questions that require attention and critical scholarship. Finally, some implications appear in this study for rhetoricians who choose to engage the topic of faith-based rhetoric and the people and organizations that make up evangelicalism.

I believe this book provides for women and men of faith, who believe they bear the image of God and are called to engage the good news of the Gospel of Jesus, a fresh theological reflection on what it means to be called into the ministry of Christ, beyond rigidly defined gender roles and ever-tightening boundary lines. I provide a renewed point of discussion to explore biblical identity and calling in ways that honor the Scripture and lived encounters with the Holy Spirit. The gap between what is typically examined as feminist concern and strict biblical interpretation is wide. This process of reflection and examination can benefit congregations and denominations inside and outside of the Pentecostal tradition to serve the world through active participation and an affirmation of all members to answer the call of the Great Commission. This shift in perspective on gender relationships and ministry service can reach beyond the purview of scholarly endeavor and provide answers for some of the most heinous injustices of patriarchy including domestic violence, pornography, and human trafficking as well as the silencing of God's daughters. To realize the full implications of gender reconciliation in the church requires from both men and women first to acknowledge that the need for reconciliation exits, the acknowledgement of past hurts and wounds, an offer of confession and repentance, and forgiveness and healing. By engaging in this very practical framework, opportunity abounds for full restitution, restoration, and fresh discourse on a shared pursuit.

I believe a book of this kind provides a launching point for further scholarly inquiry into why gender remains such a challenge within the church. In a report from the Vatican, the ordination of women was linked along with sexual abuse of children as one of the church's most serious crimes. For the first time, the ordination of women will be considered a "delicta graviora," which is the most grievous category of crimes against the church, and women will face automatic excommunication, and priests who participate in the affirmation of women's ordinations will be immediately removed from the priesthood. While the Vatican insists that this does not imply the two are in any way equivalent to one another, the statement is clear for Bishops in the United States that the "church is making a very clear statement about the core values of faith and worship."[11]

While the Assemblies of God is significantly different in its theology, doctrine, and approach to ministry from its Catholic brothers and sisters, they share the banner of Christianity and the common pursuit of the Great Commission. The challenges women face in the church are not an issue of the past, but are relevant for the ministry of the church today and going forward. How the evangelical church responds to their own perceptions of women's ordination will have a great impact on how the church universal is perceived in light of this decision from the Catholic Church. As a fellowship whose doctrine stands in stark contrast to that of the Vatican regarding

11. Burke and Richard, "U.S. Bishops Defend Inclusion," 1.

women's ordination, the Assemblies of God has an opportunity to once again consider their own rhetoric on the issue of women's roles and once again be a vanguard voice for women and the church.

I also believe there are several implications for the Assemblies of God. The Assemblies of God is facing the challenges of defining the distinctives of their doctrine and their commitment to a renewed emphasis on their core values: evangelize the lost, worship God, disciple believers, and demonstrate God's love through compassion. I identify women as a crucial link to setting their tradition apart as one that defied culture rather than succumbing to it. The reconciliation of gender in a community of faith is a powerful demonstration of the reconciliation offered by Christ to a fallen world. When once we were eternally set apart from God because of the choices of mankind, we were reconciled to God and brought into full citizenship in the Kingdom of God through the redemption of Christ on the Cross. The return of men and women to one another and to their shared responsibility in the Kingdom creates a unique opportunity for the church to demonstrate revolution rather than reaction.

Early Pentecostals were furious writers and have left a vast treasure, much of which remains unseen and unstudied. The opportunities for examination are immense, and each new scholarly endeavor provides a more complete picture of whom and what the Assemblies of God is and can be. However, a lack of critical examination particularly self-critical examination must be rectified. Pentecostals can no longer fear their own history and must understand even that which may indicate unseemliness is an opportunity for reflection, correction, and growth.

In addition to the archived materials of the past, testimony has long served as an important means of communicating God's mysterious work in the lives of Pentecostals. The testimonies, the sharing of miraculous signs and wonders, assured women a seat at the table and gave them a voice of participation in the work of the church. Further study of the rhetoric of testimony and its power to create, shape, and interpret religious experience, and how it was used to build the church will provide insight and critical examination of the unique rhetorical landscape of the Assemblies of God.

Another implication for the Assemblies of God revealed in this book and demanding of further inquiry is the hierarchical structure of the Assemblies of God and the ways this power structure is successful and the ways it inhibits potential opportunities for change or growth. One of the outcomes has been the revelation of the power of the local church and how this autonomy creates significant constraints for institutional adjustment. I avoid the term *institutional change* here intentionally. The role of women in the Assemblies of God is not a new issue that the fellowship is just now contending with and finding an ideological position on. From the moment of its inception, the Assemblies of God has grappled with how to answer the "woman question" and how to do so while still maintaining a distinctive doctrinal position that would seem to provide a clear answer to the question. If the pneumatology of the Assemblies of God is open to women and through it they are empowered for ministry service, then women must be a part of the ministry ranks in significant and visible ways.

While the national headquarters of the Assemblies of God over time has come to embrace a full empowerment for women's service and to present its position as an official doctrinal statement and reaffirm this doctrine in constitution and bylaws, a great disconnect between what is believed at the national level and what is practiced at the local level remains. When the role of women has been up for discussion, a great floor debate on where the Assemblies of God stands or should stand persists. The number of women who serve as lead pastors in the Assemblies remains dramatically low (less than 700 of nearly 9,000 credentialed women) despite efforts to raise the profile of women in General Council meetings, official publications, and by other means. Further study directed specifically at the local church and focused on the perceptions of the male pastorate are necessary to gain a better understanding of where further constraint exists and why.

Rhetorical historians and critics are provided an example of how women have effectively negotiated and renegotiated their roles within the Assemblies of God. They did so through the embracing of doctrine, which provided their empowerment not by the exhortation of mankind, but through the bestowing of a gift of supernatural power. At a time when doctrine is a polarizing topic within communities of faith and outside of these communities, rhetorical scholars must dedicate our efforts to fostering discourse and understanding on the powerful role that both epistemology and experience plays in affirming or constraining the voices of women in the church.

This analysis of the rhetoric of women's leadership in the Assemblies of God has supplied the field of rhetorical studies with an example of how women, despite constant and persistent constraint created a rhetorical space for their participation in the Pentecostal tradition and the Assemblies of God, specifically. While women on the whole have been a disenfranchised group within the church, the women who negotiated their place in the ministry of Pentecostalism were from a variety socioeconomic backgrounds, had varying degrees of education or other pedigree, but possessed something greater than what would typically define those who challenged the rhetorical landscape of a particular social movement. These women possessed a belief that they had received a supernatural empowerment for service, and they used this belief to construct a rhetorical space for their participation and their influence. For the rhetorician, this is not the typical construction of gender or social movement analysis. The supernatural dimension of religious experience provides a new and distinct avenue of rhetorical inquiry.

I hope that through this work that rhetorical studies of gender, evangelical religious movements, and reconciliation of the two is enhanced and furthered. The rhetorical landscape created and shaped by the Assemblies of God and its position on women provides a model for understanding the power of language, words and symbols, to both create and constrain. The messages created and deployed by the Assemblies of God and its women is not entirely unique to this movement and has practical implications for future rhetorical study. These are lessons, given the position of the Vatican and other religious communities that remain important and demand our scholarly attention.

Throughout my research on this topic, I have encountered narrative after narrative from family, friends, and colleagues of the impact of women in their own lives, ministries, and religious experiences. Many of these narratives serve as a source of inspiration, some of frustration, and others pure discouragement and defeat. While these narratives are varied in their successes and failures, the result of these women's engagement with Pentecostalism and their desire to be obedient to their call despite constraints, is the same: lives altered and transformed. From the former church elder raised in abuse and poverty who wandered into the crusades of evangelist Hattie Hammond to the influence of an aunt who when left widowed took up the banner of ministry and rode horseback through the mountains of Kentucky to bring the gospel of Jesus with little regard for the danger or dignity of a woman, to the daughter of immigrants who through the ministry of the Assemblies of God defied the odds to become the first women elected to a national leadership position, the narratives have one consistent strain: these women served as a catalyst for change not only in the church and the culture, but in the lives of people they encountered.

In July 2010, the Assemblies of God paid tribute to the longest continually serving pastor of a single congregation in the fellowship's history. Mary Watford Stabler pastored Faith Chapel Assembly of God in Scratch Ankle, Alabama, for 71 years and had no plans to retire. As one who began her ministry during the throes of the great depression, Stabler was viewed with great skepticism because of her Pentecostal doctrine and because of her gender. In the early days, much of the resistance to her message came because she was a pioneering female pastor. According to Stabler, "I didn't try to argue with them when they came against me. I just gave them Scriptures of women the Lord had used in ministry, and I said that I knew the Lord had called me, so I was obeying Him. I had a lot of opposition, but the Lord always stood for me."[12]

12. Kennedy, "Still Preaching and Praying," 1.

# Bibliography

Alexander, Estrelda. *The Women of Azusa Street*. Cleveland, OH: Pilgrim, 2005.

Aristotle. *On Rhetoric: A Theory of Civil Discourse*. Translated by George A. Kennedy. New York: Oxford University Press, 1991

Assemblies of God Women in Ministry Task Force. "National Conferences for Women in Ministry Slate." *General Council News*, August 2005. http://www.ag.org/ top/ events/General_Council_2005/News/2005080527_NatConf.cfm.

"As Viewed by a Missionary." *Word and Witness* (November 13, 1913) 1.

Attanasi, Katy. "Fellowship Convenes Conference for Women." *Pentecostal Evangel*, April 29, 2001. http://pentecostalevangel.ag.org/News2001/4538_conference.cfm.

Baker, Mike. "Southern Baptists Back Palin Despite View on Women's Role." *USA Today*, October 3, 2008. http://www.usatoday.com/news/religion/2008-10-02-palin-baptists_N.htm.

Barfoot, Charles H., and Gerald T. Sheppard. "Prophetic vs. Priestly Religion: The Changing Role of Women Clergy in Pentecostal Churches." *Review of Religious Research* 22 (1980) 2–17.

Bartleman, Frank. *Flapper Evangelism: Fashion's Fools Headed for Hell*. Springfield, MO: Flower Pentecostal Heritage Center, n.d.

Bell, E. N. "Questions and Answers." *Weekly Evangel* (September 2, 1916) 8.

———. "Questions and Answers." *Weekly Evangel* (March 10, 1917) 9.

———. "Some Complaints." *Word and Witness* (January 20, 1914) 2.

———. "We Fellowship All." *The Christian Evangel* (February 13, 1915) 2.

———. "Women Elders." *The Christian Evangel* (August 15, 1914) 2.

Benvenuti, Sherilyn. "Anointed, Gifted and Called: Pentecostal Women in Ministry." *Pneuma: The Journal of the Society of Pentecostal Studies* 17 (1995) 229–35.

Berg, Robert. Interview by Joy Qualls. "Reflections on the Ministry of Marie Burgess Brown." Written notes. June 22, 2009. Evangel University, Springfield, MO.

Bicket, Zenas J. "Dealing with Questions on the Role of Women in Ministry." *Enrichment* 2 (Spring 1997) 80–85.

Bitzer, Lloyd F. "The Rhetorical Situation." *Philosophy & Rhetoric* 1 (1968)1–14.

Blumhofer, Edith L. *The Assemblies of God: A Chapter in the Story of American Pentecostalism*. Vol. 1, *To 1941*. Springfield, MO: Gospel Publishing, 1989.

———. *The Assemblies of God: A Chapter in the Story of American Pentecostalism*. Vol. 2, *Since 1941*. Springfield, MO: Gospel Publishing, 1989.

————. *Restoring the Faith: The Assemblies of God, Pentecostalism, and American Culture*. Chicago: University of Illinois Press, 1993.

————."The Role of Women in the Assemblies of God." *Assemblies of God Heritage* (1987) 14–16.

————. "Selected Letters of Mae Eleanor Frey." *Pneuma: The Journal of the Society for Penetecostal Studies* (1995) 67–87.

————."Women in American Pentecostalism." *Pneuma: The Journal of the Society for Pentecostal Studies* 17 (Spring 1995) 19–20.

Blumhofer, Edith L., et al. *Pentecostal Currents in American Protestantism*. Chicago: University of Illinois Press, 1999.

Booze, Joyce Wells. "Amanda Benedict Prayed." *Pentecostal Evangel* (February 25, 1996) 13.

————. "Jesus and Women: Their Revolutionary Role in John's Gospel." *Pentecostal Evangel* (February 15, 1987) 4–6.

Booze, Melinda. "God Who Calls Is Faithful." *Enrichment: Journal for Pentecostal Ministry* (1997) 17–21.

Boulware-Wead, Janie. "Lord Send a Revival . . . So We Can Evangelize Our Nation." *General Council Main Session*. Springfield, MO: The General Council of the Assemblies of God, 1997.

Boyd, Frank M. *Women's Ministry*. Springfield, MO: Gospel Publishing, n.d.

Bradford, James T. "Summary Statistical Report." Office of the General Secretary, General Council of the Assemblies of God, 2016. https://ag.org/about/statistics.

Brekus, Catherine A. *Strangers and Pilgrims: Female Preaching in America, 1740–1845*. Chapel Hill: University of North Carolina Press, 1998.

Brock, Bernard L. "Rhetorical Criticism: A Burkean Approach Revisited." In *Methods of Rhetorical Criticism: A Twentieth-Century Perspective*, edited by Bernard L. Brock et al., 183–95. Detroit: Wayne State University Press, 1990.

Brumback, Carl. *Suddenly . . . From Heaven*. Springfield, MO: Gospel Publishing, 1961.

Brummett, Barry. *Rhetorical Dimensions of Popular Culture*. Tuscaloosa: University of Alabama Press, 1991.

Bueno, John. *A/G World Missions*. Biennial Report, Springfield, MO: The General Council of the Assemblies of God, 2005–2007.

Burke, Kenneth. *A Grammar of Motives*. Berkeley: University of California Press, 1969.

————. *Language as Symbolic Action*. Berkeley: University of California Press, 1966.

————. *Permanence and Change*. 3rd ed. Berkeley: University of California Press, 1984.

————. *A Rhetoric of Motives*. Berkeley: University of California Press, 1969.

Caldwell, E. S. "Let Us Honor Our Job-Holding Mothers." *Pentecostal Evangel* (May 10, 1981) 12–13.

Campbell, Karlyn Kohrs. "Book Review." *The Review of Communication* (2001) 194–98.

Carlson, G. Raymond. "From the Cradle to the Cross." *Advance* (March 30, 1994) 24–25.

————. "When Pentecost Came to the Upper Midwest." *Assemblies of God Heritage* (1984) 5.

Carter, Stephen L. *God's Name in Vain: The Wrongs and Rights of Religion in Politics*. New York: Basic, 2000.

Casey, Michael W. "The First Female Speakers in America (1630–1840): Searching for Egalitarian Christian Primitivism." *The Journal of Communication and Religion* 23 (2000) 1–28.

Cavaness, Barbara L. "A Biographical Study of the U.S. Assemblies of God Women in Missions." PhD diss., Fuller Theological Seminary, Pasadena, 1999.

Chambers-Gordon, Sharon. "Liberated in the Spirit: Telling the Lives of Jamaican Women in a Pentecostal/Revivalist Church." *Women and Language* 24 (2001) 52–56.

Champion, Richard. "Editor's Note." *Pentecostal Evangel* (February 18, 1990) 3.

Conley, Thomas M. *Rhetoric in the European Tradition.* New York: Longman, 1990.

Corum, Lillian. "Notes on Ministry of Rachel Sizelove." Rachel Sizelove Personal Papers, 1920–21. Flower Pentecostal Heritage Center, Springfield, MO.

Cox, Harvey. *Fire from Heaven: The Rise of Pentecostal Spirituality and the Reshaping of Religion in the Twenty-First Century.* Cambridge: Da Capo, 1995.

Credential Committee. "Dear Sister." Women in Ministry File, 1922. Flower Pentecostal Heritage Center, Springfield, MO.

Culver, Elise Thomas. *Women in the World of Religion.* Garden City, NJ: Doubleday, 1967.

Dayton, Donald W. "Evangelical Roots of Feminism." *The Covenant Quarterly* (November 1976) 54.

"Dear Brother Minister in the Lord," August 2, 1922. Flower Pentecostal Heritage Center, Springfield, MO.

Deno, Vivian. "God, Authority, and the Home: Gender, Race, and U.S. Pentecostals, 1906–1926." *Journal of Women's History* 16 (2004) 83–105.

Dresselhaus, Richard L. "The Place of Women in the Church." *Pentecostal Evangel* (February 18, 1990) 4–5.

Driscoll, Mark. *Church Leadership: Explaining the Role of Jesus, Elders, Deacons, And Members at Mars Hill.* Mars Hill Theological Series. Seattle: Mars Hill Church, 2004.

Edwards, Robert. "Woman Up for A/G Post as Doors Begin to Open." *Springfield News-Leader* (August 8, 1993) 6A.

Elliot, Elisabeth. "Why I Oppose Women's Ordination." *Christianity Today* (June 6, 1975) 16–20.

Everts, Janet Meyer. "Brokenness as the Center of a Woman's Ministry." *Pneuma: The Journal of the Society for Pentecostal Studies* 17 (1995) 237–43.

Everts, Janet Meyer, and Rachel Schutte Baird. "Phoebe Palmer and Her Pentecostal Protégées." Paper presented at the 35th annual meeting of the Society for Pentecostal Studies, Pasadena, March 23–25, 2006.

Flower, Joseph R. "Does God Deny Spiritual Manifestations and Ministry Gifts to Women?" February 1978. Women in Ministry File, Flower Pentecostal Heritage Center, Springfield, MO.

———. "Men Wanted." *Pentecostal Evangel* (April 7, 1923) 12.

———. "The Ministry of Women." *Women in Ministry*, December 28, 2007. General Council of the Assemblies of God. http://womeninministry.ag.org/roleofwim/0306 _MinistryofWomen.cfm.

Floyd, Ann. "Janie Wead—Single Mom and Missionary." *Pentecostal Evangel* (May 12, 1996) 8–9.

Frodsham, Stanley F. "Editor's General Council Notes." *Pentecostal Evangel* (May 13, 1931) 4–5.

Gardiner, Gordon P. *The Origin of Glad Tidings Tabernacle.* New York: Glad Tidings Tabernacle, 1955.

General Council of the Assemblies of God. "52nd General Council." *Resolutions,* August 8–11, 2007. http://www.ag.org/top/Events/General_Council_2007/Business/ Resolutions/ Resolutions_03.cfm.

———. "Assemblies of God Position Paper: The Role of Women in Ministry as Described by Holy Scripture." *Women in Ministry,* 1990. http://ag.org/top/Beliefs/ Position _Papers/pp_ 4191_women_ministry.cfm.

———. Executive Presbytery Minutes, 1914, 1922. Flower Pentecostal Heritage Center, Springfield, MO.

———. General Council Minutes and Reports, 1914–1999. Flower Pentecostal Heritage Center, Springfield, MO.

"General Council Meets in St. Louis." *Word and Witness* (September 1915) 1.

Gill, Deborah Menken. "Called by God—What's a Woman to Do and What Can We Do to Help Her." *Enrichment: A Journal for Pentecostal Ministry* (1997) 35–37.

———. "The Contemporary State of Women in Ministry in the Assemblies of God." *Pneuma: The Journal of the Society of Pentecostal Studies* 17 (Spring 1995) 33–36.

Gill, Deborah M., and Barbara Cavaness. *God's Women—Then and Now.* Springfield, MO: Grace and Truth, 2004.

Goff, James R., Jr., and Grant Wacker. *Portraits of a Generation: Early Pentecostal Leaders.* Fayetteville, AR: University of Arkansas Press, 2002.

Goldzwig, Steven R. "Civil Rights and the Cold War." In *Doing Rhetorical History,* edited by Kathleen J. Turner, 144. Tuscaloosa, AL: University of Alabama Press, 2003.

Goss, Howard A. "Notice to Women Missionaries." *Weekly Evangel* (May 29, 1915) 2.

Grant, A. Elizabeth. "Celebration and Commitment to Community." Conversations '08 Conference, The Network: A Called Community of Women, Phoenix, AZ, 2008.

———. "Executive Presbytery Election Speech." 53rd General Council of the Assemblies of God, Orlando FL, August 5, 2009.

Hatch, Nathan O. *The Democratization of American Religion.* New Haven: Yale University Press, 1980.

Heclo, Hugh. *Christianity and American Democracy.* Cambridge: Harvard University Press, 2007.

Hestenes, Roberta. "Women in Leadership: Finding Ways to Serve in the Church." *Christianity Today* (October 3, 1986) 4–10.

Hinman, Nelson E. "Happiness in Marriage." *Pentecostal Evangel* (November 30, 1946) 21–22.

Horton, Stanley M. "Rediscovering the Prophetic Role of Women." *Enrichment: A Journal for Pentecostal Ministry* (2001).

"Hot Springs Assembly." *Word and Witness* (1914) 1.

Hunter, James Davison. *To Change the World: The Irony, Tragedy, and Possibility of Christianity in the Late Modern World.* Oxford: Oxford University Press, 2010.

Hyatt, Susan C. "Spirit-Filled Women." In *The Century of the Holy Spirit: 100 Years of Pentecostal and Charismatic Renewal,* edited by Vinson Synan, 234–41. Grand Rapids, MI: Eerdmans, 2001.

Johns, Cheryl Bridges. "The Adolescence of Pentecostalism: In Search of a Legitimate Sectarian Identity." *Pneuma: The Journal for the Society of Pentecostal Studies* 17 (1995) 3–17.

Kendrick, Klaude. *The Promise Fulfilled: A History of the Modern Pentecostal Movement.* Springfield, MO: Gospel Publishing, 1961.

Kennedy, John W. "Still Preaching and Praying." *Pentecostal Evangel* (July 10, 2010) 1.

Kenyon, Howard W. "An Analysis of Ethical Issues in the History of the Assemblies of God." PhD diss., Baylor University, 1988.

Klaus, Byron. "Mr. and Mrs. On the Church Marquee: A Mother and Father's Ministry Example, Interview with Byron Klaus." By Loralie Crabtree, The Network for Women in Ministry, July 2005. http://www.womeninministry.ag.org.

Klaus, Martha. "He Preached Morning and She Preached Nights, Interview with Martha Klaus." By Loralie Crabtree, The Network for Women in Ministry, July 2005. http://www.womeninministry.ag.org.

Knoth, Darla. "Women in Ministry a Reality at Conference." AG News, March 19, 2004. http://www.ag.org/top/news/.

Land, Stephen J. Pentecostal Spirituality: A Passion for the Kingdom. Sheffield: Sheffield Academic, 1993.

Larson, Rebecca. Daughters of Light: Quaker Women Preaching and Prophesying in the Colonies and Abroad, 1700–1775. New York: Knopf, 1999.

Lawless, Elaine J. God's Peculiar People: Women's Voices & Folk Tradition in a Pentecostal Church. Tuscaloosa: University Press of Kentucky, 2005.

———. Handmaidens of the Lord: Pentecostal Women Preachers and Traditional Religion. Philadelphia: University of Pennsylvania Press, 1988.

———. "Transforming the Master Narrative: How Women Shift the Religious Subject." Frontiers 24 (2003) 61–75.

Lee, Joyce, and Glenn Gohr. "Women in the Pentecostal Movement." Enrichment 4 (1999) 1–5.

Marsden, George M. Fundamentalism and American Culture: The Shaping of Twentieth-Century Evangelicalism, 1870–1925. New York: Oxford University Press, 1980.

Mayo, Sam. "Who Denied the Church." Enrichment 2 (1997) 44–47.

McClung, Grant. "Pentecostals: The Sequel." Christianity Today (April 2006) 30–37.

McClure, Jennifer. "Many Roles, One Call: A Profile of Executive Presbyter Beth Grant." The Pentecostal Evangel (February 28, 2010) 10–15.

McGee, Gary B. "This Gospel . . . Shall Be Preached": A History and Theology of Assemblies of God Foreign Missions to 1959. Springfield, MO: Gospel Publishing, 1986.

———. People of the Spirit: The Assemblies of God. Springfield, MO: Gospel Publishing, 2004.

Medhurst, Martin J. "Filled With the Spirit: Rhetorical Invention and the Pentecostal Tradition." Rhetoric and Public Affairs 7 (2004) 555–72.

M. E. Frey Deceased Ministers File. Flower Pentecostal Heritage Center, Springfield, MO.

Menzies, William W. Anointed to Serve: The Stories of the Assemblies of God. Springfield, MO: Gospel Publishing, 1971.

Merritt, Steven. "Women." Midnight Cry (March 6, 1916) 5.

Moomau, N. "The Cleansing of the Temple." Pentecostal Evangel (March 31, 1923) 6.

Noll, Mark A. American Evangelical Christianity: An Introduction. Oxford: Blackwell 2001.

———. The Civil War as a Theological Crisis. Chapel Hill: University of North Carolina Press, 2006.

———. God and Race in American Politics: A Short History. Princeton: Princeton University Press, 2008.

———. The Scandal of the Evangelical Mind. Grand Rapids, MI: Eerdmans Publishing, 1994.

Palmer, Phoebe. *The Promise of the Father; or, A Neglected Specialty of the Last Days.* Boston: Henry V. Degan, 1859.

Pauley, John L. "Jesus in a Chevy? The Rhetoric of Boundary Work in Contemporary Christian Music." *Journal of Communication and Religion* 28 (2005) 71–98.

Pearlman, Myer. "The Christian Ideal of Marriage." *Adult and Young People's Teachers' Quarterly* (1944) 44–50.

Perkin, Noel. "An Appeal for Lady Missionaries." *Pentecostal Evangel* (April 12, 1947) 8.

Poloma, Margaret. "Charisma and the Institution: The Assemblies of God." *Christian Century* (October 1990) 932–34.

———. "Charisma, Institutional and Social Change." *Pneuma: The Journal of the Society for Pentecostal Studies* 17 (Fall 1995) 245–52.

Riggs, Ralph. "The Place of Men in the Work of the Church." *Pentecostal Evangel* (February 5, 1938) 16.

———. "Ralph Riggs to Kenneth Roper." January 24, 1956. Race Relations File. Flower Pentecostal Heritage Center, Springfield, MO.

Robeck, Cecil M., Jr. "National Association of Evangelicals." In *Dictionary of Pentecostal and Charismatic Movements*, edited by Stanley M. Burgess and Gary B. McGee, 635. Grand Rapids, MI: Zondervan, 1988.

Rodgers, Darrin J. *Northern Harvest: Pentecostalism in North Dakota.* Bismarck, ND: North Dakota District Council of the Assemblies of God, 2003.

Roebuck, David. "From Extraordinary Call to Spirit Baptism: Phoebe Palmer's Use of Pentecostal Language to Justify Women in Ministry." Paper presented at The Society for Pentecostal Studies, November 1988.

———. "Pentecostal Women in Ministry: A Review of Selected Documents." *Perspectives in Religious Studies* 16 (2006) 29–44.

Sanders, Cheryl J. "History of Women in the Pentecostal Movement." *Cyberjournal for Pentecostal-Charismatic Research* (October 1996) 1–7.

Sizelove, Rachel. "A Sparkling Fountain for the Whole Earth." *Word and Work* (June 1934) 1–12.

Smith, Christian. *American Evangelicalism: Embattled and Thriving.* Chicago: University of Chicago Press, 1998.

Steiner, Mark Allen. "The Liability of Enlightenment: 'Modernism' in the Relationships among Religion, Politics, and American Public Life." *Explorations in Media Ecology* (2009) 295–98.

———. "Reconceptualizing Christian Public Engagement: 'Faithful Witness' and the American Evangelical Tradition." *Journal of Communication and Religion* (October 2009) 289–319.

Synan, Vinson. *The Century of the Holy Spirit: 100 Years of Pentecostal and Charismatic Renewal.* Nashville: Thomas Nelson, 2001.

———. *The Holiness–Pentecostal Tradition: Charismatic Movements in the Twentieth Century.* 2nd ed. Grand Rapids, MI: Eerdmans, 1997.

Tackett, Zachary Michael. "The Embourgeoisement of the Assemblies of God: Changing Perspectives on Scripture, Millennialism, and the Role of Women." PhD diss., Southern Baptist Theological Seminary, 1998.

Taylor, Charles Alan. *Defining Science: A Rhetoric of Demarcation.* Madison: University of Wisconsin Press, 1996.

Tinlin, Paul B., and Edith L. Blumhofer. "Decade of Decline or Harvest? Dilemmas of the Assemblies of God." *The Christian Century* (July 10–17, 1991) 684–85.

Trask, Thomas E. "Ask the Superintendent: Interview with Thomas E. Trask." *Enrichment: A Journal for Pentecostal Ministry* (1997) 8–10.

Turner, Kathleen J. *Doing Rhetorical History: Concepts and Cases.* Tuscaloosa: University of Alabama Press, 2003.

Wacker, Grant. "The Assemblies of God." *Assemblies of God Heritage* (1987) 10–11.

———. *Heaven Below: Early Pentecostals and American Culture.* Cambridge, MA: Harvard University Press, 2001.

Weber, Max. *On Charisma and Institution Building.* Chicago: University of Chicago Press, 1968.

———. *The Sociology of Religion.* Translated by E. Fischoff. Boston: Beacon, 1963.

Wheatley, Richard. *The Life and Letters of Mrs. Phoebe Palmer.* New York: Palmer and Hughes, 1876.

Wilson, Lewis. "Book Review: *Restoring the Faith: The Assemblies of God, Pentecostalism, and American Culture* by Edith L. Blumhofer." *Pneuma: The Journal of the Society for Pentecostal Studies* 17 (1995) 119–41.

Wolfe, Alan. *The Transformation of American Religion: How We Actually Live Our Faith.* Chicago: University of Chicago Press, 2003.

Women's Movement File. Flower Pentecostal Heritage Center, Springfield, MO.

Wood, George O. Business Session. 2017 General Council of the Assemblies of God, Biennial Meeting, Anaheim, CA.

———. "Everything We Ever Wanted to Know About Women in Ministry but Were Afraid to Ask." Conversations '08 Conference, the Network: A Called Community of Women, Phoenix, AZ, 2008.

———. "Exploring Why We Think the Way We Do about Women in Ministry." *Enrichment* (2001).

———. Interviewed by Joy E. A. Qualls. Springfield, MO, November 2007.

———. *Report of the General Secretary.* Biennial Report, Springfield: The General Council of the Assemblies of God, 2005–2007.

———. "Why Credentials Are Important for Women Ministers." *Women in Ministry.* September 2005. http://womeninministry.ag.org/0509/0509_credentials.cfm.

Zarefsky, David. "Four Senses of Rhetorical History." In *Doing Rhetorical History,* by Kathleen J. Turner, 19–32. Tuscaloosa: University of Alabama Press, 1998.

———. *President Johnson's War on Poverty: Rhetoric and History.* Tuscaloosa: University of Alabama Press, 1986.